THE CLIFFORD YEARS:
The University of North Dakota, 1971-1992

By Daniel R. Rice

Published by the University of North Dakota
Grand Forks, North Dakota
April, 1992

DEDICATION

*This book is dedicated to Thomas J. Clifford,
to the many people who devoted their
lives to this University during this period,
and
to my father, Kenneth H. Rice.
He loved books.*

Publisher: *University of North Dakota*
Author: *Daniel R. Rice*
Editor: *Niomi Phillips*
Production and Design Coordinator: *James F. Penwarden*
Composition: *Mavis Ness*
Cover: *James F. Penwarden*
Printer: *University of North Dakota Printing Center*

International Standard Book Number:
0-9608700-9-1

UND Cataloging-in-Publication Data

Rice, Daniel R.
    The Clifford years: the University of North Dakota, 1971-1992 / by Daniel R. Rice ; [editor: Niomi
Phillips]. — Grand Forks, N.D. : University of North Dakota, 1992.
    viii, 198, [16] p. : ill., photos. ; 22 cm.
    Includes bibliographical references (p. 157-189) and index.
    1. Clifford, Thomas John. 2. University of North Dakota — History. 3. Universities and colleges
— North Dakota — History. I. Phillips, Niomi.

UND   LD3982.7.R5 1992

CONTENTS

PREFACE

This is an account of the people, events and decisions which shaped the University of North Dakota during a twenty-one year period from 1971 through 1992. The president of the University during these years was Thomas J. Clifford.

The University of North Dakota is the largest and oldest university in North Dakota. It was chartered as a liberal arts university and its founding in 1883 predates statehood for North Dakota. It is now the largest university in the region of North Dakota, South Dakota, Wyoming, Montana, Idaho and western Minnesota. It is a doctoral degree granting institution offering the doctorate in 16 fields. The master's degree is offered in 48 fields and the University has fully accredited schools of law and medicine. It is an important institution of higher education in the region.

Those who are alumni, former faculty and staff, and who are friends of the university will have a special interest in this account, as will those who are presently associated with the institution. Some who are interested in higher education from a scholarly perspective may find this account of interest. President Thomas Clifford has been a very popular and unusually effective president and a well regarded leader in higher education and public life in the region for many years. Interest in his life and work are important reasons, as well, for the publication of this book.

Any attempt to provide an accounting of the development of a modern university, over a period of twenty-one years, requires the making of difficult decisions. One such set of decisions concerns what to include and what to omit. In seeking to resolve that problem, I asked several key persons who were familiar with the events of the time to identify, in their opinion, the most significant developments during the period. Another difficult decision is how much detail to provide. That issue was dictated, in part, by a decision about the approximate length of this account. Beyond that practical consideration, I must admit that a multitude of subjective decisions abound. To those who have been left out of this account but who played important roles, and there are many, I can only express my regrets and apologies.

A decision which is both substantive and stylistic had to do with whether to give the account a particular focus and, if so, what that focus might be. In this instance, the decision was made to follow the pattern provided by Elwyn Robinson in his account of the University in the period immediately preceding the present account. Robinson framed his reporting around President George Starcher and gave the work the title, The

Starcher Years: The University of North Dakota, 1954-1971. The decision
to follow Robinson was made for at least three reasons. First, it is quite
common in both formal writing and in informal conversation to speak of
the terms of university presidents as eras or epochs. This is done with the
full recognition that there are many players on the stage, as well as the
individual president, and that it is often true that no single person can be
given the credit (or the blame) for certain developments. In some instances,
events seem beyond the control of everyone. Nevertheless, presidential
terms delineate some boundaries, porous ones to be sure, but identifiable
and helpful boundaries. The second reason is based upon my belief that
presidents do make a difference — for good or for ill. This present account
is not an attempt to prove the point, but it is an operating assumption. The
third reason is that following Robinson's example provides continuity and
gives those who are interested in this university a companion piece to the
earlier work. Those who wish to read the earlier history of the University
should turn to Louis G. Geiger's *University of the Northern Plains; A
History of the University of North Dakota 1883-1958.* In addition, a special
volume was published for the centennial by the UND History Department,
edited by Robert P. Wilkins, and titled *A Century on the Northern Plains:
The University of North Dakota at 100.* Both of these works were published
by the University of North Dakota.

The story of the fortunes and disappointments of a state university
must also reflect something about the state itself. That is certainly the case
with this particular university. The University of North Dakota has been
unusually vulnerable to the economic conditions of the state. This has been
the case, in part, because it is a state with a small population and because
it is especially dependent upon agriculture and energy (coal and oil) for its
economic well-being. These economic resources are highly volatile in that
both are subject to fluctuating markets. Agriculture is at the mercy of
Mother Nature, in spite of the best efforts and ingenuity of humankind,
which makes the economy of the state as unpredictable as the weather. A
university in a state such as this finds itself frequently buffeted by the same
economic forces which buffet the state. A primary challenge for the president of such a university is to take maximum advantage of available
resources during the "good times" and protect the institution as much as
possible during the "bad times." This is a story of how the University of
North Dakota has fared during the period of 1971-1992, the years of the
presidency of Thomas J. Clifford.

Elwyn Robinson, writing in *History of North Dakota,* identified
location as the most important key to understanding the history of the state.
Within that key issue six themes were identified: "remoteness, dependence,
economic disadvantage, agrarian radicalism, the 'Too Much Mistake'

(trying to do too much too fast with too little), and adaptation to environment. Every event in the history of the state is related in some way to one or more of them" (Robinson, 1966, p. vii). It is probably safe to conclude that the same holds true for the major university of this state. The reader would do well to keep these themes in mind while considering what follows.

Sources

A brief word about the use of sources is necessary. Every effort has been made to verify the accuracy of what is reported. I conducted interviews with many of those who were directly involved in the events. Original documents were consulted when available and appropriate. Some events were reported in the press and those accounts were utilized in some cases. I recognize that press accounts are not always perfectly accurate. Sources have been cited in the narrative when it seemed important to document the source for the reader. At the same time, this account has been written for the general reader as well as the more critical or scholarly reader. Therefore, an effort has been made to keep the narrative as readable as possible and unencumbered by excessive technical references. I have followed the style of the American Psychological Association (APA) for the most part. Interviews are identified in the text by the name of the person interviewed followed by the date of the interview, for example, (Jones, 3/10/90).

Acknowledgements

There are many who provided information, insights, advice, and assistance of various sorts which made this book possible. I can name only a few here. First, the invitation to write this book came from Dave Vorland, executive director of the Office of University Advancement, and I am thankful to him for this opportunity and to the staff of that office for their frequent assistance, Sara Weisgerber for searches for photographs, Mavis Ness for typing the final copy, and James Penwarden for guiding the manuscript through the graphic design and publication processes and for developing the index. President Clifford made his time available for several interviews. I am grateful to him for his full cooperation. I am indebted to Lyle Beiswenger, Alice T. Clark, W. Jeremy Davis, Alan Fletcher, Gordon H. Henry, Al Hoffarth, Edwin C. James, A. William Johnson, Bernard O'Kelly, Evan Lips, John D. Odegard, Gerald Skogley, Earl Strinden, Henry J. Tomasek, and D. Jerome Tweton for the interviews they granted to me. Interviews with a number of persons who were familiar with President Clifford and his work were conducted for my doctoral dissertation and those sources were utilized for this book, as well. These persons included, in addition to several of those listed above, John Richardson, Ed Lander, and Randy H. Lee. A number of university deans, program directors and department chairs provided information which was valuable.

Additional persons who provided assistance include Tara Nelson and Lorna Jacobson of the President's Office; Rick Collin of the Energy and Environmental Research Center; Gerri Sayler of the Center for Aerospace Sciences; Peggy Lucke, Controller; Bill Crow, Budget Director; Uta Thompson, Office of Facilities Coordinator; Doug Skipper, Sports Information Service; and Joan Kitchens, Continuing Education Division. Special thanks are due Kathleen Gershman, Niomi Phillips, Earl Strinden, Henry Tomasek, and David Vorland who served as readers of the manuscript. John Vennes read the section on the Medical School. Each reader provided many important suggestions. Niomi Phillips edited the final copy. However, any errors or lapses in quality which remain in the text are my responsibility alone.

The staff of my own office, Instructional Development, Jeanne Boppre, Rhonda Lindseth, Jeanne Anderegg, and Teresa Winker, have done much to make it possible for me to complete this project. Finally, my family has endured my preoccupation with this book for almost two years. My daughter Peggie has foregone much time with her dad while he has been secluded to write as have my older daughters, Lisa and Kristi, and their families, as well. My wife Bonnie has demonstrated remarkable patience and has provided constant support and encouragement. She has offered many valuable suggestions, as well. This sort of project reminds me of how much we depend upon others. I am grateful to everyone named and others not mentioned here who have helped me along the way.

Daniel R. Rice
University of North Dakota
Grand Forks
March 1992

BEGINNINGS

PRECEDING PAGE: On the eve of assuming the top office at the University of North Dakota in 1971, new President Thomas J. Clifford, right, conferred with retiring President George W. Starcher, left. They had worked closely for many years while Clifford was an academic dean and a vice president at UND.

CHAPTER 1

THE MAKING OF A PRESIDENT

On June 30, 1971, George Starcher, President of the University of North Dakota, and Thomas J. Clifford, Vice President for Finance and President-elect, stood side by side for the announcement of over $4 million in gifts to the University. It was also the last day of the Starcher presidency and was the threshold of the beginning of the Clifford presidency. Starcher had been president for 17 years. It had been a period of great growth and improvement for the University. It was fitting that Starcher make the announcement of such substantial gifts, as he had done so often in the past, while Clifford, his successor, looked on. Clifford would also preside over a period of great growth and improvement and would make many similar announcements in the years ahead. The torch was about to be passed.

In 1991, near the end of the Clifford years, the University was different in many respects than it was in 1971. The enrollment had increased 42 percent, from 8,395 to 11,940. Total annual expenditures had increased 610 percent, from $24.4 million to $173.6 million. Four new colleges had been established: the College of Fine Arts, the Center for Teaching and Learning, the College for Human Resources Development, and the Center for Aerospace Sciences. The state's only four-year degree-granting Medical School had been developed and was fully operational. The campus looked much different, as a host of new buildings had gone up and the physical plant had nearly quadrupled in value from $57.9 million to $223.9 million. Someone returning to the campus for the first time since 1971 would surely have been amazed at the changes. The account of this period begins with the story of the central figure on campus during these years, President Thomas J. Clifford.

Tom Clifford's Early Years

Thomas J. Clifford was born in Langdon, North Dakota, on March 16, 1921, to Thomas Joseph and Elizabeth Clifford. His mother's family had homesteaded the land before North Dakota statehood. Her family, of Austrian descent, had been successful in spite of many hardships and had expanded their interests to include a farm machinery business and banking. Clifford's father, a first-generation immigrant from Ireland, was trained in the law and was a graduate of Trinity College, Dublin. He practiced law in Langdon and engaged in business and banking, as well.

Clifford's memories of childhood are positive. He recalls having good relationships with his parents and was especially close to his maternal grandmother, from whom he learned to speak German. The young boy spent much time on the farm, especially during the summers. He enjoyed his uncles, as well, and recalls being especially influenced by uncle Les Griffith. Tom's father was a cultured person and had his son reading Shakespeare when he was only seven years old. The older Clifford attempted to govern what his son read, but the librarian, Catherine Donovan, picked out books for Tom to read — books which were often read under the bed covers at night.

Tom attended St. Alphonse, the parochial school in Langdon. Sister Mary Helen Austin, a Presentation Nun, was an especially influential teacher and further strengthened the boy's enjoyment of reading. After the eighth grade, Tom transferred to the public school in Langdon. When Tom was 13 years old his father died. The following years were not as serene as the time before. It was 1934 and the Great Depression made life more austere for everyone. Nevertheless, he enjoyed mathematics and science in school, respected his teachers and worked hard for them. He regularly read three books a week entirely on his own. Tom was athletic and participated in all sports. At this stage in his life he had not given much thought to a career, but it was assumed that he would attend college.

There had been no discussion in the family about where Tom would attend college. After high school graduation in 1938, when the time came, Tom's mother loaded him up in the car with some of his belongings, drove to Grand Forks and deposited him at the Kappa Sigma fraternity house. When asked what his major would be Tom would indicate that, like his father, he would become a lawyer. The older fraternity members would assist the pledges by filling out their registration cards for them and signing them up for courses. Tom missed home for a brief time but he made friends quickly and came to enjoy college life. Before long his family could hardly get him home.

It was Tom's good fortune to be a student at the University during a period when several excellent faculty were teaching. Professors he remembered as being especially influential were Clara Peterson (English), Raymond C. Staley (Mathematics), Orin J. Libby (History), Felix Vondracek (History), John Gillette (Sociology), and Josiah Sayer (Political Science), to name a few. Tom was keenly aware that his mother was supporting his expenses during his first year. That gave him added incentive to attend to his studies, which enabled him to make a good start on his academic career. Tom was active in a host of extra curricular activities including Collegiate YMCA, intramural sports (he did not try out for intercollegiate sports because he suffered a knee injury in high school), honors societies, service organizations, and student government. He enjoyed an active social life, and held all offices in his fraternity, including president.

A blind date during the second semester of his freshman year was the occasion for meeting his future wife, Florence Schmidt, of Ashley, North Dakota. She later accepted his fraternity pin and they dated for the next three years. They were married on January 25, 1943.

Tom had received his Bachelor of Science degree in commerce in 1942. But world events pressed in upon his life, as was the case for so many during that time. Tom decided to join the Marines rather than wait to be drafted. He had declined to join the Reserve Officers Training Corps (ROTC), as some of his friends had done, which enabled them to enter the military as officers. Tom entered as a private, was sent to Quantico, Virginia, for basic training, was selected for Officer Training School and on January 10, 1943, was commissioned a Second Lieutenant. He soon found himself engaged in combat in the Pacific theatre with the First Amphibious Corps. He saw action in the Solomon Islands, Saipan, Tinian, and Iwo Jima. He was wounded and received numerous medals including the Purple Heart, Bronze Star, and Silver Star. It took him some time to recover from the war. The experience left him a stronger person with a keener sense of values, one who had developed leadership skills and a deep appreciation for loyalty. By the time of his discharge, Tom had risen to the rank of Major.

After the war, in 1945, Clifford was thinking about attending Michigan law school. He contacted UND Accounting Professor Robin D. Koppenhaver, who invited him to teach in the Accounting Department to replace a professor who was ill. Clifford would later suggest, "If it wouldn't have been for that, I wouldn't have been at UND" (Bohn, 1991). After teaching that first semester, however, Clifford was still seriously considering law school in Michigan. This time Koppenhaver suggested that Clifford remain at UND and earn his law degree and he agreed to stay. He was promoted to associate professor in 1948 and full professor by 1949 and served as head of the accounting department. He was awarded a law degree at UND in 1948. After finishing law school, he studied for the state bar examination and the Certified Public Accountant (CPA) examination during the same year, no small undertaking. He passed both the first time (Bohn, 1991).

During the period 1946-49 Clifford also served as counselor of men and gained a reputation on campus as someone who would help students when they were in difficulty. He helped many, some with academic problems, others with financial problems, and he even bailed some out of jail. He would later learn that some had been on the verge of dropping out of college. Years later, many of these alumni, some who had gone on to become very successful, would not forget Clifford's helping hand when they had been in need.

In 1950, at age 29, he was appointed the dean of the College of Commerce. He was the youngest dean in the history of the University and holds that distinction to this day. Clifford left the University for a brief time to study at Stanford University for a Master of Business Administration (M.B.A.) degree which was awarded in 1957. He remained at Stanford an additional year as a Stanford Executive Fellow to continue further graduate study.

During these early years Clifford considered the possibility of entering private or corporate law. He discussed this possibility with University President John West. West told Clifford something which would cement the young professor's commitment to higher education. West said that if Tom would decide to practice law he would have clients, he would conclude their cases, they would pay him and that would be the end of that. But, West told him, if you help a student, that endures forever. Years later Clifford would still recall that conversation with West as a turning point in his life (Clifford, 4/25/91).

In 1959 he was appointed vice president for finance for the University. He served in that position until his selection as president of the University. During the intervening years he was very active in community and state affairs. Clifford's remarkable financial abilities were widely respected and recognized not only at UND but also across the state. His advice and assistance on financial matters was sought by many people in farming, small businesses, government, and nonprofit organizations. He helped as many as he could. He prepared federal tax returns for farmers up and down the Red River Valley and across the state as well as for many of the plant services staff at the University. He was very active in the Greater North Dakota Association (GNDA). He prepared a Manual on Uniform Municipal Accounting which was of considerable help to local governments. Clifford was a very popular public speaker and was invited to speak at numerous events. He was asked to serve as the state chair for fund drives for several charities and was very active in the leadership of the Boy Scouts.

Clifford was so highly regarded for his business acumen that in 1961 a number of people in both the private and public sectors wished to have him named the Director of State Economic Development for North Dakota. Governor William Guy asked him to serve. Clifford declined. A "draft Clifford" group continued to push for him to accept and the Governor persisted. Clifford continued to decline. He explained that he thought he could best serve the state by staying at the University.

Evan Lips, from Bismarck and a member of the Senate Appropriations Committee of the North Dakota Legislative Assembly, recalled how Clifford and Starcher made their presentations to that body:

> Dr. Starcher would make the opening statement. Then Tom Clifford would give the details of the University budget . . . He had tremendous rapport. He knew them all by their names. He made a nice presentation, not long or drawn out, but to the point . . . He had it all in his head. Then he (Clifford) would visit with them (committee members) during the breaks. (Lips, 10/19/91).

Clifford's great finesse with the Legislature was an ability that would eventually contribute to his being considered for the presidency of the University.

In January of 1970 President George Starcher announced that he intended to retire on June 30, 1971. Faculty members of the Advisory Search Committee were elected by the faculty, student members were elected by the student body and the remaining members were either selected or appointed to represent the other constituencies of the University. History Professor D. Jerome Tweton chaired the 13-member committee. Other members of the committee were William E. Koenker, Vice President for Academic Affairs; A. William Johnson, Graduate Dean; William E. Cornatzer, Biochemistry; Robin D. Koppenhaver, Accounting; Donald P. Naismith, Mechanical Engineering; Edward O. Nelson, Mathematics; Russell Peterson, Education; John L. Rowe, Business Education; Evan Lips, alumnus and Bismarck business person; Garvin Stevens, Dean at UND Williston; and two students, Harlan Fugelsten and Steven Lund.

As the Committee members discussed the characteristics they sought in a new president, some argued that the University could best be served by an external candidate with a strong traditional academic record. Others on the committee argued that the critical need was for a president who could work well with the legislature and the public as well as the faculty and students. Those who held the latter view favored the selection of an internal candidate who knew the state and the University. The UND Alumni Association favored the second position, according to Executive Vice President Earl Strinden, and supported Tom Clifford as a candidate for the presidency (Strinden 2/2/91). Clifford was an attractive candidate to many because, in addition to his other qualifications and experience, he was someone who could restore public confidence in the University after the campus unrest of the late 1960s and 1970. As an ex-Marine, his patriotism was beyond reproach and, at the same time, he was trusted by persons of all points of view.

After a national search, the Advisory Search Committee sent the names of the first five finalists to the North Dakota State Board of Higher Education, as required. All five were external candidates. The committee had been sharply divided on the selections. Four candidates were interviewed in Grand Forks. The Board asked for the sixth ranked candidate, Tom Clifford. His name was added to the list. The Board interviewed two candidates in Bismarck. Clifford was the last to be interviewed. On January 13, 1971, the Board announced the selection of Clifford. The motion to select Clifford had been made by Fred Orth of Grand Forks and the second made by Albert Haas of New Rockford. The vote had been unanimous. The chair of the Board at the time was George Sinner of Casselton. Sinner would eventually become Governor of the state. At the time of his selection, Clifford was 49 years old, the first native North Dakotan to be selected as president and the first to have completed his undergraduate degree at the University.

The selection of Clifford was greeted with enthusiasm in the North Dakota press. Students at the University were especially enthusiastic as Clifford had long been a popular figure with them. Over 300 were reported to have written, called, or personally come to his office to congratulate him and many others spoke to him during registration "where he was helping students with their schedules" (Haga, 1971). The faculty was generally pleased, as well, though there was a segment which favored the strategy of bringing in someone from the outside. The Senate of the North Dakota Legislative Assembly passed a resolution commending Clifford as the new president of the University. The resolution noted that the members of the Senate "highly respect him as an administrator and value him as a friend . . ." (*Laws of North Dakota*, 1971). Such a resolution by a chamber of a State Legislature is highly unusual and gave an indication of the strength the new president would bring to his relationship with this important body.

Historian Elwyn Robinson made the following assessment of the president-elect:

> Dean Clifford had made a habit of hard work and taking responsibility. The Board of Higher Education, after dealing with him since 1959 as Vice President for

Finance, had confidence in him. Vigorous at forty-nine, he knew the state, the students, and the University administration. These things augured well for the future. (Robinson, 1973, p. 43)

Clifford and Starcher moved quickly to begin the transition. An announcement was made that Gerald M. Skogley, business manager and comptroller, would fill Clifford's old position of vice president for finance. Loren V. Swanson, director of auxiliary services would become vice president for operations, a position newly created by Clifford. Both would assume the positions on July 1. On the same date Gordon Kroeber became assistant to the president for facilities. Clifford proposed the creation of a President's Cabinet which would include the vice presidents. Starcher had met regularly with an administrative group comprised of the deans and the vice presidents. In a memorandum, Vice President Kroeber responded to the proposal of the president-elect:

I assume that the general guide would be that those topics which are primarily academic and which have relatively little bearing on general business or financial or student affairs would be dealt with in the Council of Deans. In contrast, those which relate to business operations, public relations, student policies (non-academic), and other University-wide issues would go to the Cabinet. There would also be some issues of importance to both groups, and which should therefore receive consideration by both. (Koenker, 1971, June 1)

Koenker also suggested that the director of university relations be a non-voting member of both groups in order to keep that person informed and to provide for communication with faculty, students, and the public. This new way of conducting the administrative affairs of the University was adopted. The new administration was rapidly taking shape.

Part Two

THE FIRST DECADE: THE 1970s

PRECEDING PAGE: Christian Marvin Anderson of Wahpeton, right, was the first student to have a degree conferred by new UND President Thomas J. Clifford. Anderson, of rural Wahpeton and a 1967 graduate of Wahpeton Senior High, received the bachelor of arts degree with a political science major at UND summer commencement exercises in August of 1971.

CHAPTER 2

THE EARLY YEARS

The summer and fall of 1971 was an eventful time for the nation and the world. The U.S. Supreme Court upheld the publication of the Pentagon Papers. The news reported continued violence in Belfast, Northern Ireland. The United States and United Kingdom announced on July 24 that they were supporting a military build-up in Iran. South African surgeon Christian Barnard transplanted a heart and lung on July 25. On July 31, Apollo 15 astronauts David R. Scott and James B. Irwin took the first ride in a vehicle on the surface of the moon. The Central Intelligence Agency admitted on August 2 that it had 30,000 men under arms in Laos. George Wallace announced on August 5 that he would be a candidate for President. United States Attorney General John Mitchell officially withdrew the Kent State University case on August 13. The United States House of Representatives passed the Equal Rights Amendment on October 12. An event of special importance to North Dakota was the announcement on November 5 that the United States would sell $136 million worth of grain to the U.S.S.R. President Nixon announced on November 12 that he would withdraw 45,000 more United States troops from Vietnam by February. The People's Republic of China was officially admitted to membership in the United Nations on November 15. Nixon would visit China that following spring. Former Soviet Premier Nikita Khrushchev, once one of the most powerful people in the world, died in obscurity.

In the world of entertainment and the arts, author John Updike published the second of the Rabbit novels, *Rabbit Redux. Look* magazine announced it would cease publication with its October 19 issue. Lee Trevino won the British Open. Walt Disney World opened in Florida and "A Clockwork Orange" was one of the year's most controversial films. "Jesus Christ Superstar" was probably the most talked-about record album. Popular songs on the top 40 included Rod Stewart's "Maggie May," Carol King's "It's Too Late," Janice Joplin's "Me and Bobby McGee," and Three Dog Night's "Joy to the World." Jazz great Louis Armstrong and rock singer James Morrison both died in July.

The first year of the new administration at the University of North Dakota was an eventful one. On July 6 Clifford announced that Art Raymond would begin duties on August 1 as the first director of Indian studies for the University. Raymond was a well-known Native American educator and journalist in the Dakotas. On July 22 the ground breaking took place for the new $1.8 million Winter Sports Arena. During July Clifford announced that he would initiate a long range planning process for the University and charged the vice president for academic affairs, W.E. Koenker, with the responsibility for developing the procedures. Koenker had been academic vice president since 1962. The new president wished to begin his administration with a major planning effort which would chart a course of action for the future. On August 19, Russell Brown was named the new vice president for student affairs. The enrollment that fall was 8,395, a 3.3 percent increase over the previous year.

Vice President Koenker lost no time in impressing upon the new president the poor condition of faculty salaries at the University. He sent a memo to Clifford on July 21, 1971, three weeks into the new administration. Attached to the memo was a study of faculty salaries at other similar universities. Koenker pointed out:

> . . . how low in comparison with other Category I institutions salaries at UND and North Dakota State University really are. It would seem that this situation has some ominous implications for the future and needs to be brought to the attention of the Board, some legislature committees, etc. It may also carry the implication for a need to consolidate some graduate programs in the state.   (Koenker, 1971, July 21)

This was not entirely new information, for surely Clifford was well aware of the issue, having served as vice president for finance and as dean of the college of business and public administration. But Koenker was addressing Clifford in his new capacity where the latter was in a position to do more about the issue of faculty salaries. In addition, Koenker may have been thinking of

Clifford's excellent reputation with the Legislature, as Clifford had skillfully testified before that body many times, and hoped that now as the new president he might be even more successful with that body. Koenker's reference to the consolidation of graduate programs calls to mind Robinson's "Too Much" theme. In any event, Koenker's warning about faculty salaries was to be prophetic.

As of July 30, 1971, the UND Branch Campus at Ellendale, which had suffered severe fire damage during the previous year, was officially closed. The closing had been authorized by the legislature. Nevertheless, it was a painful matter for everyone involved, especially those on the Ellendale campus and in that community. In years to come, pundits would remark that a disastrous fire seemed to be the only way the number of higher education institutions in the state could be reduced.

That summer the commencement ceremony was the occasion for the awarding of the first Doctor of Arts degree in Teaching. This new degree had been recommended by the Carnegie Commission in a national report as a degree more fitting than the Ph.D. for those who intended to serve primarily as teachers in higher education rather than primarily as researchers. The summer commencement was also the first time for the new president to confer degrees.

The New President Tours the State

The new president announced in September that he would make a number of visits across the state in order to expand communication between the public and the University. The visits would begin in October and take the president to a total of eight communities representing every section of the state. Maps depicting services provided by the University in each county were prepared and distributed as part of the advance publicity for the visits. The tours were carefully planned by the University Relations staff and the Alumni Association and sponsored by the latter. Each day started with a breakfast meeting and often a taping session with the local radio station. A portion of the tape was typically part of the hourly news report for the remainder of the day. A visit was made to the local newspaper and television station, as well. The president spoke to a service club at lunch time. He made guest appearances at the local schools and, in some cases, students arranged a reception for him. He also visited the college campus if one existed in that community. The tours were considered a great success and actually won a national award from a higher education public relations association.

This desire to take the message of the University out to the state and to mingle with the people would become a hallmark of the Clifford presidency. He would take to the road or airways many times in the years ahead to deliver his message to the people. He always had confidence that the citizens of the state would respond if they really understood the needs of the University.

Financial Changes and Planning Efforts

In 1971, Gerald Skogley, vice president for finance, was preparing to implement the new budget in 1971 when president Richard Nixon established a Pay Board and had all wages in the nation frozen. Skogley recalls that "everyone was on pins and needles" (Skogley, 1991). Finally, the national reaction to the wage freeze was so negative that Nixon relented and the policy was abandoned.

Skogley and Clifford shared the goal of streamlining the financial operations of the University. The first main-frame computer on campus had been acquired before Clifford became president and that greatly improved the ability to improve both the accuracy and the flow of information to assist with better management at all levels of the institution.

Clifford and Skogley were also very successful in their efforts to construct new buildings. Skogley recalls that there were 14 projects under way during one year. The University would sell bonds to pay for construction costs and then would pay off the debt with income generated by the facility. While this approach was not new, Clifford achieved significant savings by knowing how to predict the bond market. And he achieved further savings by refinancing the bonds at lower interest rates when that was possible. The president's skill not only enabled the University to acquire new buildings which otherwise might not have been approved by the state, but provided for savings of large sums of money (Hoffarth, 10/24/91).

In October 1971, the recommendations for the procedures for long-range planning were received by Clifford and adopted by the University Senate. This effort would be known as the Study Committee on Planning and Evaluation (SCOPE).

Students

Also in October of that year, a tragedy struck the campus when two students died in a fire in a fraternity house. Tony W. Stein, a resident of the house, had escaped, but re-entered the house to find Pamela M. Sturn and both perished ("Fraternity House Fire . . .", 1971). The campus was deeply saddened by this loss of life.

Two additional events of special interest and importance to students in 1971 are worthy of note. The University Senate, the governing body for the University, expanded the student membership from 10 to 14 students, and in December of that year, Evan Heustis of Devils Lake became the first student, at least in recent years, to speak at a University commencement ceremony.

For Christmas that first year, President and Mrs. Clifford decided not to send out Christmas cards. Instead, they donated funds to provide a chair-lift for the Chester Fritz Library to make it accessible to the disabled. This gesture would signal a determined effort by the president to make the entire campus accessible to the disabled during his presidency. This goal would take many years and significant resources, but it reflected Clifford's genuine and deep commitment to this important need. In this respect, the University was well ahead of most other campuses in the state.

At its December meeting, the North Dakota State Board of Higher Education discussed the possibility of elevating the Medical School at UND to a four-year degree granting program. The program at that time was providing only the first two years of study and North Dakota students were required to transfer to out-of-state programs to finish the medical degree. The development of a degree granting Medical School would become one of the new president's major goals.

New Colleges Organized

The development of a new college within a university is an important and relatively infrequent event. These early years would see the development of three new colleges at UND: the College of Fine Arts, the Center for Teaching and Learning, and the College for Human Resources Development. Most of the programs already existed in some form on the campus. The new colleges were developed as the result of realignment. Nevertheless, these realignments represented important programmatic as well as administrative changes.

In September of 1971, the State Board of Higher Education gave approval for a plan to form a College of Fine Arts (President Starcher presented the plan during the previous April). Starcher had long held the view that a College of Fine Arts was essential if UND was to flower into a complete liberal arts university. President Clifford continued to support that view.

The College of Fine Arts included Music and Visual Arts, which were transferred from the College of Education, while Theatre Arts was moved from the College of Arts and Sciences. William Boehle served as the acting dean of the College of Fine Arts from 1971 to 1972. The College was governed by a faculty committee during the 1972-73 year and in 1973 John Rogers was named dean.

Discussions had been under way for some time to consider how to reorganize the College of Education and the New School of Behavioral Studies in Education, two separate entities. Dean Vito Perrone, of the New School, which had been organized in 1968 as an alternative to traditional teacher education, had been seeking a way to move that unit from experimental status to a more lasting structure. Such considerations were necessary in light of the fact that much of the funding for the New School came from temporary federal grants. In addition, the New School had generated some controversy around the state because of some of its progressive and unusual methods. Perrone, a former college wrestler, was a gifted speaker and writer and made an unusually articulate spokesperson for school reform. President Starcher had appointed a committee on "Teacher Education for the 70s" which proposed the creation of a new unit to be called The Center for Teaching and Learning (CTL). The new Center would replace both the New School and the College of Education. Clifford received the second report from the committee in October of 1971. The University Senate supported the plan and it was approved by the State Board of Higher Education in January 1972, for implementation beginning July 1, 1972.

In February Perrone was appointed the dean of the new Center for Teaching and Learning. Dean Martelle Cushman of the College of Education had been at the University for 18 years and was deeply committed to the college and the philosophy which had guided it. He did not support the creation of the Center for Teaching and Learning and it must have been a painful time of transition for him. Nevertheless, Dean Perrone has acknowledged that Cushman cooperated with the transition. Perrone reports that the two corresponded several times during the following decade and Cushman continued to be greatly interested in CTL and the university which he had served for many years (Perrone, 1983, p. 37-38).

The combination of the School of Education and the New School resulted in a new alignment of several programs. The College for Human Resources Development (HRD) was conceived as a college devoted to programs that prepared students for careers in human services. The new college would include Physical Education and Recreation, Counseling and Guidance, and Industrial Technology, all from the College of Education, as well as Social Work from the College of Arts and Sciences, and Occupational Therapy from the School of Medicine. Dr. Henry Tomasek was recruited from the Political Science Department to serve as the dean. Library Science would be transferred to the College for Human Resources Development in 1973. The Business and Vocational Education Department was reassigned from the College of Education to the College of Business and Public Administration. Dr. Clair Rowe had been appointed dean of the College of Business and Public Administration when Clifford assumed the presidency.

SCOPE

On January 10. 1972, Clifford spoke to a group of 240 people to "kick-off" the Study Committee on Planning and Evaluation (SCOPE) effort. The strategy called for two stages, one to recommend plans for the next four or five years and a second stage to recommend plans projected into the 1980s. The new president's planning effort was under way.

Project Lignite

The research mission of the University received a boost when, in March of 1972, Project Lignite, directed by Donald Severson, received a $3.3 million grant from the United States Office of Coal Research. The purpose of the grant was to develop new methods of utilizing lignite coal. Western North Dakota was rich in lignite coal, but that particular type of coal had limited commercial uses. According to Severson, bituminous coal produces over twice the heat per ton as does lignite coal. The UND project focused on the liquefaction of lignite coal as a method to make it more commercially viable (Nelson, 1976). Dean of the School of Engineering and Mines Alan Fletcher would later remark that the Engineering Experiment Station, which included Project Lignite, was one of the most beneficial economic development activities in the state during this period (Fletcher, 10/17/91).

A Vote of Confidence

During the second year of the new administration, Vice President for Academic Affairs William E. Koenker sent a personal letter to Clifford which must have been much appreciated. Koenker had been the academic vice president for 10 years and was considerably older than Tom Clifford. Koenker's letter was dated October 2, 1972.

> Dear Tom:
>
> Before I leave on vacation, let me say some things that I have thought about during the past year and a quarter. I have had more real satisfaction from my work and there has been more of a challenge than there was previously. The sense of working at the vice president's level and with the deans in a coordinated effort makes part of the difference. Another part is your appreciation of our efforts and your willingness to express this appreciation. Your openness to exploring alternatives and your example of dedicated commitment also plays a part.
>
> I knew you could bring some very important strengths to the presidency. Your commitment during the past year makes me recognize that these potentialities have been and will continue to be attained to an extent exceeding even the best of our expectations. Let

me mention a few specifics. Your courage in doing the most difficult things and making the hardest decisions, but taking great care where some people are adversely affected to minimize this and the "hurt" involved. Your concern about people has always been characteristic and this continues to come through as your decisions affect a wider range of people. You must have given some careful thought to ordering your priorities as to time and attention because you seem to have time for the important concerns and yet dispose of the details.

One suggestion — a return of one you have made to me. Take care of yourself. Apart from your family and personal considerations, and looked at from an accountant's or an economist's point of view, your health is a principal University asset, non-insurable and protected only by minimizing all avoidable risks. Even with your stamina and discipline and keeping yourself in good physical condition, you can't keep up your recent pace. You, too, need some time away from the constant pressure and harassment.

Sincerely,

(signed)

William E. Koenker
Vice President for Academic Affairs

New Buildings

The first two years of the new administration saw the completion of major building projects. In 1971 the Upson I facility for engineering, named after Maxwell Mayhew Upson, was completed at a cost of $1.5 million. The building was constructed southeast of Harrington Hall. A new auditorium, which was named in honor of university benefactor Chester Fritz, was completed in 1972 and was to become the center of major cultural events on the campus and the Grand Forks community. The auditorium was built on the west side of the English Coulee along and south of University Avenue at a cost of just over $3 million. It is an imposing structure which dominates the west side of the campus. The auditorium features a lovely open foyer reaching four stories high in which hangs a Dalambert chandelier made in Italy. The chandelier was donated by their many friends in honor of President and Mrs.

Starcher. The auditorium seats 2,300 on the main floor and in two balconies. The dedication of the Chester Fritz Auditorium in October of 1972 was a gala event attended by approximately 2,400 people.

Another major event that year was the dedication of the new Winter Sports Center in January. The Center was built just east of the Memorial (football) Stadium and south of Second Avenue at a cost of nearly $2 million, and replaced the old "barn," as it was affectionately known to Sioux hockey fans. The last series played in the barn was in March of 1972. The new facility provided a much warmer and more modern setting for the major intercollegiate and only Division I sport at the University. It is interesting to note that there was very little state funding involved in these building projects.

In February of 1972, in a letter to alumni, the president announced plans for the addition of a new library to the law school building. The library would be named in honor of Dean Emeritus Olaf Thormodsgard. The same letter carried the announcement for the construction of a new rehabilitation hospital to be located in the medical park which was being developed along Columbia Road south of the campus. The letter also announced that the doctoral program in psychology had been accredited for the first time and the physical therapy program had been accredited, as well. The accreditation of all of the professional programs at the University was to become one of the president's major goals.

The Inauguration of the President

As is often the case, the official inauguration of the president took place some months after his assuming the office. The inauguration for Clifford was held on April 14, 1972. It was a festive event with over 300 people marching in the procession. The charge to the president was given by the Reverend Peter Hinrich, chair of the North Dakota State Board of Higher Education and the new president was welcomed by Student Body President Bill DiBrito. In his speech Clifford explained his understanding of the meaning of the event by saying, "I prefer to think of this inauguration as a symbolic event, with the importance of the ceremony the historical continuity of the University" (Retallic, 1972). He clearly acknowledged that one of the strengths of his appointment was that he represented continuity for the University. In his remarks Clifford said,

> I recognize as my first responsibility the continued effort
> to maintain an intellectually stimulating environment,
> and outstanding faculty, imaginative and productive
> research activities, and dedicated supporting staff.
> (Retallic, 1972)

Clifford also noted that "the watchword for the seventies will be accountability." He was certainly correct in that assessment.

Yearbook Discontinues

In April the Board of Student Publications brought an era to an end when it voted to discontinue the Dacotah Annual yearbook. Ralph Perkins, a member of the Board, noted that "no applicants for next year's editor, a lack of interest, and the limited finances here" led to the decision ("BOSP Discontinues . . ." 4/21/72). The demise of the yearbook was a sign of the times as such things were out of style.

The Chester Fritz Professorships

During this same period, an exchange of letters took place between Clifford and benefactor Chester Fritz. Fritz was living abroad at the time. A balance existed in the account which had been set aside for the construction of the auditorium and a decision needed to be made about an appropriate use for those funds. A plan to do something to honor the outstanding faculty of the University began to take shape. Fritz wrote to Clifford on April 13, 1972, with a proposal that the funds be " . . . paid to such members of the faculty who have been selected by a committee, to reward them for exceptional instruction to students." Clifford wrote back on May 11, saying that he liked the proposal, suggesting that the awards be known as the "Chester Fritz Distinguished Professorship" and expressing his belief that the awards " . . . would have a real impact on the quality of instruction in the University. . . ." A letter dated May 12 from Fritz to Clifford outlined the specific financial arrangements which were to be made, including the bank where Fritz wanted the funds to be administered. Fritz made the observation that he was especially interested in this project " . . . because the greatness of any University depends, to a very great extent upon the quality of its individual faculty members." While it was clear that Fritz valued academics, as his gift to the library certainly indicated, this new program would serve as a symbolic reminder of Fritz's belief that the University would only be as great as the individual members of the faculty.

The arrangements were made and Clifford notified Fritz in June that the first awards would be made during the 1973-74 academic year. The president went on to note that those involved in the discussion at UND were very enthusiastic about the idea. The plan was carried forward and the following spring the first faculty members to receive the honor were selected and announced at the annual Founders Day banquet and ceremony. Clifford wrote to Fritz on May 2, 1973, to inform him of the names of those selected and to describe the event. The three professors selected were Dr. William E. Cornatzer of Biochemistry, John L. Rowe of Business Education, and Donald E.

Severson of Chemical Engineering. All three were chairs of their departments.

The awards would be given every year thereafter (except for 1986 for which no records could be found). Faculty are eligible to receive the award more than once and several have. The Chester Fritz Distinguished Professorship has become the highest honor the University bestows upon a member of the faculty. Those who have received this high distinction, through 1991, are listed here, followed by the years in which the award was received and the person's rank and academic department.

Robert Beck, (1975, 1976, 1977), Professor of Law

Richard E. Beringer, (1988), Professor of History

William F. Cornatzer, (1973, 1974), Professor of Biochemistry and
    Molecular Biology

Kenneth J. Dawes, (1987), Professor of Social Work

Ronald C. Engle, (1989), Professor of Theatre Arts

Carla W. Hess, (1987), Professor of Communication Disorders

Harvey Knull, (1988), Professor of Biochemistry and Molecular Biology

Richard G. Landry, (1991), Professor of Education

Robert W. Lewis, (1990), Professor of English

Frank N. Low, (1975, 1976, 1977), Professor of Anatomy

Robert C. Nordlie, (1974, 1975, 1976, 1985), Professor of Biochemistry
    and Molecular Biology

Lewis W. Oring, (1987), Professor of Biology

Surendra S. Parmar, (1989), Professor of Physiology

Brian O. Paulsen, (1990), Professor of Visual Arts

Russell Peterson, (1984, 1985), Professor of Education

John L. Rowe, (1973, 1974), Professor of Business and Vocational
    Education

Donald E. Severson, (1973, 1974, 1978, 1979, 1980, 1981, 1982, 1983,
    1984), Professor of Chemical Engineering

William F. Sheridan, (1991), Professor of Biology

Virgil I. Stenberg, (1977, 1984), Professor of Chemistry

D. Jerome Tweton, (1989), Professor of History

Stephen K. Wikel, (1987), Professor of Microbiology and Immunology

Sharon C. Wilsnack, (1989), Professor of Neuroscience

Progress on Several Issues

A number of developments during the early 1970s indicated that the University and President Clifford were sensitive to the issues of the day and the changing responsibility of higher education. During the summer of 1972, for example, a Committee on Indian Awareness was formed (Jeanotte, 2/1/91).

Some members of the committee and others expressed concern that some of the imagery which had developed around the "Fighting Sioux" logo was inappropriate. There was agreement that the name "Sioux" for teams was not a problem. However, a cartoon caricature of an Indian with crossed eyes and a feather in his hair, known as "Sammy Sioux," was considered to be offensive. The character was removed by the Athletic Department and a new logo was designed and approved by the committee and the University. Only officially sanctioned logos would be permitted in the future. The Native American student organization started sponsoring an annual powwow on campus and that tradition has continued for some 20 years up to the present.

The summer of 1972 saw the beginning of construction on the new Rehabilitation Hospital. It was the first building to be located in what would become the Grand Forks Medical Park located on south Columbia Road. That same summer Ruby McKenzie, who had served as Registrar and Admissions Director, concluded 42 years of service to the University and retired.

During February of 1973, a Women's Center was opened in Budge Hall. The Center was staffed by volunteers during the early days of operation. Women's issues continued to receive attention on campus during the years ahead. Eventually the Center found a more permanent home and a paid staff person was provided. Later that spring the student body granted authority for the Student Senate to be expanded from 14 to 26 members. The new members represented each of the academic units on campus. Another event of note that same spring was the awarding of a grant from the United States Department of Health, Education and Welfare (HEW) to assist in developing a campus television station. During that summer a new director for the Chester Fritz Library was secured as Edward Warner arrived from Baltimore. Warner served in that capacity for most of the remainder of the Clifford years.

The report from the SCOPE planning committee, presented to the president on March 15, 1973, was 63 pages long and represented extensive involvement by 42 subcommittees with membership from the many constituencies of the University. As the introduction to the report noted, 350 persons took part in the planning process including 180 faculty, 100 staff, 70 students, as well as alumni, representatives from the community and the State Board of Higher Education. Copies of the report were circulated widely on and off campus. To the extent that adequate involvement in the planning process was an important goal, the process had clearly succeeded. The report contained 246 recommendations.

Clifford Appointed to Two Boards of Directors

In June of 1973 President Clifford was elected chair of the Council of Presidents. The Council was made up of all of the presidents of the institutions governed by the North Dakota State Board of Higher Education. Clifford soon became an influential member of the Council. That same year Clifford was elected as a director to two regional boards, the board of the Bush Foundation and the board of Otter Tail Power Company. Clifford's acceptance of the position on the Otter Tail Board stirred a minor controversy. The Farmer's Union and the Minot newspaper raised questions about a possible conflict of interest for a president of a public institution serving on a corporate board. That view gained little support across the state and at the next meeting of the State Board of Higher Education the entire issue was ignored.

In November of 1973 President Clifford was elected to serve on the board of directors of the Bush Foundation, the largest philanthropic foundation in the region. Later, Clifford became the chair of the Bush Foundation Board and provided valuable leadership to the Foundation as it awarded significant grants to institutions of higher education in the Dakotas and Minnesota. It became evident to most that these posts were expressions of the high regard held for the president's leadership ability, business acumen, and public spirit. He had also served as the chair of the North Dakota Easter Seal campaign and other charitable causes. If the cause was a good one, Clifford was not above some public antics. In that spirit, he supported the local Muscular Dystrophy fund drive by swallowing a goldfish. Various persons had pledged donations totaling $1,000 to the fund drive for each goldfish consumed.

The Need for Open Communication

President Clifford was greatly concerned about communication with students during these early years. This was the period in which there had been much student unrest on many campuses. At Kent State University on May 4, 1970, the Ohio National Guard had fired into a crowd of protesting students, killing four and wounding nine. At about this same time an incident took place at UND involving then Vice President Clifford. A student group had gathered in front of the Reserve Officers Training Corps (ROTC) facility on campus to protest the Vietnam War. In order to mediate the situation, Clifford stood in the doorway of the ROTC building and addressed the crowd. A serious altercation did not develop, perhaps because of Clifford's intervention. Now, as president, Clifford wanted to keep the channels of communication open on the campus and so announced that he would meet with students on a scheduled basis for a series of "Chats with the President" during the 1973-74 academic year. A similar series was also scheduled for the faculty. These sessions gave faculty and students alike the opportunity to ask questions and make suggestions and also gave Clifford the opportunity to test ideas and explain his decisions. These sessions continued for several years until interest waned. Clifford recognized the importance of communication with internal constituencies as well as with those external to the University.

Lawrence Welk Visits the Campus

On September 24, 1973, band director and television personality Lawrence Welk visited the University for a day. Originally from Strasburg, North Dakota, Welk was probably the best known native of the state. He visited music classes and directed the University Band in a special concert at the Chester Fritz Auditorium. The sponsors of the visit underestimated the response and the auditorium was filled to capacity. Realizing that the brief program which had been prepared with the band would not be adequate for such a crowd, Welk sent for his accordion and played several numbers himself. The Lawrence Welk Foundation made a significant gift to the UND Alumni Association.

The College of Engineering

In the early 1970s the College of Engineering began formal and informal efforts to support the entry of more women in the field of engineering. Even though the first woman graduate in engineering received her degree in 1916, the total number of women graduates had reached only eight by 1971. In 1974 a Student Section of the Society of Women Engineers was chartered on the UND campus. The organization has been highly successful. It received recognition as the best student section in the region for four years (1982, 1986, 1988, and 1989) and national recognition as the best student section for three years (1982, 1986, 1989). It was the first in the nation to receive the distinction of winning the national award three times. The most telling evidence of success is that 180 women have graduated from the UND engineering program as of the spring of 1990 and, at that time, 14 percent of the enrollment in the college were women (Medalen, 1991). President Clifford, Vice President Alice Clark, and Dean of Engineering Alan Fletcher, all gave their enthusiastic support to the organization. Clifford was made an honorary member in 1989. Joyce I. Medalen served as the director of the Women in Engineering Program during all of these years.

The existence of two engineering schools within the state, one at UND and another at North Dakota State University (NDSU) in Fargo, had long been a source of some contention and another example, in some minds, of the "Too Much" problem in the state. At the October 1974 meeting of the State Board of Higher Education, the presidents of the two universities had reported that discussions were under way to devise a plan which would coordinate the two programs and share one dean between them. By the time of the December meeting, however, Clifford and President Laurel Loftsgard of NDSU reported to the Board that discussions had failed. Alan Fletcher, dean of the UND School of Engineering and Mines at that time, has indicated that he and Clifford never withdrew their support for the plan (Fletcher, 10/17/91). The existence of two engineering schools within the state emerged as an issue from time to time subsequently but a solution remained illusive.

An Accreditation Profile of the University — 1973

The documents which were prepared for the accreditation of the University in 1974 provide a portrait of the institution at that time. The total (full-time equivalent) enrollment for the 1973-74 academic year was 7,476. The subtotals by degree level were 6,494 undergraduates, 632 graduate students, and 350 professional students. The mean ACT score for entering freshmen in the 1972-73 class was 22.3, compared with 21.6 at other North Dakota four-year institutions, 22.2 for similar types of institutions nationally, and 20.0 for all colleges and universities nationally. UND seniors and graduates who took the Graduate Record Examination, a test utilized for admission to graduate schools, also scored somewhat above the national norms (Basic Institutional Data for North Central Association Review, 1974, pp. I, 1-4; II, 5-9).

The faculty profile indicated 460 full-time faculty at the instructor rank and above, 408 excluding medicine, according to the Office of Institutional Research. Women held 83 of these positions for 20 percent of the total, excluding medicine. The doctoral degree was held by 237 or 52 percent of these faculty. In addition, the University employed 43 part-time faculty at the instructor rank and above. The average salary for full-time faculty at the full professor rank was $17,979; at the associate professor rank, $13,944; at the assistant professor rank, $11,905; and at the instructor rank, $9,499 (Basic Institutional Data for North Central Review, 1974, p. III, 10). The Chester Fritz Library reported a total of 302,923 books (p. V. 17). Total expenditures by the University were $27,666,105 (p. IV, 14). The value of the physical plant was reported at $62,167,038 (p. IV, 15).

These data reflected a healthy and growing institution which was fiscally sound. The one exception, which seemed to be a constant through the years, was the inadequate support for faculty salaries. UND continued to lag far behind both regional and national averages for similar institutions in this one important respect and in spite of the best efforts of capable administrative leaders. Robinson's theme of "economic disadvantage" was familiar to the faculty and staff during these years, as it had been in the past.

Native American Programs

The 1970s was a time when there was growing concern about the role of minorities in our society in general and in higher education in particular. The primary concern at the University of North Dakota was for the American Indian population of the state. In the late 1960s an American Indian Student organization had been formed on the campus. It began with just a handful of members but grew over the years until it was one of the largest student organizations on the campus by the 1980s. In 1971 the Legislature approved an Indian Studies program at the University. This legislative action indicated a recognition that the University was regarded as the campus in North Dakota with a particular mission to serve American Indian students. In 1976-77 two additional developments took place which sharpened this role: The Legislature approved and funded a Native American Programs unit within the Division of Student Affairs at the University, and the Indian Studies Program was granted departmental status within the College of Arts and Sciences, a move which further validated the place of the program in the academic sector of the University.

Early in the discussions within the University, there was agreement that any effective effort to focus on American Indian programs would have to proceed on two fronts, the academic front and the student services front (Jeanotte, 2/1/91). Both would be essential in providing a well rounded and successful program, not only for the American Indian students themselves, but also in order to fulfill this important mission of the University. In the early years, the Native American Culture Center was housed in the old depot building which later became the parking office. The location was given the name "Anashinobay Aki" which is Chippewa for "Land of the Original People." In June of 1972 the program moved to the present location at 2419 Second Avenue North, east of the Memorial Stadium. The new location was named "Metu Ta Tunke" which means "East Village." American Indian students urged that a staff person be added in the Division of Student Affairs and in 1974 Flo Wiger was appointed the first assistant to the vice president for Student Affairs for Native American Programs.

A host of special support programs on campus and special outreach programs off campus were developed during these years. Within the Division of Student Affairs a Student Opportunities Program was developed which provided an array of support services for Native American students. Later that program was merged into the Student Support Services program. The services included tutoring, career counseling, financial counseling and support, and job placement. The Upward Bound and Trio Programs provided outreach to minority and low income high school students and brought them to the campus during the summer. These and other services were deployed in an effort to reach students early and provide the necessary support for them through the college experience to the point of employment. This strategy seems to be effective as evidenced by retention and graduation rates when UND is compared to other similar institutions.

Several academic programs were also developed during this same period.

Most were supported by federal funds. The list is impressive and includes the Medex Program (physician assistant), the INMED Program (discussed in more detail later), the Teacher Corps (a cooperative project between the Center for Teaching and Learning and the schools on the Turtle Mountain, Standing Rock and Devils Lake Sioux reservations), Future Indian Teachers, the Bilingual Education Program, and special programs for Native American students in counseling, geography, library science, education, educational administration (Project IDEAL), and engineering. The Satellite Program at one point had an entry level educational program located on each of the reservations in the region. Some of these efforts survived reductions or total elimination of federal funding, but tight budgets at the University did not permit the continuation of many. Project IDEAL, led by Professor Donald Lemon, prepared American Indian school administrators at the graduate level and lasted well into the 1980s. Twenty-seven graduates of the program were identified in a final report, a majority of whom had returned to administer schools in the region (Lemon, 1988). The good that these programs accomplished can only be estimated. It is clear, however, that they greatly strengthened educational opportunities in the Native American communities as well as at the University. It is unfortunate that the support for such important efforts has been greatly reduced at the federal level. These programs provided benefits in both directions. The University has been greatly enriched by the presence of American Indian students and the presence of these programs on the campus.

African American Program

An organization for African American students took shape during the same period. In 1973 a house owned by the University and located at 2315 Second Avenue North was made available for a Black Student Center. In 1974 there were approximately 40 African American students at UND. By 1977 there were approximately 60 African American students on campus. In 1979 the Center was moved to a house on University Avenue near the Memorial Union and was renamed the Era Bell Thompson Cultural Center in honor of the UND graduate who had become a well-known journalist and an editor for *Ebony* magazine. President Clifford read the formal dedication statement during Black History Week, February 11-16, 1979. During this period several prominent African American leaders came to the campus to speak during Black History Week including United States Congressmen John Conyers of Michigan (1975), and Ron Dellums of California (1977); Minnesota Vikings football great Alan Page (1976), and television newscaster and journalist Ed Bradley (1979). In 1980 an athletic scholarship was established by the local Masonic Lodge in honor of Jack Mayfield, African American boxer and long-time resident of Grand Forks.

Changing Student Lifestyles

The 1970s was a time of changing values and lifestyle for students. The old legal concept of "in loco parentis," which had granted parental authority to college and university officials, was passing away. Students demanded to have more freedom and wished to take more responsibility for their own lives. President Clifford was sympathetic to the desire of students but left the development of specific policies to the appropriate student affairs processes (Henry, 1/28/91). Similar to campuses all across the nation, policies began to change at UND. Residence halls were open to 24 hour visitation rather than having restricted visiting periods. Sexist policies that imposed strict hours only on women students were lifted. Coeducational residence halls were established. These changes met with disapproval by some citizens of the state, but many others found it difficult to disagree with the argument made by students that if they were capable of fighting a war in Vietnam, they should be free to decide what time to return to their rooms or whether they might choose to reside in a residence hall which housed members of the opposite sex.

The College of Nursing

Important changes were also taking shape in the nursing program at UND during the 1970s. The program had been growing and was housed in two locations, in parts of Robertson and Sayre Halls. Quarters were cramped and faculty were doubled and sometimes tripled in one office. Efforts had been under way by Dean Margaret Heyse and others to secure funding for a new building, but funds at both the federal and state levels had not been forthcoming. Finally, in the spring of 1974 funding in the amount of $1.4 million was awarded by the federal Department of Health, Education and Welfare (HEW), thanks to the work of the North Dakota Congressional delegation, especially the senior Senator Milton Young (Cory, 1982). On June 2, 1975, ground was broken near Robertson Hall for the new building. The building was occupied in 1976, just one year before the retirement of Dean Heyse. She provided distinguished leadership to the University and the nursing profession in the state and region for some 19 years. During the 1977-79 biennium, special appropriations were approved by the state to increase the size of the faculty in the College of Nursing from 33 to 40. Dean Elisabeth Zinser was instrumental in securing these additional resources for the college. President Clifford provided additional funds to the college for recruitment of new faculty. The program continued to flourish, and in 1978 the college received a grant from the Bremer Foundation to study the feasibility of developing a master's degree program. During subsequent years the Legislature provided additional funding to establish a graduate program in nursing. (Merrill, 2/28/91).

Athletics

The football teams of the early 1970s did very well under Head Coach Jerroll "Jerry" Olson, a native of Hoople, North Dakota. The 1971 team won the North Central Intercollegiate Athletic Conference (NCIAC) title with a 5-1-0 record. The thriller of the season, of course, was the game against major rival North Dakota State University (NDSU) in Fargo with a 23-7 Sioux victory over the Bison. Adding sweetness to the victory was bringing to a halt the Bison's 36 game winning streak, the longest in the nation, according to Lee Bohnet, UND Sports Information Director. Linebacker Jim LeClair was named to the Little All American team and went on to play for the Cincinnati Bengals. Head Coach Ruben Bjorkman's hockey team finished third in the Western Collegiate Hockey Association (WCHA) that year.

The 1972 football team missed a perfect record by a single loss to NDSU. The conference ended in a three way tie between UND, NDSU, and the University of South Dakota. UND was selected to represent the conference in the national Camellia Bowl game at Sacramento, California, where the Sioux defeated California Polytechnic-San Luis Obispo by a score of 38-21. Mike Deutsch was later named to the Little All American team. The hockey team that year opened the season in the new arena but skated to a disappointing seventh place in the conference. The 1974 football team finished with another three way tie for the conference title behind outstanding players Bill Deutsch, Dale Kasowski, and Ron Gustafson. Bill became the second Deutsch to be named to the Little All American team.

Coach Dave Gunther's 1974-75 basketball team won conference and regional titles with notable performances by Mark Lindahl and Jim Goodrich. The team swept for the third consecutive season to the NCIAC and regional titles in 1975-76. The 1975-76 football team made it to the national playoffs undefeated but lost that game before a home crowd to Livingston (Alabama) University. Predictions that the frigid North Dakota weather would assist the Sioux proved to be false.

Leonard Marti, who had been serving as athletic director since 1958, retired in June of 1976. A search for a new athletic director produced Carl R. Miller from neighboring South Dakota. The football team that year struggled through a tough season but Gunther's cagers rose to a 42 year best season with a 26-4 record and a fourth straight NCIAC championship.

A changing of the guard in two top coaching slots marked the next academic year. Olson resigned after another tough year on the gridiron and new Athletic Director Miller promoted Eugene V. Murphy, a UND graduate and member of the coaching staff for 12 years to the head spot. Likewise, Bjorkman resigned after another disappointing year for the skaters and Miller named another UND graduate and member of the coaching staff, John "Gino"

Gasparini, to the head spot. The *Grand Forks Herald* sports staff was embarrassed by its prediction that Ned Harkness, a former coach for the Detroit Red Wings, Cornell, and Rensselaer Polytechnic, would receive the top hockey post at UND (Bohnet, p. 109).

A high point of the 1978-79 year was the remarkable season of the hockey team which won the last game of the season against Minnesota to win the Western Collegiate Hockey Association (WCHA) title. The team sailed through the playoffs undefeated and went on to the National Collegiate Athletic Association (NCAA) tournament in Detroit where they eliminated Dartmouth. The Minnesota team finally gained revenge as they defeated the Sioux by 4-3 for the championship. Center Kevin Maxwell and goaltender Bob Iwabuchi were named to the All American team.

The 1979 football team regained its footing and won the NCIAC title but fell in the first game of post season play. Paul Muckenhirn made the All American team. It was another championship year, however, for the hockey team when they emerged victorious from the nationals at Providence, Rhode Island, where they defeated both Dartmouth and Northern Michigan. Doug Smail scored four goals in the championship game and Mark Taylor and Howard Walker made the All American team.

Women's athletics at UND in the 1970s were ahead of many programs in the region but still were not strong. Helen Smiley made a considerable effort to build the programs during this period. Patricia Warcup coached women's basketball during the 1960s and into the 1970s, but the going was slow without the advantage of being able to offer scholarships to excellent players (Bohnet, p. 115). Dietta "Dee" Watson provided leadership for field hockey and basketball teams for five years during the mid 1970s. Margaret Peterson took over the field hockey program for the 1977-78 season and strengthened that sport to the point where the 1980-81 team had a 28-7 record and placed sixth in the Association for Intercollegiate Athletics for Women (AIAW) national tournament at Southern Illinois University.

The UND Alumni Association

The UND Alumni Association would undergo a significant reorganization during the middle and late 1970s. J. Lloyd Stone, long-time director of the association, retired in 1973. Earl Strinden, Stone's assistant, had been on the staff at UND since 1969 and was selected as the new executive vice president of the Alumni Association. (Coincidentally, Strinden had been the assistant house majority leader in the North Dakota Legislative Assembly under house majority leader Bryce Streibel until 1974 when Streibel stepped down and Strinden was elected the new majority leader.) With the reins of the Alumni Association in his own hands, Strinden began to make some sweeping changes.

In 1975 the old UND Development Fund was dissolved and a new University of North Dakota Foundation was established. The Foundation was a separate, not-for-profit corporation. However, it would share the same executive director and the same board of directors with the Alumni Association. Strinden had observed alumni operations at other universities and had learned from their successes and their mistakes. He noted that this dual organization under one executive and board was "carefully crafted" because he had observed that when the two were entirely separate "there was animosity and a breakdown in communication and cooperation between the two organizations" at other campuses. "I was determined that would not happen here" (Strinden, 1991). The incorporators of the new corporation were Earl Strinden, Tom Clifford, and Gerald Skogley.

These organizational changes, the computerization of the records systems, the change in the format of the *Alumni Review*, the revitalization of on- and off-campus alumni events, and the comprehensive deferred and planned giving program, along with promoting the establishment of named endowments, were significant changes which strengthened the Alumni Association and alumni and friend support for the University of North Dakota. The UND Development Fund had $350,000 in assets in 1974 (Rylance, 1983). By 1982 the Foundation had $12 million in assets. In the 1990-91 Annual Report the assets were listed at $38.7 million.

There is some indication that during the Starcher and Stone administrations some tension had existed between the University and the Alumni Association. While both were certainly working for a common purpose, the Alumni Association had a strong and independent board of directors who were not always as responsive to Starcher's wishes as he would have liked. In addition, Starcher and Stone may not have had the closest of working relationships, themselves. The Clifford and Strinden period was characterized, on the other hand, by a very cooperative and congenial relationship between the University and the alumni organizations. Strinden has said, "I have not stuck my nose into Tom's business, interfered or interjected myself into what Tom Clifford was doing as president of the University nor has Tom interfered, interjected or usurped in any way what I do — our working relationship has been very good" (Strinden, 2/2/91). The fact that Clifford was an alumnus, himself, and a very popular one at that, and was an active member of the boards of the Association and the Foundation, was a major asset. Clifford knew alumni from several generations and knew them well. He often traveled to alumni gatherings across the nation. Clifford understood the importance of a strong and effective alumni association and foundation. Strinden's own ability to relate well to alumni should not be underestimated. He was a master at treating people well and making them feel confident that their gifts were both appreciated and would be administered in the most effective and professional manner. The entire operation was simply a first-class act.

Strinden was in a potentially difficult situation with his dual role with the Legislature and the UND Alumni Association. While he always had the best interests of higher education and the University in mind, he has explained that he could not be the house majority leader in the Legislature "carrying water for one institution" but had to keep his eye to balancing the entire state budget (Strinden, 2/2/91). While some may have wondered if Clifford and Strinden plotted behind the scenes to further the aims of the University with the Legislature, there is no evidence to support such a view. In fact, Strinden was known for his ability to fashion budget compromises during the legislative sessions. In these "Strinden budgets," higher education and the University took their share of adjustments along with other state programs and agencies. Strinden has commented that Clifford always "respected and understood my role" in the Legislature and there was never any "heavy handed or high pressure lobbying by UND" (Strinden, 2/2/91). There can be little doubt that Clifford's skill with the Legislature and Strinden's strategic position in the same body were vitally important during these years. One can only speculate as to how the University and higher education might have fared during this period had either of these two figures been absent from the North Dakota scene.

The economy of the state improved during the middle 1970s and this translated into catch-up salary increases for the University. The grain sales to the Soviet Union were a boon to North Dakota farmers and the energy market was more favorable than it had been. The state appropriations to the University increased form $18.57 million for the 1973-74 biennium to $27.85 million for the 1975-76 biennium, a 50 percent increase. This was the best year for funding for higher education in many years and would be the watershed biennium during the Clifford years. The University would never see such a large increase, or anything near it, during the 1980s.

Professor D. Jerome Tweton, chair of the History Department since 1965, in reflecting on the early years of the new administration, concluded that the theme was continuity. In fact, he observed, these early years could be described as the "Starcher-Clifford years" because of the extensive continuity with the previous administration (Tweton, 10/22/91).

The continuity of personnel in many administrative positions, for example, is certainly accurate in many respects, and yet it is important to recognize the significant new developments which took shape during these early years. One of the most far-reaching and significant, the development of a four-year medical school, deserves a more detailed account and is the subject of the next chapter.

CHAPTER 3

THE SCHOOL OF MEDICINE: NORTH DAKOTA'S OWN

The Clifford years were especially significant for the School of Medicine. A history of the Medical School, *The History of UND School of Medicine: 1979,* written by Vonda Kay Redman (Somerville), was utilized extensively for this account (Redman, 1979). Edward E. Waldron's (1987) *From House Calls to HMOs: A History of Organized Medicine in North Dakota,* and A.D. McCannel's (1956) *Medical Milestones in North Dakota* are two additional written records which include references to UND's Medical School. The most significant change during the Clifford years was the transformation of the School of Medicine from a two-year transfer program to a four-year degree-granting program. Yet this change took place in stages over a lengthy period of time and is a story of political skill, personal dedication, and dogged persistence. Only some of that story can be told here.

It is difficult to know when the idea of a four-year medical school for North Dakota was first considered. No doubt many had harbored such a wish for many years, even if it seemed difficult if not impossible to achieve. North Dakota lawmakers legislated and later rescinded a four-year program as early as 1953 (Vennes, 1991). The two-year program in place at UND in the early 1970s seemed to be working fairly well. When President Clifford took office, according to Redman, he reviewed the condition of the several colleges on campus and thought to himself, "Well, there's a two-year program over at the Medical School that's running well and is pretty well funded. That one's not going to be a problem" (p. 10). But, wrote Redman, Clifford added with amusement that this situation lasted all of three months.

External events were mounting pressure on the UND medical program and others similar to it. The Carnegie Commission on Higher Education produced an influential report *Higher Education and the Nation's Health: Policies for Medical and Dental Education* (1970), recommending that all two-year programs be phased out or converted to degree-granting programs. Partly in response to this report and related concerns, Senator Pell of Rhode Island sponsored legislation and the Congress provided appropriations for "conversion grants" for medical programs which were willing to make the transition (Vennes, 1991). At the same time the American Medical Association was attempting to counter the growing tendency of physicians to focus on narrow specializations by developing a new specialty in family practice. This new specialty would be especially suited for the practice of medicine in North Dakota. In addition, the Medical School staff began to learn that the out-of-state programs, to which UND students transferred after the second year of medical study, were projecting that they would soon be unable to accept such transfers. Medical education was in a state of considerable transition. These developments provided the context for the events which transpired in North Dakota in the 1970s.

Within North Dakota important developments were taking shape as well. Three staff members in the School of Medicine, Drs. Robert Eelkema, Wallace Nelson and John Vennes, became concerned about the future of the Medical School and initiated discussion with key constituents around the state. Dr. Willard A. Wright, who had practiced medicine in Williston, was serving as the executive director of the North Dakota Regional Medical Program, an agency of the North Dakota Medical Association. Dr. Wright shared that concern and took steps to secure approval for a study. The report which resulted from that study, known as the *Dunn Report,* outlined the alternatives faced by the state. The consultant, Gary Dunn, noted that in his interviews across the state there were about as many physicians who opposed the idea of a degree-granting program at UND as supported the idea (Redman, p. 12). The report presented the consequences of the various alternatives, and in May of 1972, the North Dakota Medical Association reached a conclusion and endorsed the concept of a degree-granting program at UND. A 16 member liaison committee was appointed to work with the University and the Legislature to further this goal (Redman, p. 13). The North Dakota Legislature was aware of the issue, and in December 1971, the Legislative Council established a Committee on Medical Education and Services to study the matter and make recommendations to the Legislature. Bryce Streibel, legislator from Fessenden, was the chair of the Legislative Council at this time and was instrumental in gaining support in the legislative assembly for the upgrading of the Medical School.

President Clifford established a Medical Affairs Committee for the University on July 10, 1972, and asked Eelkema, Vennes, and Nelson to serve on the committee. Their charge was to study all of the alternatives and make specific recommendations to the president. Clifford also gave them the authority to represent the University with external groups on this issue. Eelkema, the chair of the committee, announced shortly that task forces would be established in Minot, Bismarck, Fargo and Grand Forks. These task forces would be called upon to provide valuable information and advice.

In August of 1972, a delegation from the state, which included representatives of the University, the Legislature, and the medical profession, attended a conference at Michigan State University on the organization and implementation of a degree-granting medical school. The dean at the Grand Rapids campus was Dr. Tom M. Johnson.

The federal Department of Health, Education and Welfare (HEW) announced a new program in 1972 which would provide funding for the development of Area Health Education Centers (AHECs). The AHECs were to serve as decentralized medical education centers and could be especially appropriate for states which were willing to phase out their two-year medical programs. The UND School of Medicine submitted a proposal to HEW in June of 1972. The AHEC concept would come to play a monumental role in the development of the medical program in the years to come. But many hurdles remained.

The Medical Affairs Committee, appointed earlier by Clifford, developed their proposal and urged a four-year program in which some students would transfer out of state after the second year of medical study and the remaining 40 students would complete their third year in one of the AHECs. The fourth year would be completed at a number of sites, depending upon the specialty. The budget for this program would cost $7.5 million for the biennium (1973-75) with $5.3 million of that coming from the state (Redman, p. 13). Because the budget for the previous biennium was only $2.6 million, the Legislative Council requested yet another study to be conducted by an outside consultant. The new study confirmed the basic findings of earlier studies but offered a new alternative. This alternative, which came to be known as the 2-1-1 plan, provided for the first two years of study at the University, the third year in Minnesota for the clerkships, and the final year back in North Dakota. The 2-1-1 plan was viewed by some as a way to allow more time to develop the resources to enable a fully developed four-year program entirely in-state. During the time the new study was taking place, the University received notice that it had been awarded one of the 10 AHEC grants made nationally by HEW. The timing could not have been better.

President Clifford and John Vennes from the University; Dr. Robert Painter, Grand Forks physician and member of the State Board of Higher Education; Ken Raschke, Commissioner of Higher Education; and Oscar Solberg, member of the Legislature, made two trips to Minnesota to negotiate agreements for North Dakota students to attend the third year at either the University of Minnesota or the Mayo Medical School. The agreements were reached but the plan still had to be accepted by the Legislative Council Committee. A hearing was held on January 19, 1973. The Committee refused to accept the additional cost created by the residencies within the state. It seemed clear that this cost was the final stumbling block to the acceptance of the idea of a four-year program. The University team went back to the drawing board and developed a revised budget. On January 22, 1973, the Legislative Council Committee supported the 2-1-1 plan and the legislation which would be introduced at the next session of the Legislative Assembly. Senator Evan Lips (Bismarck) introduced the legislation in the Senate and Vennes represented the University by giving testimony before both the Senate and House Appropriations Committees. The legislation was adopted on March 29, 1973. Redman notes that the sequence of events was significant in that the State Board of Higher Education did not act on the Medical School issue until after the Legislature acted (p. 15).

A word of explanation needs to be provided on the role of the dean of the Medical School, Theodore Harwood, in these developments. It seems that Dean Harwood held the view, which was shared by many of the faculty, that the two-year program was functioning rather well and should not be altered in any dramatic way. The efforts to carry forward the plan for a four-year degree-granting program were led by a relatively small core of dedicated and determined leaders within the University including Clifford, Vennes, Eelkema, and Nelson, and by an equally dedicated and determined group of physicians, health care professionals, and citizens around the state. As so often happens, significant change comes about this way rather than through a massive ground swell of support. There were many who doubted that the state could or should mount the necessary effort to implement such a plan or would continue to support such a plan. Those who were willing to take a risk and work for change have prevailed. Since that time, the University has had to continue to make the case for expansion and has had to fight a rear-guard action at times because of those who see the Medical School as a target for reductions in state expenditures.

The medical program would see continued change and development in the years ahead. Dean Harwood took an early retirement in 1973 and Dr. Vennes was appointed as acting dean until 1975. The School of Medicine received a Veteran's Administration grant for approximately $12 million to allow the development of the third and fourth year programs and the residency programs at the Veteran's Administration Hospital in Fargo (Vennes, 1991). Richard E. Davis served as dean for a brief and difficult term from 1975-76. Neil J. Thomford served briefly as acting dean shortly thereafter. Thomford presided over the first graduation in 1976 and President Clifford gave the commencement address. That same year the medical program received accreditation from the Association of American Medical Colleges (AAMC) and the American Medical Association (AMA). The Nurse Practitioner Program received accreditation from the AMA the same year. Tom M. Johnson (the same met by the delegation to Michigan in 1972) would serve as dean from 1977-1988. Dean Johnson's tenure would bring a period of much needed stability to the leadership of the school.

When Tom Johnson was appointed dean, Vennes stepped down as academic dean and returned to his teaching post. Wallace Nelson resigned as associate dean of students shortly thereafter, and the new dean began to develop his own team. An Office of Medical Education and Evaluation and an Office of Rural Health were established. The residency programs were developed further and the organization and administration of the AHECs was tightened up by making the dean the director of the AHECs. Formerly, there had been a separate director. As the medical program expanded, facilities became an increasingly difficult problem. The merger of the Deaconess Hospital with St. Michael's Hospital, and the construction of a new hospital facility on south Columbia Road, presented the University with the opportunity to acquire the old St. Michael's facility which is located on the north edge of the campus.

A humorous story has become attached to this event. According to the story, President Clifford attended a meeting with the religious order which owned the St. Michael's facility. The discussion focused on how to dispose of the facility. President Clifford returned from the meeting and said, "I think I just bought a hospital! Now I have to find the money!" In fact, the St. Michael's facility could provide the University with much needed space in a convenient location and at a cost considerably below what it would have cost for construction. The new space available in St. Michael's, known now as the North Unit, allowed the opportunity for several offices to move to that facility. The Medical Library was expanded into the east end of the old Medical Science Building.

It would take four more years (until 1981) for the Legislature to authorize the third year of study to return or be "repatriated" to North Dakota and another three for it to be implemented. In order for that authorization to take place, some 13 different studies and reports were conducted, over several years, to explore various aspects of the medical program. Dozens of legislative hearings and numerous meetings took place around the state. It must be said that if there was ever an educational program in North Dakota which was subjected to rigorous study and massive public input, this was it! The length of time it took to make the full transition to a totally in-state program reflects the cautious nature of the North Dakota Legislature. In the minds of some observers, it also reflects the tendency of that body to oversee and sometimes even to manage the operation of higher education in the state. On the other hand, there were those in the Legislature who believed that it was essential that the Legislature be involved in the development of the plans in order to increase the prospect that the final plan would be approved (Strinden, 1992, January 14).

Dean Johnson resigned in 1988 and Dr. Edwin James, chair of surgery, was named acting dean and after a national search, as the new dean of the School of Medicine and vice president for Health Sciences. Another important administrative change occurred when Dr. Dwayne Ollerich, associate dean for Academic Affairs and Research, resigned in 1989. John Vennes was named the associate dean and served for the remainder of the Clifford years. Judy DeMers served as associate dean of Student Affairs and Admissions beginning in June 1983. Writing in *The Review*, a School of Medicine publication, James noted that 51 students graduated on May 12, 1990, bringing the total number of graduates since the authorization of the four-year degree to a total of 650. James further noted that in the 1990 class, 27 percent of the graduates were entering family medicine. Of the 126 medical schools in the United States, the UND School of Medicine ranked 11th in the percentage of graduates entering family medicine (James, 1990). In 1990, nearly one-half of the physicians practicing medicine in the state were alumni of the UND program (Campaign for Excellence, p. 8). In the rural areas of the state, three out of four physicians are graduates of the UND program. The state enjoys a higher physician-to-population ratio, 146 per 100,000, than several surrounding states -- South Dakota 126, Iowa 135, Wyoming 126, Montana 142 (p. 16). The Center for Rural Health has been instrumental in placing physicians in at least 24 communities in the state (p. 17).

The change in the funding patterns for the Medical School over the period of the Clifford years is instructive to examine. The general fund appropriation for the 1971-73 biennium was $641,760; for the 1981-83 biennium, $19,605,739; and for the 1989-91 biennium, $24,769,290. It is evident that the largest increase came in the first decade when the school made the transition to a degree-granting status. The one-mill levy and tuition revenue changed very modestly over this same period of time with a total of $1,417,000 in the 1971-73 biennium, $2,758,000 in the 1981-83 biennium, and $4,705,620 in the 1989-91 biennium. The level of federal and non-state-appropriated funds increased significantly from $2,207,100 in the 1971-73 biennium, to $12,413,946 in the 1981-83 biennium, to $23,410,169 in the 1989-91 biennium. The total expenditures for the School of Medicine have grown from $4.2 million in the 1971-73 biennium, to $34.7 million in the 1983-83 biennium, to $54.9 million in the 1989-91 biennium (Eken, 1991).

The general fund appropriations from the state for the School of Medicine have made the greatest gains, reflecting both an effective effort by the University with the Legislature and a substantial level of support for the program within the Legislature. Perhaps one could conclude that this level of legislative support also reflected growing support for the School of Medicine by the people of the state. This support by the public is exhibited by the fact that the Medical School "is the only higher education program supported by a statewide mill levy which the voters put on themselves and refused to remove, even when they had the chance" (Strinden, 1992, p. 9). On the other hand, the portion of revenue from non-state sources had increased steadily until by 1991 over 50 percent of the total revenue of the Medical School came from non-state sources. One could say that for every one dollar the state spent on the medical program, another dollar was matched from other sources. This development reflected considerable effort by the Medical School to attract outside funds for program development and research. This was a remarkable effort considering the growing competition for a declining pool of resources at the national level during this period.

One of the programs in the Medical School, the Indians Into Medicine Program (INMED), initiated with federal funding in 1972, has developed a national reputation for successfully graduating American Indian students from Medical School. Five slots were originally added to every class for INMED students and the number was increased to seven. The program was initiated by Drs. Robert Eelkema and Lionel deMontigney and received support from the National Institute of Health and the Office of Economic Opportunity. Dr. deMontigney is the first American Indian medical graduate from UND. Careful planning and involvement with the tribal leaders on 22 reservations in the region and the development of an all-American Indian Board of Directors has been a key to the success of the program. INMED students enroll in programs of nursing, medical technology, clinical psychology and other health specialties as well as medicine. One out of every five American Indian physicians in the United States is a graduate of the UND INMED program (Campaign for Excellence, p. 12). The program has graduated a total of 67 American Indian physicians and 31 other health care professionals. The retention rate of the program is approximately 70 percent for pre-professional students and 85 percent for professional students. The staff of the INMED program provide intensive support services for students in the program. The program has been so successful that it has been cited as a prototype in Congressional legislation and in the latest reauthorization of the Indian Health

Care Improvement Act. Duplication of the program at two additional universities was endorsed by the legislation. In 1990, a satellite office was established at the University of South Dakota. In 1991 the program received a federal grant as a Center for Excellence. The INMED program is one more example of how the University has taken seriously its unique mission to serve American Indian students in North Dakota and the region.

In 1991 the Medical School and the UND Foundation launched a "Campaign for Excellence" to raise $8 million in a capital fund drive. The goals included $3.5 million for a state-of-the-art Bio-Information Learning Resources Center which will be connected to the south side of the present North Unit. In addition, plans were developed for a Medical Research Center which would be connected to the north side of the unit. In fiscal year 91 and fiscal year 92, the U.S. Congress appropriated $2.8 million and $4.4 million, respectively, towards the project in the bills for the farm and agricultural-related agencies. The new funding and facility would lead to the creation of the UND Institute for Agricultural Health Sciences and Rural Medicine.

Within the Campaign for Excellence, another $4.5 million will be dedicated to the endowment, increasing it by one and one-half times. The endowment would support research, scholarships, and unrestricted monies for developing needs in the medical education programs. The new campaign will upgrade the facilities and place the programs on a more solid financial base to insure a secure future.

It has taken many years and the imagination, dedication, and labor of many people for the UND Medical School and its programs to have finally reached the present level of excellence and maturity. This latest effort will help insure the preservation of the gains which have been made and will enable continued improvement into the future. President Clifford's assessment of the progress of the Medical School is that it has probably done more good for the people of North Dakota than almost anything one could imagine.

In reflecting on the development of the four-year medical program, Vice President James noted that prior to the four-year program, one in five graduates returned to practice in North Dakota. Since the four-year program, one in two graduates return to practice in North Dakota (James, 1/28/91). Describing President Clifford's role, James observed that, "He has been the key individual in developing the four-year Medical School . . . without his support and strong leadership, it would probably not have made it" (James, 1/28/91).

CHAPTER **4**

THE CENTER FOR AEROSPACE SCIENCES: SEIZING OPPORTUNITY

We must step back in time to trace the beginnings of what would become one of the most remarkable stories of the Clifford years. The story begins in 1968 when Clifford was still dean of the College of Business and Public Administration. A young assistant professor, who happened to be teaching accounting and data processing in the Accounting Department came to Dean Clifford and asked permission to teach an aviation ground-school course on an overload basis. Clifford gave his permission. Twelve students took the class. That young faculty member was John Odegard. Some 20 years later Odegard was dean of the Center for Aerospace Sciences which began with that one class and grew to an academic unit with 917 student majors (1991 academic year) in four departments, a flourishing multifaceted research program, and facilities built at a cost of more than $44 million. A visionary and determined leader, good timing, the support of key political figures, and a president who was willing to take some risks, brought all of this into being.

From the very beginning there were many obstacles to the development of a full-blown aerospace program. The Aviation Department was established in 1969 with Odegard as the chair, but only after much controversy on campus. Not everyone thought this was such a good idea, including Vice President Koenker who had some skepticism as to whether aviation was a proper academic subject. Clifford and Odegard decided to reverse the usual process and see if the idea could gain acceptance at the state level and, if it could, then perhaps it would receive a warmer welcome on campus. They talked to members of the State Board of Higher Education, cultivating their interest, and finally won their approval.

Next Clifford and Odegard talked to Governor William Guy who was excited about the fledgling program. However, the governor saw no chance of funding for any new program and suggested that the concept be included in the Governor's budget as a non-funded program. The Governor insisted that the new program had to be self-supporting from the very beginning. The program now had the support of both the Board and the Governor, though without any promise of funding. Even then, the University Curriculum Committee defeated Odegard's request for approval. It took many months of persuading and cajoling to finally gain permission for the program to go forward. A new curriculum was then developed for the major in Aviation Administration which combined the technical field of aviation with the field of business.

But now the struggle began on a different front. Odegard recalls, "When the fixed-base operators (private flying companies) found out we'd be giving flight instruction, they went wild" (Youngblood, 1979). It took several months to quiet this new source of opposition. Less persistent players might have just given up. Clifford could have pulled the plug on the program rather than face opposition both on campus and out in the state. Some of the private air service operators went as a group to the State Board of Higher Education to voice their opposition to the aviation program at UND. A member of the Board staff phoned back to UND. Clifford and Odegard flew at once to Bismarck and passed the private operators in the doorway leaving the Board meeting. After hearing from Clifford and Odegard, the Board was convinced that the program should go forward and they dismissed the objections of the private operators.

The next problem was to find additional aircraft. When the University put out bid requests to lease aircraft, none were received. Those with aircraft to lease may have been hesitant to work with the University for fear of antagonizing some of the private operators. Odegard recalls returning from an especially discouraging meeting. As he and Clifford flew back to Grand Forks, they both sat in silence looking out the windows of the airplane. All at once Clifford snapped his fingers and said, "I've got it. I know what we can do!" (Odegard, 2/2/91). Not long thereafter the UND Alumni Association came to the rescue and provided the financing for two planes. The program eventually repaid the Association which, in turn, put the same funds back into a scholarship for aviation students. Two additional planes were donated by Ernie Fox of Billings, Montana, who had prospered in the oil business and whose tax preparer had been Tom Clifford. Fox later contributed funds for scholarships for aviation students. Bryce Streibel, North Dakota legislator and friend of UND, donated $10,000 to establish the first scholarship endowment fund for aviation. The program was making progress. Later, Fred Orth, the Fellows of the University, and the Robert D. Campbell Foundation bought the first simulators.

The city of Grand Forks allowed the Aviation Department to lease the city hangar at the airport. Space to store, service, and warm the small fleet of aircraft was essential because of the North Dakota weather. A temporary maintenance area was constructed in the large hangar by hanging canvas over a wooden frame and a gas heater was used inside this makeshift structure to keep the mechanics warm during the cold winter months. Another important need was for an air traffic control tower at the airport. U.S. Senator Milton Young provided assistance to secure federal funding for the FAA staff for the tower. The City of Grand Forks provided the control tower. The tower was obviously essential to control the rapidly increasing air traffic at the Grand Forks airport, but it also was critical to enable a program in air traffic control for students.

An important development took place on another front when in 1973 a contract was awarded from the U.S. Bureau of Reclamation for $285,000 to conduct weather modification research. The National Science Foundation provided support for pilot training for weather modification. Once again a North Dakota official, someone who had often assisted the University, was in the right place at the right time. Bryce Streibel, the majority leader of the North Dakota Legislature, had been appointed to the National Weather Modification Board and was an advocate for the UND program. The weather modification award would mark the beginning of a number of grants and awards for a growing research enterprise in the years ahead. With the weather modification project off to a good start, in 1978 a $3.3 million contract was awarded from the Bureau of Reclamation to continue and expand the project. A Piper Cheyenne II aircraft was acquired and retrofitted with special equipment to carry out research. By 1980 the number of aviation majors was up to 650, a degree in meteorology had been added to the program, and a large 10,000 square foot hangar had been constructed.

Sometimes a misfortune for one group proves to be fortunate for another. When the Professional Air Traffic Controllers Union (PATCO) went on strike in 1981, President Reagan fired the strikers and created a crisis in the air service system. That crisis presented an opening for the Center for Aerospace Sciences program at UND. North Dakota Senator Mark Andrews was to become an important player in the developments which followed and he became an avid supporter of the UND effort. Odegard has noted that "Andrews had tremendous respect for Tom Clifford" (Odegard, 2/2/91). After the PATCO strike, Senator Andrews announced that UND had been awarded a $4 million grant from the Federal Aviation Administration (FAA) to construct a 55,000 square foot building for Airway Science. Ground was broken for the new Center for

Aerospace Sciences (CAS) facility in 1983. Major research projects on wind shear and aircraft icing were supported by the FAA, and when the new building was dedicated in 1984, FAA Administrator Admiral Don Engen was the featured speaker at the ceremony. The program at UND was receiving national attention and support.

There were many personalities who came to play important roles in the development of the CAS program over the years. Lee Barnum was the first flight instructor. "Lee was a cantankerous sort of guy but he taught the students a lot and they loved him," according to Odegard (2/2/91). Don Smith was "the first real faculty member," according to Odegard, and was instrumental in developing the program in Airport Management. Smith would become the chair of the Aviation Department and eventually the associate dean of the Center for Aerospace Sciences. George Hammond, a retired Air Force Commander, "essentially developed the entire airport operation," according to Odegard (2/2/91). He retired in 1984 but returned to campus to fly with students for several months every summer. Bill Shea was the associate administrator for airports for the FAA before coming to CAS. He chaired the Aviation Department for five years before returning to the FAA. Les Severance was the North Dakota FAA officer in Fargo and was an early and enthusiastic supporter of the program at UND. Odegard reported that whenever he became discouraged about the future of the program, Severance reminded him that "the program was a great idea and we shouldn't give up!" (Odegard, 2/2/91). Severance and Gordon Amundson of North Central Airlines, who taught airlines operations for the UND program, were eventually given Presidential medals by Clifford. Astronaut Buzz Aldrin joined the faculty in 1985 and helped to develop the Space Studies program. Aldrin opened many doors at NASA. His association with the program gave it even more national recognition and exposure. Aldrin brought David Webb from NASA to serve as the first chair of the new Space Studies program. Charles Wood, another NASA staff person, would later replace Webb. These are just a few of the many persons who would devote their talents to do the development of this unique venture at the University.

President Clifford and John Odegard decided in 1985 to establish a UND Aerospace Foundation, a non-profit legal entity. Clifford had brought his legal and financial expertise to bear on similar situations in the past. The development of a free-standing foundation provided for an entity which could make agreements with industry in ways which were much more effective and less cumbersome than attempting to administer everything through the highly bureaucratic system imposed upon the University by the state. The purpose of the Foundation is "to promote University-industry joint ventures and technology transfer. . . ." (Center for Aerospace . . ., p. 7). The Foundation would support many important projects including a helicopter training program, aerospace physiology training, and the ACT-2000 air traffic control simulation system.

In May of 1985 the University Curriculum Committee and the University Senate approved degree-granting status to CAS and President Clifford named Odegard dean of the Center for Aerospace Sciences. The Center had finally reached full academic status as a college of the University. The UND Flying Team won first place at the National Intercollegiate Flying Association airmeet in 1985 and would win the national contest for each of the next seven years. That same year, when former astronaut Buzz Aldrin joined the CAS staff, the first Young Astronauts program in the nation was initiated in Grand Forks. The new Computer Science wing of the CAS Building, which was funded by an FAA grant, was completed in 1986 at a cost of $2.3 million and word was received that the Computer Science undergraduate degree program had been accredited. In May the atmospheric research division officially became the Atmospheric Science Department within CAS.

A joint program between Northwest Airlines and CAS was announced during 1986. The joint venture had been in the making for two years and President Clifford had played an important role in negotiations with the top management of the airline. The plan was for the development of an advanced pilot training program which would be operated by Northwest Aerospace Training Corporation (NATCO), a subsidiary of the airline, and would be housed in a new facility to be constructed near the CAS facility. NATCO would provide state-of-the-art flight simulators which would be used by the Northwest pilots and would be made available to students in the University program. The construction of the facility was completed in 1988 at a cost of $5 million. A new program which emerged from the NATCO venture was titled SPECTRUM and it took students with no experience to entry-level standards for regional airlines within a period of 16 months. Another new program was under development for some time by David Webb and colleagues and in 1987 was announced as an interdisciplinary master's degree program in Space Studies.

The NATCO/CAS venture proceeded rather well for a period of time but difficulties began to develop. Speaking later about the program, Dean Odegard's analysis was that the difficulty was that they were attempting to merge two entirely different and contrary cultures (Odegard, 2/2/91). Conflicts in personalities and management style may have contributed to the difficulties, as well. Whatever the reasons for the problems, tensions rose to the point of a disruption and finally a break in the relationship. UND may have learned what other universities have, which is that marriages between universities and private corporations can end in divorce. Divorce settlements can get a bit contentious and so it was when NATCO withdrew from the program. The UND Aerospace

Foundation agreed to purchase the NATCO 50 percent of the SPECTRUM program. While the separation was being negotiated, however, NATCO attempted to remove its simulators from the facility. CAS refused to allow the simulators to be removed until an agreement was reached about the lease on the NATCO half of the building. Finally, CAS permitted the removal of the simulators and NATCO locked up its half of the building, which now stands empty. Was it worth it? Odegard believed that the SPECTRUM program, which took 12 months to develop, was the finest training program in the world and its development was well worth the cost and difficulty with NATCO.

The UND Aerospace Foundation announced a new venture in February of 1991 which would expand regional commercial air service. The Foundation had developed a plan with Great Lakes Aviation, Ltd. of Spencer, Iowa, to expand service in the region by that air carrier, utilizing the students from the UND SPECTRUM program as co-pilots. These students, who would be fully qualified pilots, would be able to earn advanced qualifications and experience by their flying time with the regional air carrier. The students involved in this program were Chinese students from Taiwan, preparing for eventual service as crew members for China Airlines (Schmidt, 2/10/91). The airlines paid the UND Aerospace Foundation approximately $167,000 per student for tuition and expenses.

Air training at UND started from a handful of students with two donated aircraft and an accounting professor providing flying lessons after hours. By 1991, it was a full-fledged degree granting college, the third largest in the University, with students majoring in 12 degree programs. The academic departments encompassed Aviation, Atmospheric Sciences, Computer Science, and Space Studies. The total research income over this period exceeded $60 million. The Center employed approximately 680 persons, 65 of whom were faculty members. The programs were housed in three impressive facilities located on the west side of the campus and in an extensive complex at the Mark Andrews International Airport. This was certainly one of the most remarkable chapters in the history of the University.

CHAPTER **5**

A NEW VICE PRESIDENT, A NEW PLAN: 1976-1980

Vice President for Academic Affairs William E. Koenker had been appointed in 1962, by President Starcher, as the first to serve with that title. He had served the University prior to that as a professor and chair of the Economics Department. During the 1975 academic year, he made it known that he planned to retire the following year. Koenker, like Clifford, had gained a reputation as an expert in economic affairs and his advice was sought throughout the state. He had written papers on the potential of the coal and oil deposits in the state. He had made many trips to the North Dakota Legislature to plead the case for the University. As a native, he understood the people of the state and had chosen to spend virtually all of his academic career in North Dakota and at the University. In a parting interview with the *Grand Forks Herald* he reiterated:

> Koenker said that one of his most difficult tasks had been convincing state officials and legislators "of the need to have classroom people who are truly on the forefront of their fields — not just people who can make assignments and do some evaluation of students . . ." The University has some faculty like that, he said, and "the modest amount of money needed" to attract more "would be one of the best investments the state could make." (Haga, 1975)

It is clear that Koenker felt that the communication of this message was one of the greatest challenges of his office. It was difficult to convince pragmatic, rural legislators, many of whom did not have a college education, that attracting and keeping professors was an investment which made good economic sense for the state.

During 1975 another change in a top administrative post took place when A. William Johnson, dean of the Graduate School took a leave. Alice Clark of the Psychology Department was asked to fill in as the acting dean and did so for 18 months until Johnson's return.

A New Vice President

The national search for a replacement for Koenker began. After many months of effort, the recommendation was made to President Clifford by the Search Committee to offer the position to Conny E. Nelson, assistant vice president for Academic Affairs at the University of Nebraska. Clifford accepted the recommendation and Nelson accepted the offer, his duties to begin July 1, 1976. Nelson was a very different person than Koenker. He was young, 43 years old. He was a professor of English with a Ph.D. in English and Comparative Literature from the University of Washington. He had taught at Washington, Washington State, Purdue, and the University of Wisconsin-Green Bay before going to Nebraska. Nelson recognized that there were marked differences between himself and Koenker, and he was very open about this in an interview the month after he began his new position at UND.

> "Bill Koenker was a very big man," Nelson said. "He had intimate, broad knowledge of the University and all of its programs, indeed all of its people. No one, let alone me, could hope to continue in his style. An outsider just doesn't have his intimate knowledge. Yet we've got to start administering, right now." (Kenner, 1976)

During that interview Nelson identified three priorities for the academic sector of the University: decentralizing the decision-making process, developing a long-range academic plan, and increasing academic excellence.

Nelson came with a very clear agenda and lost no time in beginning to implement that agenda. As for the priority of decentralizing, Nelson's plan was to shift more of the authority, including that for budgets, down to the dean's level in the University structure. The need for a long-range academic plan would be addressed in what would finally result in the document, *A Strategy for the 80s*. The drive for excellence, however, would be more elusive. In the same interview in August of 1976, Nelson had already sized up the situation at the University and made this assessment:

> The problem I have noticed is that resources available to the University are indeed limited, and I have really be [sic] impressed by the tightness of the budget. There are many demands made on every area of the University. The University tries to meet these responsibilities with too few faculty members or other resources. This situation makes the high morale of the faculty even more impressive.   (Kenner, 1976)

Echoing the concerns expressed by Koenker during his last days in the office, the interview with Nelson continued:

> He said faculty salaries are below average for a university of "this size, admission, and importance as a state university. But I understand there has been significant improvement the last few years. That is good but there is room for more improvement." (Kenner, 1976)

It was evident that Nelson would be clear in his intentions and direct and forthright in his comments about how he viewed the University and the state. These qualities would bring significant changes to the academic sector of the University. However, Nelson's actions ruffled some feathers and led the director of University Relations to refer to Nelson as President Clifford's "sometimes controversial chief adviser" in academic affairs and one whose actions sometimes generated "heated discussion on and off the campus" (Vorland, 1979, p. 12). History Professor D.Jerome Tweton later observed, "Conny Nelson upset the apple cart! Especially for administrators. He shook up the deans. . . . He wanted them to justify what they were doing." Tweton noted that Nelson "had some very good ideas." But, added Tweton, "He was very blunt. He didn't have much tact and that was his biggest shortcoming" (Tweton, 10/22/91). In spite of his controversial manner, Nelson was responsible for significant accomplishments during a relatively brief period of time.

Office of Research and Program Development

One of Nelson's early accomplishments was the establishment of an Office of Research and Program Development (ORPD) which was designed to assist faculty in seeking external grants and other sources of funding for research and for program development. Nelson believed that it would be essential for the University to develop these sources of funding in light of the uneven record of state support and because this was the course many other universities had taken with some success.

A New Plan

Another major accomplishment during the Nelson term as vice president for Academic Affairs was the successful completion of the long-range planning process which produced the document, *A Strategy for the 1980s*. While the effort was directed by Nelson, during the pre-planning period, the president issued a brief but detailed statement of "Presidential Planning Priorities." Unlike the prior planning effort, this one seemed to have been given a more specific set of "marching orders" by the president. The presidential document was attached to the University newsletter. A faculty member recalled the first time he saw the document and his thought at that time: "Why go through all that . . . when the president has already issued his plan" (Rice, 1986, p. 86). He later concluded, however, that the statement had actually given focus to the effort rather than detracting from it. He noted that the Presidential statement was attached to later reports and that it seemed to "still maintain a separate identity" (Rice, 1986, p. 86).

On September 1, 1977, the president called a general meeting of the faculty to "explain the need for planning, outline the planning process, and formally initiate the overall planning effort" (*A Strategy for the 1980s*, p. 1). Once again, the planning process was extensive and involved many people on the campus. The final report was presented to the president in August of 1979 and contained two parts. Part One contained the recommendations of the vice president for Academic Affairs. Part Two contained the priorities of the various colleges and schools of the University.

This extensive effort and the resulting recommendations required action. On September 19, 1979, the president appointed a planning council to review the document and he gave them a specific charge. The council was to "designate those goals and actions which deserved priority attention and to suggest means for achieving the goals" (*Toward the Second Century*, p. 1). The council included 21 faculty members and four students. The dean of the Graduate School, A. William Johnson, was appointed as the chair. The final report from the council was submitted to the president on January 8, 1980, and was titled, *Toward the Second Century: A Report of the President's Planning Council.*

These were major planning efforts undertaken by the University at its own initiative. In the late 1980s, the North Dakota State Board of Higher Education would require that all of the colleges and universities in the state undertake such planning. UND had taken that responsibility seriously many years earlier and had gained considerable experience at institutional planning.

Clifford viewed these planning initiatives as an important part of the historical development of the University. He viewed the first plan, which was initiated shortly after he took office, as necessary after the "chaotic period of the 1960s" when there was change in university governance and limited decision making. His purpose at that time had been to put many people, including students, into the planning process. The result was a "shopping list" of things to do. His perception was that the vast majority of the plan had been put into effect.

The second cycle was in a period when governance was more set. It was a period of conserving resources and so the process could not be opened up for another "shopping list." From his perspective, the later study reflected a more "mature university setting." He, too, noted that the "Presidential Priorities" statement continued to be a guiding document (Rice, 1986, pp. 88-89). It is interesting to note that these planning efforts at the University took place during the period when the business world was deeply involved in what was called "strategic planning." That approach to institutional management would not become popular in higher education until the 1980s (Keller, 1983). In this respect, UND was ahead of many other campuses.

It should be noted that these planning documents were utilized by the president during the following years. Such reports often seem to simply gather dust on the shelf. When the Interim Joint Appropriations Committee of the Legislature held a hearing on the UND campus during the late 1980s, President Clifford recommended to the committee that the University be granted authority to build an addition to Abbott Hall (Chemistry), build a Communication Building, and acquire the St. Michael's Hospital North Unit. Recommendation 231 of the report of the Study Committee on Planning and Education (SCOPE) stated:

> Construct the following new buildings: Biology Building, Chester Fritz Library Addition, College of Nursing Building, Women's Physical Education Building, Communication Building, Behavioral and Social Science Building, Center for Teaching and Learning Building, Chemistry Addition, Laundry Building and Warehouse.
> (p. 43)

Two of the three requests made by the president to the Legislature were on the SCOPE list and four of the projects had been completed previously. In most cases, a very lengthy time-line was required for new buildings due to limited funds at the state level and because projects at the University had to be considered along with projects from the other campuses in the state. At the time of this writing, some of the building projects on the SCOPE list have not been approved. Nevertheless, the planning documents continued to give direction to these decisions.

University College

In 1978, D.J. Robertson, dean of University College and founder of that academic unit, announced that he would retire as of June 30 after 23 years as dean. President Clifford announced the appointment of the chair of the Speech Pathology and Audiology Department, Professor George W. Schubert, to the post. Schubert had been serving as the official faculty athletic representative since 1973 and was president of the Western Collegiate Hockey Association (WCHA) from 1976-77. University College was and remains an academic division in which all freshmen students are enrolled at UND. The enrollment in University College for the fall of the 1977-78 academic year was 2,563, 27 percent of UND's 9,363 students. Although Robertson was retired, he continued to serve the University in the next few years in various ways. The University found a way to honor Robertson for his many years of loyal service by naming a new scholarship the "D.J. Robertson Academic Achievement Award." This new award would go to first year students who had achieved a straight A average (4.0) after the first year at UND.

Continuing Education

During this period, the Division of Continuing Education was led by several persons, some of whom served relatively brief terms. George Wasinger served from 1969-72, John Penn served from 1973-75, and Orlo Sundre served from 1975-79. Finally, Robert Boyd was promoted from within the Division to the position of dean in 1979 and served for the remainder of the Clifford years. That same year the University purchased the old Phi Delta Theta house located on the south bank of the English Coulee. Renamed Gustafson Hall, in honor of long-time director of extension, Bernhard G. Gustafson, the facility was restored and remodeled and became the new home for Continuing Education.

Dean Boyd's tenure produced much change and expansion of the Division and significant increases in enrollments in a host of educational activities off-campus. The Extension program provided many opportunities for school teachers across the state to upgrade their skills and knowledge and earn graduate credit. Correspondence Study served hundreds of students not only in North Dakota but across the nation. The Conferences and Institutes unit provided non-credit training activities for both governmental agencies and the private sector. A Weekend College made courses available for many nontraditional and working students who could not attend classes during the regular weekday schedule. The Division delivered courses and degree programs to the Air Force Bases at both Grand Forks and Minot. Many military personnel and their families earned degrees through these UND programs. Both the programs and the staff of the Division increased significantly during this period.

The Flood of 1979

The spring of 1979 will long be remembered for the serious flooding which spread across the Red River Valley. The Red River flows north into Lake Winnipeg and often floods because the spring melt backs up as it encounters the yet frozen river and lake to the north. Grand Forks is the first major city along the Red River to receive this water as it backs up. The 1979 flood was especially severe. The river grew quickly into a massive lake. The English Coulee, normally nothing more than a modest stream, one which barely moves at that, quickly expanded beyond its banks and flooded everything in the area. Hundreds of homes and parts of the University itself were in peril. Volunteers sandbagged at a furious pace in an effort to protect as many structures as possible. UND students responded in large numbers to assist with the sandbagging effort not only at the University but in the community. It was a heroic effort. President Clifford announced that students would be excused from classes to assist with flood work. The president also announced a policy on May 1 which provided for special arrangements for missed examinations and completion of course work. Such tragedies often bring communities closer together and this was certainly true in Grand Forks. It must be said that relations between the University and community have been very good over the years, but certainly people came to a renewed sense of appreciation for each other during this period of crisis.

Office of Instructional Development

Near the end of his term as vice president, Conny Nelson was instrumental in the planning and writing of a proposal to the Bush Foundation to establish an Office of Instructional Development (OID), which would assist faculty with the improvement of their teaching and with curriculum development and related concerns. A planning committee was formed for this purpose and a proposal submitted to the foundation. It was funded. The Office of Instructional Development was designed to serve as a counter-balance to the increasing emphasis on research at the University. Robert E. Young was selected to head the office after a national search. Young served the office for seven years from 1980 to 1987. He developed several successful programs, brought national experts to the campus, and built a solid base of faculty support for the office. Establishing a free-standing office to support teaching was another instance of the University being ahead of the times. This approach would not be implemented on most campuses until the later 1980s or early 1990s. The Office of Instructional Development, as well as the Office of Research and Program Development (ORPD), continue to function to this day.

Further Leadership Changes

Loren F. Swanson, the Vice President for Operations, died suddenly on February 24, 1979. Swanson had done much to make the campus a more attractive and comfortable place for everyone. He had led a significant reorganization of the operations sector. He was deeply devoted to the University and close to President Clifford. Someone once observed that Swanson was so familiar with the many buildings that he could find the fuse box in every one on campus. It was fitting that the newest residence facility on campus, built in 1985, was named in his honor. Vice President for Finance Skogley supervised the Operations area until he left the campus in 1983.

On June 18, 1979, President Clifford announced that Gerald Hamerlik, director of Financial Aid, was given the additional title and assignment of dean of Enrollment Services. The new unit, replacing the high school relations program, was designed to provide information to prospective students and to assist them in their enrollment at the university. Hamerlik became a regular member of the small group which Clifford used to represent the University to the Legislature. Also in June, John Penn, dean of Summer Sessions, retired. The responsibility for Summer Studies was shifted to George Schubert, dean of University College. These changes allowed for the allocation of two full-time positions for academic advisors in University College, the unit responsible for advising freshmen and sophomores.

Nelson made some internal changes in the vice president's staff, as well. Margaret Davenport had served as Koenker's secretary and loyal assistant for many years. Upon her departure, Nelson, following Koenker's advice, sought an assistant vice president to help carry the rapidly growing administrative duties of the office. Nelson had been impressed with the work of Alice Clark during her time as the acting dean of the Graduate School and selected her from the applicants for the position. Clark served as assistant vice president for Academic Affairs for two years. She was then promoted to associate vice president. David Bowen, a former Air Force officer who dealt with financial management, was added to the staff.

Professor D. Jerome Tweton, History Department, was a department chair under both Koenker and Nelson and, during an interview, offered some reflections on the two. Tweton compared how financial matters were handled with the deans and departments. "Koenker," he noted, "held the purse strings and you'd go bargain with him. Nelson, on the other hand, would say, 'Here's your money. You decide what to do with it'" (Tweton, 10/22/91). Tweton also commented on Nelson's relationship to the academic departments. "Nelson took an interest in the departments. He was the only vice president I have known who would pop over, without being obtrusive. He was chattish. He would meet with your department if you wanted him to. This side of him was very positive" (Tweton, 10/22/91).

As is often the case when following an administrator who was in the position for many years, Nelson did not stay long at UND. He left in 1980 to become the chancellor of the University of Michigan-Flint. It was an opportunity for Nelson to be the chief administrator of a campus. Though Nelson's time at UND was not lengthy, many of the changes he brought to the academic life of the campus have proven to be effective and enduring. The UND campus was shocked and saddened to learn that Conny Nelson died of cancer on May 2, 1983, at 53 years of age. His many friends at UND felt a great sense of loss. That sorrow was heightened because of the realization that he was still relatively young, really at the peak of his abilities.

Nelson's resignation in 1980 required a new search for a vice president for Academic Affairs. This time the University would turn to an internal candidate, after a national search, to fill its highest academic post.

THE SECOND DECADE: THE 1980s

PRECEDING PAGE: Growth in enrollments, programs, and the physical plant of the University that marked the 1980s required astute planning and resource acquisition and allocation in the face of continuing budgetary problems. The campus spread eastward (foreground) with the acquisition of what is today named the Energy and Environmental Research Center from the federal government. Westward expansion (background) came in the form of the burgeoning Center for Aerospace Sciences facilities, which may be seen more clearly in an aerial view in the photo section of this book.

CHAPTER **6**

INTO THE 1980s: A TIME OF GROWTH AND CHALLENGE

With the departure of Conny Nelson from the campus, Associate Vice President Alice Clark was appointed as the acting vice president for Academic Affairs while a national search was mounted. A search committee was appointed with Clair Rowe, dean of the College of Business and Public Administration, as the chair. After their initial deliberations, the committee interviewed six finalists including three internal candidates: Alice Clark, A. William Johnson and Henry Tomasek. At the conclusion of that process, Clark emerged as the candidate who was selected by President Clifford. Clark, as noted earlier, had served as dean of the Graduate School while Johnson was on a leave and subsequently served as associate vice president for academic affairs. She became the third vice president of Academic Affairs for the University.

The New Vice President Begins

One of Clark's first tasks was to find a new associate vice president. Of the internal candidates, five would become finalists and from those Clark selected Gene Kemper. Kemper was a professor in the Mathematics Department and had been serving in an administrative capacity in the University Computer Center. Clark saw that technology was looming on the educational horizon and she saw in Kemper the knowledge which could provide that expertise in the office. Kemper's expertise would serve the University and the state very well, indeed, in the period which was to follow. He would provide leadership in the development of the computer resources of the University and the development of the computer network for the North Dakota higher education system. Kemper came with considerable skill in the budget and finance area, as well.

The year was 1981 and Alice Clark was the first woman to serve as the chief academic officer at the largest institution of higher education in the state. She was the leading woman administrator on campus for the remainder of the Clifford years and, except for Clifford, held the most important administrative post on the campus.

Clark was interviewed by the *Dakota Student* early that fall. "'For several years we've experienced an increase in enrollments,' Clark said, 'but the Legislature fails to fund us in the posture of growth. It's very difficult to deal with'" (Stjern, 1981). Echoing her two predecessors, "'You just can't run a college and maintain quality without sufficient resources,' she said" (Stjern, 1981). When asked about the movement away from interest in the arts and humanities toward the professional programs, Clark confirmed that trend but added a caution. "'It's extremely important to the general health of the University,' Clark said with intensity, 'to maintain a broad, general education'" (Stjern, 1981).

Clark's general approach to the academic programs of the University was to seek to make improvements on several fronts. For the first time an annual review was conducted of every college on campus. Each dean was required to present both a written and an oral annual report to the president and vice president. The Graduate School had been following a rotating cycle of reviews of all graduate programs. Clark instituted a seven-year cycle of program review for all undergraduate programs, to begin during the 1986-87 academic year. All academic personnel policies and practices were reviewed and regularized and affirmative action policies were designed and put in place for the academic sector. The need for more and better data for academic decision making resulted in changing a half-time Institutional Research position to full time (Clark, 1991).

The College of Fine Arts

The College of Fine Arts changed deans in 1980. John Rogers left the University and Bruce Jacobsen, who had been the chair of the Theatre Department at Montana State University, was selected to become the new dean. Jacobsen served in that position for the remainder of the Clifford years. The smallest of the colleges of the University, Fine Arts had 79 students in 1980. The College, in spite of its small size, provided important general education classes for all students and necessary course work for the training of teachers, in addition to majors and minors in the disciplines of the fine arts. The importance of the contributions of the College to the cultural and artistic life of the University during these years cannot be overestimated. The Music Department provided concerts and performances by the instrumental and vocal groups as well as many individual faculty and student recitals. The Visual Arts Department sponsored many exhibitions of art and each year loaned original student works for display in the many offices across the campus. The Theatre Arts Department produced regular productions of first-rate plays and took six different productions on tour between 1976 and 1990.

State Funding and a Major Gift

Fortunately, the 1979-80 biennium was a very good one for state appropriations for the University. The appropriations rose from $36.91 million for the 1977-78 biennium to $50.98 million for the 1979-80 biennium, an increase of 38 percent. Funding from the state for the following biennium was strong, as well, as it was increased to $66.24 million, an increase of almost 30 percent. The economy of the state was stronger and oil prices were high. The high inflation during this period, however, eroded some of the gains which were made by these higher levels of funding.

In 1980, UND Alumni Association executive vice president Earl Strinden was invited to the Racine, Wisconsin, home of alumnus W. Ken Hyslop, a member of the class of 1906. Hyslop, born in Inkster, North Dakota, was prepared to finalize his will. He willed approximately $6 million worth of Red River Valley farm land to the University. The value of the land, combined with other gifts made then and earlier, brought his total contribution to approximately $8 million, the largest amount ever received by the University from an individual. Interestingly, Hyslop's father donated to the University during 1895-1896 when such support literally kept the University open (Rylance, 1983, p. 135).

Accreditation

President Clifford had long aspired to have all of the professional schools and programs of the University fully accredited. The 1980s would be the time when this aspiration would finally come to fulfillment. To get to that point took a great effort by many dedicated faculty and staff and required considerable expense. Accreditation is one of the marks of a quality program and is a sign of the academic maturity of an institution of higher education. In addition, accreditation helps to attract excellent faculty and students to a campus. The University set its sights on this goal with renewed determination during the 1980s. During the early years of the new decade the programs which achieved accreditation or reaccreditation were Visual Arts by the National Association of Schools of Visual Arts (1983), Social Work by the Council on Social Work Education (1983), Home Economics Coordinated Undergraduate Program in Dietetics by the American Dietetics Association (1984), Athletic Training by the National Athletic Trainers Association (1984), Physical Therapy by the American Physical Therapy Association (1985), and the Engineering programs in Chemical, Civil, Electrical, Geological, and Mechanical Engineering by the Accrediting Board for Engineering and Technology (1985).

Oxford House Restored

The Alumni Association and UND Foundation found a new home in 1981. The old Oxford House on University Avenue, which had been the home for four presidents from 1903 to 1954, had been vacated. In fact, the building had fallen into disrepair for a time after serving as a dormitory and as a facility for the art department. Some on campus concluded that the building was a "fire trap" but, by good fortune and foresight, a group on campus led by Bill Blaine had been successful in having the building listed on the National Register of Historic Places in 1973. If not for that protection, the building might have been demolished. An effort to rejuvenate the building was organized, funds raised, and in 1981 it was occupied by the Alumni Association and UND Foundation. The first floor was not used for office space but was restored to reflect the decor of the original house. Furnishings from the period were gathered from around the campus and many antiques, some donated, others purchased from the estate of Ken Hyslop, returned the house to its original charm. The largest share of the cost, $340,000, was provided by private donations, with federal grants covering $200,000 and state appropriated funds covering $100,000 of the total cost of $640,000. The restored building was dedicated during Homecoming in 1981 and was named the J. Lloyd Stone Alumni Center in honor of the director who had served the association well for so many years (Rylance, 1983, p. 33).

Budge Hall Destroyed

One of the oldest buildings on campus, Budge Hall, constructed in 1899, suffered severe water damage in 1981 when a small fire set off the water sprinkler system and flooded the building over a weekend. The structural damage was such that the building had to be demolished. The cause of the fire was reported by the police to be associated with a forced entry into the third floor office of English Department graduate assistant Steve Weiler (Gornowicz, 1981). A story developed in the English Department, but was never substantiated, that the fire resulted from the burning of Weiler's grade book by a disgruntled undergraduate. The basement of Budge Hall had served many purposes over the years as an "auditorium, gym, armory, YMCA, bookstore, and student union ('Nodak Center')" before it was converted to classroom space (Vivian, 1983, p. 138).

Student Humor
Student life during this period was not always devoted exclusively to academics. The staff of the *Dakota Student* created a stir when they entered a turkey in the contest for 1981 homecoming queen and placed her picture and report of a supposed interview on the front page of the paper. The interview began, "Betty Gobbler, who appears to be this year's front-runner in the homecoming queen contest, said it all started when 'I got tired of being cooped up on the farm . . .'" ("Gobbler Unruffled . . .," 1981). No doubt some people were offended while others were amused by the prank.

The UND Graduate Center at Bismarck
An important off-campus development took shape beginning in 1981. The University had been offering graduate courses at various locations around the state for many years. Some means of regularizing those offerings and making programs more accessible to place bound students in the western part of the state had been considered but not resolved. Under President Clifford's guidance, the Division of Continuing Education developed the concept of a Graduate Center at Bismarck. The plan was approved by the State Board of Higher Education. Dean of Continuing Education Robert Boyd employed Donald Piper, chair of the Educational Administration program in the Center for Teaching and Learning, to serve as the first director of the UND Graduate Center at Bismarck. Piper devoted the next three years to making the local arrangements at Bismarck, including a cooperative agreement for the Center to be housed on the campus of Bismarck Junior College. Piper developed the policies and the many procedures which established a solid beginning for the Center.

In short order, master's degrees in Educational Administration, Public Administration, and Business Administration were available to students in that area of the state. Faculty would board a UND airplane at Grand Forks early in the morning on Saturday, teach classes and meet with students all day, and fly back to Grand Forks in later afternoon or early evening. The Graduate Center became an important means by which the University was able to more effectively carry out its mission to the entire state and, more specifically, its mission as a graduate institution. In subsequent years, programs in Elementary Education and Nursing would be delivered to Bismarck as well as several cycles of Educational Administration and Business Administration. Many students, most of whom were already employed in the Bismarck area, were able to earn advanced degrees through the programs at the Center. While the North Dakota State Board of Higher Education had approved establishing the Center, it never appropriated any funds for its operation. President Clifford provided significant financial support from non-state funds to establish the Center and, subsequently, to sustain its operation each year. The Division of Continuing Education provided important logistical and financial support, as well.

The School of Law

The School of Law underwent a time of transition in the late 1970s and early 1980s. Robert Rushing served as dean until 1979, when ill health required him to step down and he returned to the faculty. The search for a new dean ended without success and Law Professor Randy Lee served as acting dean for the 1979-80 academic year. Karl "Pat" Warden served as dean for two years from 1980 to 1982. UND Law Professor W. Jeremy Davis was appointed interim dean for the 1982-83 year and was subsequently named dean. President Clifford was an ardent supporter of the Law School during this period. Faculty positions increased from nine (tenure track) in the early 1970s to 12 (tenure track) plus three non-tenure track and a librarian for the law library by 1991.

In the early 1980s, the Law School received significant support and encouragement from the president for funding of computers for the law faculty. Legal research was being revolutionized by computer technology. Clifford secured non-state funds to provide the necessary support for this vital project. Dean Jeremy Davis noted that "He (Clifford) recognized the need." And Davis added that this technology and its subsequent updating has meant that the UND Law School is "better equipped than 90 percent of the law schools in the United States" (Davis, 1992).

The Law School began an exciting exchange program with the Faculty of Law at the University of Oslo, Norway, in 1982. Dean Davis initiated the plan. Thirteen UND law students spent six weeks in Norway. Students from Norway likewise spent a similar period of time at UND studying law. The students paid tuition and fees to the home institution, which made the program simpler to administer. Credits taken by visiting students at each law school counted toward graduation and thus caused no delay in completion of the degree.

As the state's only School of Law, the UND school and its faculty served many important functions. Faculty served on many important committees. For example, Larry Kraft served on the Rules Committee of the Supreme Court, and Randy Lee and Barry Vickrey served on the committee which wrote the Code of Professional Responsibility. Dean Davis served on the Board of Governors of the North Dakota State Bar Association, the board of the North Dakota Trial Lawyers Association, and on the Court Services Advisory Committee. President Clifford, a lawyer, was very popular with and well regarded by the State Bar Association. The Legal Aid Association, funded largely by federal funds, provided a clinic in which law students practiced under the supervision of three full-time attorneys. The program provided legal services to many who could not afford to retain private counsel. The Law Library was a valuable research resource for attorneys in the region. Davis estimates that approximately 75 percent of the approximately 1,600 attorneys in the state of North Dakota are graduates of the UND School of Law.

Student Housing: The Old and the New

An era passed in October of 1982 when the last of the "tin huts" were torn down. One of the huts was left standing for ceremonial purposes that year. The "huts" were brought to campus from military bases as temporary quarters for married students in 1947. At that time, of course, many veterans of World War II were enrolling at the University. These meager facilities subsequently housed veterans from the Korean and Vietnam Wars as well as other students and their families for the next 35 years. Gail Hand, a former resident of a hut, was interviewed at the time they were being demolished. "Hand mentioned several 'endearing' traits of her tin hut, including weeds through the cement floor, frost on the walls, a huge pot-bellied stove . . ." and residents were free to decorate as they pleased and could have pets (Brodshaug, 1981). The glass door knobs from some of the huts were saved and mounted on oak boards to make coat racks. These were given as mementos to selected alumni who had lived in the huts. The door knobs were the only items worth saving, according to LeRoy Sondrol, director of Plant Services (Sondrol, 11/3/91).

Over a period of a decade spanning the 1970s a series of modern units known as "the Greens" had been constructed for student family housing. Several of these units had been constructed west of the Chester Fritz Auditorium and several more just south of the Gallery Apartments.

President Clifford was very concerned that student families have quality, comfortable, and affordable housing. The president was intimately involved in the planning, the approval process, and the funding. These facilities, similar to other projects on campus, were funded primarily by bonding and received little or no state funding (Hoffarth, 10/24/91). The Gallery Apartments were deeded as a charitable remainder unitrust by Francis D. "Fritz" and Verona Mikkelson and Larry K. and Jean Johnson to the UND Foundation. The University purchased three privately owned apartment buildings known as "Virginia Rose," "Williamsburg," and "Mt. Vernon," which are located along University Avenue. This array of housing for student families surely must be one of the finest at any university of comparable size. The development of extensive student family housing presaged the significant increases in non-traditional students during the decades of the 1970s and 1980s.

An Accreditation Portrait — 1983

The accreditation of the entire University by the North Central Association (NCA) was up for review in 1983. President Clifford and Vice President Clark turned to Dean Vito Perrone of the Center for Teaching and Learning to chair the accreditation committee. Perrone, the members of the committee, and many others contributed a great deal of work to the development of the self-study report which was required prior to the site visit by the NCA team.

The documents which were prepared for the accreditation provided a portrait of the University at that time. The total (full-time equivalent) enrollment for the 1982-83 academic year was 9,554 (compared to 7,476 in 1973-74). The subtotals by degree level were (with the 1973 figures following each category), 8,315 undergraduates (6,494), 730 graduate students (632), and 509 professional students (350). The mean ACT score for entering freshmen was 21.2, down somewhat from the 1973 mean of 22.3 (Data Forms, North Central Association, 1983-84, pp. 4, 7).

The faculty profile indicated 427 full-time faculty, excluding medicine, at the instructor level and above, up from 408 in 1973-74. Women held 110 of these positions for 25 percent of the total, excluding medicine, up from 20 percent in 1973. The doctoral degree was held by 249 or 58 percent of these faculty (up from 52 percent in 1973-74). In addition, the University employed 42 part-time faculty at the instructor rank or above (43 in 1973-74). The average salary for full-time faculty (followed by the 1973-74 amount) at the full professor rank was $33,050 ($17,979), at the associate professor rank was $27,189 ($13,944), at the assistant professor rank was $22,341 ($11,905), and at the instructor rank was $19,318 ($9,499) (p. 10). The Chester Fritz Library reported a total of 436,229 books, up from 302,923 in 1973-74. The total expenditures for the University in 1981-82 were $91,744,633, up three-fold from $27,66,105 in the earlier report (p. 14). The value of the physical plant was reported at $131,134,900 more than double the $62,167,038 reported earlier (p. 15). It is important to note that while the full-time equivalent enrollment had increased by 27.7 percent from 1973, the University actually had only 4.6 percent more full-time faculty in 1983. This disparity resulted from the fact that the University was not being funded by the state at 100 percent of the budget formula. This chronic underfunding of the formula during the decades of the 1970s and 1980s meant that the University never had the proper number of faculty positions for the size of the enrollment. The University was able to capture the tuition generated by the additional students by making a request to the Emergency Commission. However, tuition covers only about 30 percent of the cost per student.

Nevertheless, the accreditation was renewed for 10 years, the maximum period of time possible. Robert Dolphin, chair of the NCA team was complimentary about the University in his final summary and noted that "... this is a stable institution that can carry out what it intends to do. . . There is no question in our minds about that" (Vanvig, 1983). He went on to identify institutional strengths as "a sensitive administration, qualified faculty and dedicated staff" and "students who are well qualified and highly motivated" (Vanvig). He warned, however, that "Lack of salary increases over the past two years threatens morale" (Vanvig). In spite of the actual increases reported in salary averages, it should be remembered that the intervening period was noted for unusually high inflation rates. UND would continue its long history of being an accredited institution of higher education.

Administrative Changes

Gerald Skogley, vice president for Finance and Operations, left the University in 1983 to become the financial officer for the Bush Foundation in St. Paul. Lyle Beiswenger, who had been the university comptroller since 1979, was named the new vice president for Finance. Clifford had placed Operations under Skogley after Swanson's death. With Skogley's departure, Clifford split the positions again and appointed Al Hoffarth, who had been the associate vice president for Operations, as the new vice president for Operations. This structure would stay in place during the remainder of the Clifford administration.

Diversity on Campus

The University continued to support diversity issues on the campus through the Native American Programs Office, the Black Student Union, and the Women's Center. By the 1980s there were several American Indian student organizations reflecting the different concerns and backgrounds of the students. President Clifford had been instrumental in establishing a Native American Endowment through the UND Foundation. The endowment provided for scholarships for American Indian students. Leigh Jeanotte, assistant to the vice president for Student Affairs for Native American Programs and a UND doctoral graduate, noted that the president had been instrumental in the development of UND's strong Native American program. "It couldn't have happened without him," said Jeanotte. "Thank goodness he had the vision to help design and support these programs. Our campus stands above others in the upper Midwest on sensitivity to Native American issues." The president has been "sincerely and truly committed to Native American students," he noted (Jeanotte, 1991).

The role of women on campus continued to receive attention. In November of 1981 the *Dakota Student* featured a lengthy "Supplement on the Roles of Women at UND" in which it reported that the percent of women on the faculty that year was exactly the same as it had been in 1918, 22 percent (Kreir, 1981). Progress on this issue seemed to many to be painfully slow.

Experimental Program to Stimulate Competitive Research: EPSCoR

The 1980s was a time of heightened effort and success by the University in acquiring grants. The National Science Foundation (NSF) announced a new program for states which were generally disadvantaged in seeking grants from that agency. UND and North Dakota State University (NDSU) joined together to develop and submit a proposal but the effort was unsuccessful the first time. However, the group persisted and a second proposal, dated March 5, 1986, was submitted and this time it was one of eight successful proposals out of a total of 12 submissions. The program, titled Experimental Program to Stimulate Competitive Research (EPSCoR), provided $3 million and required a match of an equal amount from the state of North Dakota. The two universities had planned well and had organized a State Relations Committee which included Higher Education Commissioner John Richardson, the Office of Management and Budget Director Richard Rayl, former Governor Guy, and important business leaders from Grand Forks and Fargo to get support for the state matching funds. The essential support of Governor Sinner was solicited and received. The strategy was successful and the state agreed to provide the match. UND Professor Lewis Oring was selected to direct the project for both universities. This program provided the opportunity for faculty at both institutions to engage in significant sponsored research when the odds would have been heavily against them if they had applied directly on their own to the NSF.

The Last Will of Chester Fritz

Chester Fritz, North Dakota native and student at UND from 1908 to 1910, died on July 28, 1983, in Lausanne, Switzerland, at the age of 91. Up to that time, Fritz had already made gifts to the University of nearly $3 million. Included in his will were five bequests to the University which he remembered with such fondness. The largest bequest was the division of his residual estate between UND and the University of Washington, where Fritz earned a degree in economics in 1914. The actual value of the estate could not be determined at the time, and according to his attorney, it would probably take many years before the full value could be known but it could total several million dollars. Additional bequests to UND included $700,000 for the construction of a chapel, $50,000 to be added to an endowment for scholarships, and $5,000 to the UND Alumni Association's annual sustaining fund drive, and the transfer over time of his collection of Oriental art.

During his declining years, Fritz had not been able to keep in touch with the University from Monte Carlo as well as he had before. President Clifford became concerned about the possible deterioration of this important relationship. Clifford decided to send history professor Dan Rylance to visit Fritz to collaborate with him on the writing of Fritz's biography. Fritz had led a fascinating life, growing up in North Dakota and making his fortune as a gold and silver trader in China and Europe. The Fritz biography, titled, *Ever Westward to the Far East: the Story of Chester Fritz,* was completed by Rylance and Fritz and published by UND (1982). The continuation of a working relationship with Fritz at that stage in his life may have been a critical factor in maintaining his interest in the University and his desire to provide for it in his will.

Athletics

Many important developments took place in athletics at the University during the 1980s. Athletic Director Carl Miller announced his resignation in 1983 to accept a post in California and Assistant Director Helen Smiley was named acting director by President Clifford. A faction on campus advocated Smiley's selection as the new athletic director, not only because she was highly regarded as an experienced and capable athletic administrator, but because it gave the University the rare opportunity to name a woman to the athletic director post. When the search process was completed, however, President Clifford announced on October 4, 1984, that he had selected UND's head hockey coach, John "Gino" Gasparini. No doubt Gasparini's excellent coaching record and popularity made him a favorite with many Sioux fans. Gasparini continued as hockey coach and added the athletic director position. The combination of the two positions was rather unusual and some were concerned about whether one person could or should attempt to carry the heavy duties of both positions. Smiley left the campus shortly to accept another opportunity at Western Illinois University.

The 1980s began with a new head coach for football when Eugene Murphy resigned late in 1979 and Patrick Behrns, a five-year veteran on the coaching staff, was promoted to the top position. The team finished second in the North Central Intercollegiate Athletic Conference (NCIAC) with a 5-2-0 record. Todd Thomas made the Little All American team. The basketball team made a strong finish by winning the championship at the NCIAC post-season tournament, the seventh in eight seasons, but lost in the championship round at the National Collegiate Athletic Association (NCAA) regionals.

The hockey team began the new decade with a slow start by finishing fifth in the Western Collegiate Hockey Association (WCHA) with a 21-15-2 win-loss-tie record. The Sioux rebounded in the 1981-82 season with championships in both the Western Collegiate Hockey Association (WCHA) and the

NCAA and a 35-12 record. With three national championships to their credit, more Sioux players were recruited into the professional National Hockey League (NHL) than from any other college team. They included Kevin Maxwell, Doug Smail, David Christian, John Marks, Marc Chorney, Phil Sykes, Cary Eades, Troy Murray and Craig Ludwig (Bohnet, p. 112). Mark Taylor and Howard Walker made All American in 1980 and Marc Chorney in 1981. James Patrick made All American from the 1983 team. The team placed third in the NCAA in 1984 and John Casey made All American that year.

The Sioux had some outstanding athletes in individual sports during the 1970s and early 1980s. In golf, UND won NCIAC championships in 1974, and every year from 1979 to 1982. Jeff Skinner became UND's first All American golfer. Some outstanding wrestlers emerged during the same period and made All American including Rick Lee (1975), Ken Gabriel (1976), Harvey Kruckenberg, Paul Marquart, and Jerome Larson (all in 1980), Jeff Tescher (1981), and Jerome Larson (1982).

Two former Sioux women athletes were the first to be named to the University Athletic Hall of Fame in 1981. Era Bell Thompson, for whom the UND Black Student Center would later be named, had been a superior athlete in all sports during the 1920s. Grace Osborne Rhonemus had been an outstanding athlete during the same period and both she and Thompson held state track records. Rhonemus had been a well-known teacher of dance and physical education at the University for 33 years when she retired in 1975 (Bohnet, p. 112).

A team that was not considered a major sport at the University and consequently did not have the advantages enjoyed by other programs was Margaret Peterson's women's field hockey team. However, the team made an excellent showing in 1980-81 having a 28-7 record and placing sixth in the national American Intercollegiate Athletics for Women (AIAW) tournament. The sport was dropped from the UND program after the 1985 year because of increasing difficulties in fielding a team.

The Energy and Environmental Research Center

A federal research facility had existed on the eastern edge of the campus since 1951. It was significant, yet not large. Known as the Charles R. Robertson Lignite Research Laboratory, it employed 25-30 people and was funded at the $1-2 million level by the U.S. Department of the Interior. The laboratory was one of only a few in the nation doing research on coal. It grew steadily and by the early 1980s employed 150 people and received annual funding in the range of $7-12 million from the U.S. Department of Energy (Energy and Environmental Research Center, University of North Dakota, Project Plan and Supporting Documents, undated, p. 2). The size of the operation gave it a significant economic impact on the Grand Forks community and, in addition, the research being done had considerable long-range implications for economic development of the coal deposits in the western part of the state. However, in 1982, the operation was targeted to be closed as a result of the Reagan administration's reduction in federal programs.

Dean Alan Fletcher of the School of Engineering and Mines (SEM) recalls that Senator Mark Andrews came to President Clifford with the idea of the facility being acquired by the University (Fletcher, 10/17/91). Clifford was very receptive to the idea and sought Fletcher's opinion. Fletcher was equally receptive and the decision was made to go forward. With the assistance of both North Dakota Senators Mark Andrews and Quentin Burdick, the necessary federal officials were persuaded to allow the Department of Energy to begin negotiations with the University for a possible transfer. Dean Fletcher was appointed by the president to be the chief negotiator for the University. In April of 1983 the transfer was made. The State Board of Higher Education was persuaded by President Clifford to make the research center a part of the School of Engineering and Mines (SEM) within the University. This was a logical arrangement, for according to Fletcher, "SEM had related to it intimately for years" (Fletcher, 10/17/91). Ironically, in fact, the Center had originated many years earlier within the Chemical Engineering Department when it began as a spinoff (Fletcher, 10/17/91).

A cooperative agreement was negotiated with the Department of energy whereby that agency would provide $7 million each year for three years in order to facilitate the transfer from dependence on federal support. With the acquisition completed, the facility was named the Energy and Mineral Research Center and George Wiltsee, a staff member at the Center, was named the first director. The task before Wiltsee was a difficult one. While the federal funds provided the Center with a grace period, the effort to win contracts from the private sector had to begin at once. Dean Fletcher wrote to the president, "UND must plan to bring in enough outside research to be able to sustain the Center's programs without support from the Department of Energy . . ." (Fletcher, 1983).

Perhaps even more challenging, according to Dean Fletcher, were the changes which would have to take place in the culture of the Center. The staff had become accustomed to the culture of an agency of the federal government. Now they would have to quickly change to a "contract research culture," a culture which was entrepreneurial and characterized by risk. Not only that, they would have to both understand and adopt some of the values of yet a third culture, the "academic teaching and research culture" of the University. "They are different!" according to Fletcher (Fletcher, 10/17/91).

The acquisition of the Center was, in many respects, a remarkable achievement for the University, the Grand Forks community, and the state. In addition, this venture would greatly expand the research capacity of the University in the years to come and would have significant impact on the community and the state. The strategy of cooperation between the University, the Grand Forks community, the state government, and the Congressional delegation, which had proved so effective in the development of CAS, produced impressive results again and proved to be the key to success.

In 1986 the Center was awarded a contract by Union Carbide to do research on the disposal of polychorinated biphenyls, a toxic substance known as PCBs. Very small amounts of the substance were to be destroyed in a high temperature incinerator in an effort to develop a safer method of disposal. The incinerator at the UND Center was one of only two of its type in the world. Some residents in the area of the facility as well as others were concerned about possible contamination and registered their concern with University authorities and state health officials. UND student Kathy Williams was an active leader of the opposition to the project. A series of public hearings were held. Finally, in order to avert any possible hazard and to prevent any further tension between the Center and the community, the State Health Department withdrew the permit and President Clifford announced that the tests would not be conducted and the contract to conduct the research would be rescinded.

The controversy surrounding this project probably contributed to some rethinking about the Center, its mission and its organization. Wiltsee resigned as the director. Gerald Groenewold, director of the North Dakota Mining and Mineral Resources Institute within the School of Engineering, was named the new director. The Institute was merged with the Center. Later the Center was renamed the Energy and Environmental Research Center (EERC) to reflect a broader mission within the context of a philosophy which recognized the importance of environmental concerns. The new mission statement read, in part:

> The Energy and Environmental Research Center (EERC) at the University of North Dakota, features an integrated systems approach to energy and environmental research and technology development beginning with fundamental evaluation and characterization of earth resources, followed by research and development of innovative technologies to extract and utilize these resources in an efficient and environmentally acceptable manner, and culminating in the utilization or safe disposal of wastes generated in using natural resources. (Energy and Environmental Research Center, University of North Da-

kota, Project Plan and Supporting Documents, undated,
p. 4).

Under new leadership and with a new and expanded mission, the EERC
rapidly expanded its acquisition of new grants and contracts. Groenewold
attempted to insure the financial security of the Center by negotiating a new
cooperative agreement with the Department of Energy which provided $3
million in annual income plus $2.5 million for projects with industry (Energy
and Environmental Research Center, updated). This financial base provided
the foundation from which the Center began to build a large and impressive
portfolio of research projects with both governmental agencies and the private
sector.

CHAPTER 7

THE CENTENNIAL YEAR: 1983

The centennial anniversary of the University in 1983 had been eagerly anticipated. The president turned to D.J. Robertson, retired dean of University College, to chair the effort. Robertson had chaired the 75th anniversary celebration so had ample experience for such an event. Robertson's appointment was announced in the fall of 1976, well in advance of the centennial celebration. The Alumni Association organized a planning effort, as well, chaired by Warren Hanna, a member of the Association Board of Directors and the first president of the UND Foundation. The Foundation provided significant resources to fund the celebration.

The occasion of the centennial was seen by President Clifford as an unusual opportunity for increasing the endowment for the University and so a goal of $25 million in new gifts was set, a goal which some thought to be rather optimistic. The plan for the fund drive was drawn up by Earl Strinden, Bonnie Sobolik and other members of the staff of the Alumni Association. Arley Bjella, UND alumnus and Minneapolis businessman, was selected to serve as national chair of the fund raising drive. The drive had received an early and substantial boost when the first contribution was made in December of 1977. The pledge was for $10,000 and was made by the First Federal Savings and Loan of Grand Forks. The check was delivered by Ed Christenson, president of the Savings and Loan, to President Clifford and members of the fund-raising committee.

The celebration was kicked off on January 13, 1983, with a party in Bismarck attended by virtually all of the elected officials of state government, the national congressional delegation, and a host of other dignitaries and members of the general public. Ethel Crary Davis of the class of 1906 was the honorary chair. Similar though smaller events were staged in other communities around the state in the following weeks.

The centennial was a time to celebrate the arts at UND. In January a full-scale production of the musical, *South Pacific*, directed by Peter Webb of New York, was produced on campus. Additional stage productions featured during the centennial included the world premier of Daniel Pinkham's *The Dreadful Dining Car* and a production of *Brigadoon*. A special two-week class titled, Maxwell Anderson's Theater World, was conducted by the English Department. Anderson was a UND graduate. A three-day Festival of Ethnic Music Traditions in North Dakota, held in July, was especially well received. The festival featured dozens of musicians from throughout the state. A published program and documentary, 68 pages in length, was edited by festival director Tamar C. Read. UND faculty member Kathryn McCleery designed and fired a limited edition of centennial plates which were given as gifts by the president to a few selected persons.

A special collection of historical photographs of the University and university life had been selected and was placed on exhibit on the campus as well as sent on a traveling show around the state. *A Century on the Northern Plains: The University of North Dakota at 100*, a collection of essays and photographs, was written and produced by several members of the History Department, edited by R.P. Wilkins, and published by the University of North Dakota. On October 2, 1983, the laying of the cornerstone for Old Main was re-enacted, complete with a procession of horse-drawn carriages and the burial of a time capsule. Another feature of the celebration was the writing of departmental histories for nearly all of the departments of the University. These histories continue to be available in the Special Collections section of the Chester Fritz Library.

The centennial was to be a time of intellectual renewal and stimulation and so the Centennial Symposiums, a series of lectures by distinguished speakers, was established. The list was an impressive one and included Lutheran theologian Robert D. Preus, writer Elie Wiesel, philosopher Mortimer Adler, writer and psychoanalyst Rollo May, social critic Max Lerner, and educator Ernest Boyer. Former UND faculty who were invited to return for lectures included historian Louis Geiger, author of *University of the Northern Plains: A History of the University of North Dakota 1883-1958*, and Harvard Business Professor Theodore Levitt. Featured as well were Chancellor of the University of North Carolina at Chapel Hill, Christopher Fordham III; Yale

Law Professor Geoffrey Hazard Jr.; Rockwell International Vice President Stephen Spence; Director of the Energy and Chemical Process Laboratory for Allied Chemical, George S. Hammond; and Columbia Philosophy and Education Professor Maxine Green.

An impressive three-day Technology Fair was held in February. A gala for the Grand Forks community was hosted by the UND Alumni Association on Sunday, February 27, and featured birthday cake, a dance, and an original stage production, *Beacon Over Our Western Land*, an account of the history of the University.

It was a special year for athletics, as well. The National Collegiate Athletic Association Division I hockey championships were played in Grand Forks in March and the visitors from across the nation gave their hosts high marks for hospitality. The Sioux did not make the playoffs that year, a great disappointment, especially as they had been the national champions the previous year. In February the new addition to the Winter Sports Arena, made possible by a donation from W.K. Hyslop, had been dedicated. Homecoming during the centennial was a special time, of course. A "Sioux Rendezvous" for all former Sioux athletes was held in July.

Older graduates must have been especially touched by the resurrection of one of the great traditions of UND, the Flickertail Follies. This talent show, which had once been an annual event, was held in the Chester Fritz Auditorium for two nights in April. The speaker for the May Commencement that spring was UND's own Tom Clifford. The spring graduates that year numbered 1,353. The speaker for the Law School graduation, selected each year by graduating students, was U.S. Supreme Court Justice Harry Blackmun. While the selection created some reaction because Blackmun had written the Roe v. Wade opinion on abortion, the University explained, as it had done in the past, that an important purpose of a university is to provide an open forum for different points of view.

A 36-page newspaper insert was published in May and provided as a supplement to the *Grand Forks Herald* and nine other major newspapers in the state. The publication titled *UND: A Centennial Portrait*, was produced by the Office of University Relations and was paid for by the Alumni Association and the Gold Seal Company of Bismarck and Medora. It was an impressive publication which contained historical as well as contemporary information and photographs. In addition to this publication, David Vorland and the staff of the Office of University Relations managed a massive public relations campaign which included several projects, including a television movie about the University which was seen by approximately 200,000 North Dakotans on television, alone. The movie was funded by the UND Foundation.

The centennial year was a great success by any measure. On October 12,

1985, an "Over-the-Top" celebration for the $25 million fund drive was held. Those who had considered the goal to be optimistic must have been both surprised and pleased. These funds would provide a margin of support for important programs and needs of the University during what was certain to be an uncertain future.

Centennial Chair Robertson was assisted with the University planning by a host of persons including Henry Tomasek who served as coordinator. Hazel Heiman organized the symposia. Volunteers for the Alumni Association activities included Barb and Ed Lander for the cornerstone ceremony, Shirley and Dan Goodwin for the stage productions, Jayne and Jim Kennelly for homecoming, Judy and Rob Larson for publicity and special projects, and Earl Strinden and Sharon and John Marshall for the community gala. Over 60 events took place in North Dakota and around the nation. The staff members of both the Office of University Relations and of the Alumni Association worked many extra hours to support the centennial celebration. The planning and execution for such a multitude of events was an enormous undertaking. It was well done. It was a year to remember.

CHAPTER **8**

INTO THE SECOND CENTURY: THE MIDDLE AND LATE 1980s

The College of Business

One of the professional colleges which had been striving to gain accreditation was the College of Business and Public Administration (BPA), the second largest college in the University. In July of 1984 the undergraduate business program finally realized that goal and was accredited for the first time by the American Assembly of Collegiate Schools of Business (AACSB). AACSB is the traditional accrediting body for business programs in higher education and is noted for its rigorous standards. Only approximately 300 business programs in the nation are accredited by AACSB. Clair Rowe had been serving as the dean of the College of Business and Public Administration from the time Tom Clifford had left the post. The accreditation of the Master of Business Administration (MBA) program, the largest graduate program in the college, had yet to be accredited. Rowe retired from the deanship in 1985 and Dr. W. Fred Lawrence, who had been director of the MBA program and associate dean, was asked to serve as acting dean. After a national search, Lawrence was selected to be the new dean. The accreditation of the MBA program was his top priority. It would take time, great effort, and considerable expense to achieve that goal. The president took more than a casual interest in the fortunes of this college where he had served as the dean, himself.

Student Affairs

The Division of Student Affairs experienced significant leadership changes during this same period. William Bryan had been serving in the dual capacity of vice president for Student Affairs and dean of students. Bryan left UND in 1983. He had done much to reorganize and strengthen the student affairs program at the University. Lillian Elsinga, an associate dean of students, was appointed by the president to serve as the interim vice president while a national search was conducted. The candidate favored by the Search Committee, which included a strong contingent of students, was the second associate dean of students, Gordon Henry. Clifford received the recommendation of the committee and appointed Henry, effective February 1, 1984. One of Henry's first actions was to split the two positions, vice president for Student Affairs and dean of students, which had been joined during Bryan's term, and he appointed Lillian Elsinga dean of students. Henry would bring a philosophy of caring for students to his leadership of the Division of Student Affairs. Henry was a North Dakota native, was well known around the state, and would become an important member of the president's legislative team.

International Education

International education emerged as an important issue during the 1980s as universities across the country developed and expanded programs to assist both faculty and students in this regard. The issue was not a new one to UND but it was faced with more intentionality during these years. Each year President Clifford had set aside $5,000 of private funds which he had raised to provide for study abroad by University students, especially undergraduates. A small faculty committee received requests and interviewed the students and made recommendations to the president. Some funds from the Bush Foundation monies which supported the Office of Instructional Development and local funds from the Office of Research and Program Development enabled faculty to travel abroad to do research and study. State regulations and University policy prohibited the use of any state appropriated funds for foreign travel. Such a policy seemed inconsistent for a modern university. The consequence of the regulation was to severely limit the ability of faculty and students to travel abroad at a time when internationalization was not only becoming a more significant part of higher education generally but also one of the missions of the University. President Clifford continued to provide some non-state funds for foreign travel for faculty, but the need greatly exceeded available resources. An Office of International Student Programs had been established within the division of Student Affairs largely to assist foreign nationals who had come to study at the University. But the time came when it seemed necessary to consider more systematically what might be done to increase international opportunities for those at the University.

Vice President for Academic Affairs Alice Clark and Vice President for Student Affairs Gordon Henry jointly appointed an International Education Task Force on August 5, 1985. The 21-member task force was given the charge "to recommend . . . the directions and actions the University should take in the area of international education over the next five years" ("International Task Force Final Report," p. 2). Jeremy Davis, dean of the Law School, served as chair of the Task Force and led the group through several meetings through the 1985-86 academic year. In January a mission statement for international education was adopted as follows:

1. To offer to our students, the community and the region a broad, integrated perspective on global events and trends and an appreciation of cultures other than their own.

2. To make our university a resource for students and scholars from foreign lands. ("International Task Force" . . ., 1986, pp. 4-5)

The final recommendations included three options. Each option included the appointment by the president of a Committee for International Programs and the establishment of an Office of International Programs. The options differed only in the levels of staffing for the office. The recommendations were received and efforts to implement them began.

The results included the development of a major in International Studies, which was eventually approved by the Board of Higher Education, the appointment of a half-time director of International Academic Affairs, and the reinstatement of a half-time international student advisor. The entire program moved into one of the houses on University Avenue across the street from the Memorial Union. President Clifford's view was that in order for North Dakota students to be prepared for the international marketplace, more emphasis would need to be placed on the study of foreign languages (Clifford, 5/23/91).

A Profile of UND Students — 1986

Each fall UND freshmen students took part in a national survey sponsored by the American Council on Education. The 1986 report provided an interesting portrait of UND students during that period as well as a comparison with students nationally. The new UND class was 53 percent male and 47 percent female. Nationally, the entering class was 49.9 percent male and 50.1 percent female. At UND 13 percent of the class were over 20 years of age while the national sample only 1.6 percent were over 20 years of age. The UND class was 94.8 percent White and the remaining 5 percent was divided between

Native Americans (3 percent), Asian Americans (.8 percent), Blacks (.2 percent), Mexican Americans (.1 percent), and "others." Nationally 89 percent of the entering class was White, followed by 4.8 percent Black, 4 percent Asian American, 1.5 percent Mexican American, 1.1 percent Native American and "others" (1.6 percent). American citizens accounted for 97.9 percent of the UND class and 99.6 percent nationally. As for religious preference, the UND students reflected the immediate region with 39 percent Protestant and 37.9 percent Catholic; .1 percent were Jewish; 17.9 percent selected some other religion, and only 5.1 percent indicated no religious preference though many students did not respond to this question. In this respect, the class was unlike their national counterparts wherein 33.2 percent were Protestant, 31.6 percent were Catholic, 4.6 percent were Jewish, 17.6 percent indicated some other religion, and 13 percent had no religion preference. Slightly fewer of the UND students' parents had a college degree than was true nationally.

Slightly more of the 1986 UND freshmen class were planning to major in business or a professional program than was true of their national classmates and fewer UND students were interested in a major in the arts and humanities. In terms of career interests, somewhat fewer UND students were interested in careers in engineering, law, and medicine than their national counterparts. Somewhat more UND students were interested in accounting, nursing, and physical, occupational, and speech therapy. UND students saw themselves as somewhat less likely to earn a doctoral degree than did the national group.

UND students were somewhat more pragmatic than their national classmates in that they were slightly more inclined to attend college to get a better job (85.8 percent UND, 82.2 percent national) and were slightly less likely to indicate that learning more, gaining a general education, preparing for graduate school, or becoming more cultured were reasons for attending college. The reasons why students selected UND were very similar to those of other students elsewhere in that "good academic reputation" and "graduates get good jobs" were the top two reasons for both groups. UND students were much less likely to have chosen UND because of its social reputation than were their national counterparts (28.5 percent UND, 38.1 national) and were much less likely to have selected on the basis of low tuition (14.4 percent UND, 32.1 national).

UND students seemed less confident of their academic abilities in spite of the fact that they were generally better prepared for college and scored higher on the ACT test. UND students were also more likely to work at an outside job while attending college. The objectives of UND students were quite similar to their national classmates in many respects "to be well-off financially," "to be successful in own business," "to be an administrator." However, UND students were less likely to have objectives such as developing philosophy of life, promoting racial understanding, participating in community action, influencing politics, or engaging in creative arts.

The political leanings of UND students indicated that fewer were on the "far left" (.8 percent UND, 1.7 percent national), they were less likely to be "liberal" (17.6 percent UND, 23.7 percent national), there were more likely to be "middle of the road" (62.8 percent UND, 53.4 percent national), but they were less likely to be "conservative" (17.7 percent UND, 20.1 percent national) and about the same ratio were "far right" (1 percent UND, 1.2 percent national). On some specific social issues, UND students were more "conservative." For example, UND students tended to agree more with the view that homosexual relations should be prohibited (56.4 percent UND, 45.6 percent national) and disagreed with the view that abortions should be legalized (52.7 percent UND, 65.8 percent national). On the other hand, UND students took a more "liberal" position than their national counterparts in their agreement with the position that the wealthy should pay more taxes (75 percent UND, 70.3 percent national) and their support for national health care (57.4 percent UND, 55.8 percent national). (Could these views reflect a residue from Elwyn Robinson's themes of "economic disadvantage" or "agrarian radicalism"?) UND students were much more likely to support busing for racial balance in schools (61.5 percent UND, 51.4 percent national) but one suspects that the common experience of North Dakota students riding school buses would make them more accepting of this practice. In summary, it seemed that UND students tended to be rather practical and "middle of the road" in most respects and did not follow a consistent "liberal" or "conservative" line on specific social issues. In this respect they may not have differed greatly from their parents (All data from Schieve and Driscoll, 1987).

A Master's Program and Full Accreditation for Nursing

The College of Nursing went through some important developments in the middle of the 1980s. Efforts had been under way for several years to develop a master's degree program. Both the Legislature and the president had provided extra funding in the late 1970s to upgrade the faculty. A grant from the Otto Bremer Foundation in 1978 provided the resources to conduct a feasibility study. The degree program was finally established in 1982 with a specialization in Adult Health Nursing. Dean Elisabeth Zinser had done much to strengthen the college and the credentials of the faculty by 1981 when she left the University. Judith Plawacki served as acting dean for 1981-82 and as dean for 1981-83. After Plawacki's resignation, Inez Hinsvark was brought to UND, out of retirement, to serve in the position after a two year search. She served until 1986 when Lois J. Merrill was appointed dean.

It was with special pride that the College was able to announce in 1987 that the master's program had received initial accreditation from the National League of Nursing (NLN). The program was the only NLN accredited graduate program in nursing in the state and the region. By the late 1980s the master's program had four specializations and the College was responsible for the Statewide Psychiatric Nursing Education Program at the North Dakota State Hospital in Jamestown. With both the undergraduate and the graduate programs fully accredited by the NLN, the UND College of Nursing was clearly the premier nursing program in the state as well as the immediate region.

A Time of Contrasts

The late eighties was a period of contrasts for the University. While enrollments reached an all-time high, swelling to a peak of 12,321 for the fall term of 1989, a taxpayer revolt wiped out much needed additional revenues. Many years of an open door policy to high school graduates was reversed by the North Dakota State Board of Higher Education with little opposition. The western side of the campus, the location of the Center for Aerospace Sciences, expanded with new programs and new buildings, and the eastern side of the campus, the location of the Energy Center, was engaged in frenetic grant acquisition activity and frequently made the headlines. The traditional undergraduate liberal arts sector of the University, located at the geographical center of the campus, as well as at the center of the mission of the University, seemed to recede into the background. National studies of student attitudes reflected continued strong interest in business and professional careers that promised financial reward. North Dakota students reflected much the same attitudes as their national counterparts. The 1980s at the University reflected, in many ways, the mood and trends of the Reagan era.

President Reagan Visits the Campus

In the fall of 1986 President Ronald Reagan came to North Dakota and the University on a campaign swing. A visit to a campus by the president of the United States is always an extraordinary event. President John Kennedy had visited the campus in 1963. When the University learned that President Reagan planned to make a campaign stop at UND, the campus and the community were filled with excitement. Air Force One landed at the Mark Andrews International Airport on October 17, 1986, and President Reagan traveled to campus in what must have been the most impressive motorcade ever witnessed in the area. The Presidential campaign rally was held in the Hyslop Sports Center before a packed house. The same facility had been the scene for speeches in the past by President Kennedy and Vice President Richard Nixon. President Clifford joined President Reagan and a host of dignitaries on the platform and classes were suspended from 10 a.m. until 2 p.m. Reagan was in the state to shore up the troubled campaign of Republican Senator Mark Andrews. Andrews had been a good friend of the University and had been especially helpful with securing funding for programs in the Center for Aerospace Sciences and the Energy Center. Clifford had been careful, however, to notify the campus that "The University believes that it is its obligation to make a platform available for the nation's leader, regardless of political affiliation" (Clifford, 10/9/86) and pointed out that the facility had been rented by the organizers of the visit. The visit was certainly a momentary boon to the Grand Forks economy as the town filled with people from miles around. Incidentally, Senator Andrews lost the election to Democratic Tax Commissioner Kent Conrad in one of the closest Senate races in the state's history.

Enrollment Increases

University enrollments hovered at just over 11,000 full-time students for much of the 1980s. Enrollments moved upward for the fall term in 1988-89 to 11,860 and again for the fall term in 1989-90 to 12,321, the largest in the history of the University. The most substantial gains were in undergraduate enrollments which jumped from 9,551 for the fall term of 1987-88 to 10,166 for the fall term of 1988-89 and to 10,650 for the fall term of 1989-90. Enrollments in the Center for Aerospace Sciences (CAS) accounted for much of the increases. During this period, graduate enrollments moved up slightly from 1,223 in 1987-88 to 1,269 for 1988-89 but then fell to 1,240 for 1989-90. The record enrollment of 1989 contained a factor which would sound a warning, however, in that the size of the freshmen class actually declined for the first time in several years.

These enrollment increases had important budget implications. Because the University budget was funded on the basis of full-time equivalent enrollments (FTEs), when more students arrived on campus than expected, the University was able to go to the State Emergency Commission to request permission to receive and spend the additional tuition revenue which had been generated. President Clifford exercised that option for each of those years when enrollments exceeded the FTEs which had been utilized to calculate the budget. The president's requests were granted in each instance. In spite of the fact that the Legislature never funded the University budget at 100 percent of the higher education formula, this method of retrieving the additional tuition revenue provided the University with critical funds to function during this period. It seems clear that the increases in undergraduate enrollments were providing the University with a critical margin of much needed revenue.

At the same time as these larger enrollments generated much needed revenue, they placed a severe strain on some segments of the University. University housing was bursting at the seams and, for the first few weeks of classes, dozens of male students were housed in local motels until spaces opened on campus. Some classes were filled to capacity and closed to students who attempted to register which forced these students to settle for second choices. Some class sections were large by North Dakota standards, even if not as large as at many other universities. Part-time lecturers were hired to teach additional sections of high-demand classes, especially in English composition and mathematics. The picture which emerges was one of a growing, thriving University which was, at the same time, resting upon a fragile financial base, one which was inadequately funded by the state. The stage was set for difficult times to come.

A book, *A Guide for Parents and Freshmen Students*, published in 1989, was authored by George Schubert, dean of University College and Summer Sessions, and Douglas Munski, associate professor of geography. The book was written specifically for UND parents and freshmen and was designed to provide practical information and advice to both. The book fit the need for a free-standing advisement tool as the University faced steadily growing enrollments.

Integrated Studies

During the middle 1980s a relatively small but very significant academic innovation began to take shape at the University. Faculty members Pat Sanborn and Gerald Lawrence had become increasingly dissatisfied with the way in which general education courses were being conducted. Most students seemed to be either apathetic or even hostile toward many of these classes which were required of all entering students. Students did not understand why they were expected to take these courses when they wished to get on with a major and prepare for a career. Sanborn wrote ". . . the general education courses were unrelated to each other, often very large in size, and frequently asking relatively little in the way of active thinking and sensible writing" (Sanborn, 1991). Sanborn and Lawrence began the process which would lead to the development of what would become the Integrated Studies Program. They studied alternatives to general education which had been developed at other campuses and received a start-up grant from the Office of Instructional Development at UND. Then, during the 1985-86 academic year, they prepared a grant proposal to the National Endowment for the Humanities even though such grants were very competitive. To their credit, the proposal was funded at $207,000 for three years from October 1986 through August 1989. The first teaching semester was the fall of 1986 and five departments responded (Economics, Geology, English, History, and Humanities). Jack Barden was employed to serve as coordinator.

The curriculum was imaginative and interdisciplinary. Each semester

Thomas J. Clifford taught his first accounting classes in 1945 while still wearing his U.S. Marine Corps uniform. By 1992, he had served longer than any other employee of the North Dakota University System.

Passing the key to the office on to his successor is George W. Starcher, left, president from 1954 to 1971. President Starcher relied heavily upon the management and fiscal acumen of his vice president for finance, Thomas J. Clifford, who served simultaneously as dean of the College of Business and Public Administration.

Clifford meets with the Council of Deans in July 1971. Only Bernard O'Kelly, nearest the camera, still served on this body in 1992. Others, pictured counter-clockwise from O'Kelly's right, are D.J. Robertson, University College; President Clifford; Donald P. Naismith, Engineering (acting); W.E. Koenker, vice president, Academic Affairs; Clair Rowe, Business and Public Administration; Margaret Heyse, Nursing; A. William Johnson, Graduate School; Robert K. Rushing, Law; Martelle Cushman, Education; Theodore Harwood, Medicine; and Vito Perrone, New School of Behavioral Studies in Education.

The new president and his first vice presidential team. From left, W.E. Koenker, academic affairs; Russell Brown, student affairs; Clifford; Loren Swanson, operations; and Gerald Skogley, finance.

Florence Clifford (above, center), first lady of the University until her death from cancer in 1984, is remembered as a gracious hostess and as a gifted musician and piano teacher who helped to promote the fine arts at UND.

Clifford is interviewed on television during the 1971 statewide tour organized by the UND Alumni Association to introduce him to citizens of the state.

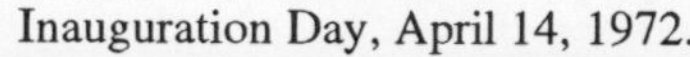

Inauguration Day, April 14, 1972.

Monthly open meetings with students (or "raps," as they were then termed) were a regular part of Clifford's first years as president. Students soon learned that his office door was always open.

ABOVE: One of the best-received celebrities to visit the campus was musician Lawrence Welk, who in 1973 played the accordion and lectured to a history class in popular culture.

BELOW: Students lined up outside Twamley Hall at the beginning of the 1973 semester. During the Clifford presidency, enrollment grew from 8,395 to a high of 12,321.

ABOVE: The World War II-vintage "tin huts" disappeared during the Clifford administration. BELOW: Just one new residence hall was constructed: Swanson Hall (below), opened in 1985, features air conditioning and other amenities.

A scene from the 1970s that has become history: mass registration at the Fieldhouse. Today, many students sign up for classes via telephone.

Clifford, here presenting UND's budget to the State Senate, became legendary for his effectiveness in advocating the University's case.

ABOVE: Robert McCarney, left, North Dakota's maverick politician and "referral king," was an outspoken critic of UND during the 1970s. But McCarney and President Clifford eventually settled their differences, and McCarney became a contributor to UND's scholarship fund. BELOW: Restoration of the historical Adelphi fountain in 1976 was emblematic of Clifford's long-time interest in beautifying the campus.

Students, faculty and staff worked around the clock to fight the great flood of April 1979.

One of the most revolutionary changes at UND has been the adaptation of the campus to the needs of the physically disabled.

Clifford and Alice Clark, who Clifford appointed vice president for academic affairs in 1980, when she became the highest ranking woman administrator in the system.

Academic events, a massive public relations effort, a successful $25 million fund-raising campaign, and social festivities marked the University's Centennial in 1983.

UND's venerable Memorial Stadium saw new artificial turf, installation of an Olympic quality running track, the temporary return of a marching band, and mixed results in the fortunes of the football team.

The average age of UND's students has grown steadily older. Ed Clarke, 81, was UND's most elderly student in 1984, shown here in a class in money and banking.

UND initiated a variety of programs for Native Americans during the Clifford years, especially in medicine and education. The annual Wacipi and Time-Out continue to give Indian students the opportunity to share their culture.

Despite the demands of the presidency, Clifford continued his success as a champion handball competitor and was still an active player upon his retirement at age 71.

Thomas and Gayle Clifford shortly after their marriage in 1986.

The restoration of the old president's mansion, renamed the J. Lloyd Stone Alumni Center, in 1981 gave UND an elegant headquarters for its Alumni Association and Foundation.

Although UND vastly increased its research activity during the Clifford years, good teaching remained the highest institutional priority.

The two best known coaches during the Clifford years were probably John "Gino" Gasparini, hockey (above), who also served a simultaneous stint as athletic director, and Dave Gunther, basketball (right).

Women's basketball was a growth sport at UND, by the late 1980s capable of packing the Hyslop Sports Center.

Ralph Engelstad, alumnus, former hockey player and Las Vegas businessman, on the occasion of the naming of the winter sports center in his honor in 1988.

This picture, taken during President Ronald Reagan's visit to UND in October 1986, was published in newspapers and magazines around the world.

This view of the English Coulee, graced by the Hughes Fine Arts Center and the Chester Fritz Auditorium (both opened during the Clifford years), is one of the most photographed scenes in eastern North Dakota.

The newest cultural addition to the campus is the North Dakota Museum of Art which, thanks to more than $1 million in gifts and grants, has first class quarters in the refurbished former "West Gym."

Perhaps the most striking milestone of the Clifford presidency has been creation of the Center for Aerospace Sciences. This 1991 air view shows the CAS complex on the west side of the campus; extensive facilities serving the largest training fleet in North America are located at Mark Andrews International Airport.

UND's internationally known Energy and Environmental Research Center resulted from UND's bold response to the Reagan Administration's threat to close the federal coal research facilities adjacent to the campus.

The 1980s and early 1990s saw the widespread adoption of new teaching and research technology at UND, including a lead role in development of a systemwide interactive video network.

Unlike many of its counterparts around the country, the University Senate remained an influential and activist governing body during the Clifford presidency.

The opening of the Olympic pool in the Hyslop Sports Center (formerly the fieldhouse) in 1984 helped put UND on the map in competitive swimming and provided new recreational opportunities for students.

President Clifford and his wife Gayle enjoy a Homecoming banquet dedicated to them in 1990. Most alumni thought he would retire in June of 1991, but a moonlighting assignment as interim chancellor of the North Dakota university system kept him at his post for another year.

Five key figures in the Clifford administration. From left, Earl Strinden, who for much of his tenure as executive vice president of the UND Alumni Association also served as majority leader of the North Dakota House of Representatives; John Odegard, who with Clifford's firm backing created with little state funding UND's enormous Center for Aerospace Sciences; Tom Johnson, who as dean at a crucial period completed the conversion of the School of Medicine from a two-year basic sciences sequence to an M.D. granting program; the late Conny Nelson, vice president for academic affairs who in a brief tenure from 1976 to 1980 brought long-lasting changes to the way UND administered itself; and Vito Perrone, innovative dean of the Center for Teaching and Learning who until his departure in 1986 often was called upon by Clifford to lead University-wide projects such as the self study in 1982 for UND's successful re-accreditation by the North Central Association.

Captions by David Vorland, Office of University Advancement. Photographs, unless otherwise indicated, by Richard Larson, David Vorland, and Audrey Stewart, Office of University Advancement, and Jerry Olson, Academic Media Center.

was organized around a different theme. In the fall of 1986 the theme was "People and the Land"; in the fall of 1987, "The City"; in spring of 1988, "Fact and Imagination"; in fall of 1988, "Time and Change"; and in the spring of 1989, "Power and the Powerless." Extensive readings in original sources, writing assignments, and discussions were focused around these themes. While special presentations were made by the faculty, lectures were generally limited. Special attention was given to carefully developed writing assignments. Faculty worked closely with small groups of students in cooperative learning groups, and laboratories were used to provide the scientific connections to the theme. This format evolved over time but was based upon careful planning by the faculty involved in the program each semester and was an attempt to employ the best in learning theory. From its inception, 14 different faculty taught full-time for a semester in the program; about half of those taught two semesters, and another eight faculty participated in more limited roles. Students earned from 10 to 16 credits, which met specific general education requirements, depending upon the semester.

When the grant expired, the University assumed the cost of the salary for the program coordinator and a part-time secretary. The vice president for Academic Affairs, the dean of Arts and Sciences, and the Office of Instructional Development provided support for the program, also. A problem for the program continued to be the fact that faculty who taught in the program were not replaced in their own departments and this created difficulty with the coverage of those classes. In addition, there was concern that, because UND was a research university and faculty were rewarded and promoted largely on the basis of their research and publications and less so on the basis of their teaching, those who devoted much time to this program might risk falling behind in their research.

There were some efforts to disseminate the experience of the UND program. The Integrated Studies staff and faculty sponsored a conference in November of 1989 to which all of the two-year colleges, both state and tribally controlled in the state, were invited. Representatives of six institutions participated to learn more about how such an approach might be developed on their own campuses. A paper on the UND Integrated Studies Program was presented by program coordinator Jack Barden at the Association of American Colleges in January of 1988. While the program adopted elements from such well-known programs as Meiklejohn's Experimental College at the University of Wisconsin, the curriculum at Evergreen State, and the Great Books programs, the UND program adapted and added its own unique elements. Students who participated in the program, numbering over 400, returned to campus to testify about how much they had learned and how the program had helped them develop both intellectually and socially.

Another Branch Campus?

The 1987 legislative session produced an unusual dilemma for the University. Bismarck legislator Robert Martinson introduced a bill which would have made the Bismarck State Community College (the name had just been changed by the State Board of Higher Education from Bismarck Junior College) a branch campus of the University. The campus at Williston had been a branch of the University for several years. The bill was jointly sponsored by nearly all of the Bismarck representatives. While the proposal had some merit, it actually reflected a deep division in the Bismarck community and a sharp difference of opinion over the future of the college. One group, represented by Martinson and most of the delegation to the state Legislature, actually favored a plan to make the college a four year institution. This group thought that a four year college would be better for the community and would allow more public educational opportunities at a lower cost to citizens in the second largest city in the state and the surrounding area. Sympathetic to this group were the Bismarck Chamber of Commerce and many community leaders. Another group in the community was a strong supporter of the University of Mary, formerly Mary College, a Catholic private school located on the outskirts of Bismarck. This group saw any move toward a public four year program as a direct threat to the fortunes of the University of Mary. In fact, the University of Mary had become more vocal in opposition to the presence of graduate programs from UND which were being offered at the UND Graduate Center on the Bismarck State campus. UND had been delivering graduate programs to Bismarck with the State Board of Higher Education's approval for many years before the University of Mary began to provide graduate offerings. Ironically, when Martinson offered his bill in the Legislature, the president of Bismarck State, Kermit Lidstrom, joined forces with the University of Mary to oppose the "branch bill" and head off any move that could lead to the eventual expansion of the college. Lidstrom was an ardent advocate of the community college concept and was, no doubt, wary of any possible loss of autonomy for himself and the college.

To complicate matters even further, many of the faculty at Bismarck State favored the idea of becoming a branch of the University. The State Board of Higher Education and Commissioner Richardson opposed the "branch bill" and any effort to expand Bismarck State beyond a two year program. President Clifford attempted to remain above the fray. When asked what his position was, he simply stated that he did not oppose the idea but that UND was not actively seeking for Bismarck State to become a branch. He had to be careful not to take a position contrary to the Board, but neither did he want to alienate a large segment of the Bismarck community, especially the segment which supported public higher education. It was an impossible situation in many respects. Martinson's bill passed the House but ran into opposition in the Senate.

The plot thickened as legislators from Dickinson were concerned about the prospect of having another four year institution within the radius of Dickinson State College, as did representatives from Minot who had the same concerns for Minot State. In addition, some representatives from Fargo were worried that having a branch in the state Capitol would give UND a power base there which could disadvantage North Dakota State University. It became evident that all of these forces together would block his bill and Martinson withdrew the reference to the branch concept and reworded his bill to simply change the name of the college by dropping the word "community." The new name would be Bismarck State College. The branch idea died. Politics does make strange bedfellows.

Ironically, Senator Charles Mertens from Devils Lake, thought the branch idea was a good one and introduced a bill which would make the Lake Region Community College a branch of the University of North Dakota. The bill passed and was enacted. The campus was renamed UND-Lake Region. In the same bill the colleges at Dickinson, Mayville, and Valley City were named "universities." Whatever the political reasons for naming these colleges "universities," the title made no sense to anyone who knew anything about higher education. Nevertheless, after the dust settled, UND had another branch campus, though a different one than had been expected at the beginning of the legislative session. It should be noted that President Clifford had always related to the Williston campus as a semi-autonomous campus rather than as a true branch campus. He followed the same practice with the Lake Region campus.

The Graduate School

A significant change took place on the administrative team of the University when A. William Johnson, dean of the Graduate School since 1968, and only the second graduate dean in the history of the University, announced in February 1988 that he would step down and return to the Chemistry Department. Johnson's tenure as dean could be characterized as a period of development and maturity for the Graduate School. Prior to his time the Graduate School had been administered "as a relatively private affair," according to Johnson, with no graduate faculty involvement and decisions being made within the dean's office (Johnson 2/11/91). "I wanted to open it up with a Graduate Faculty, a Graduate Committee, an open public agenda, with bylaws and a restructured membership and a public level of debate the faculty wanted" (Johnson). The staff in the Graduate School office was upgraded and areas of special responsibility assigned. A Summer Research Professorship program was developed and funded for faculty and a similar program for graduate students. The number of scholarships was increased with special attention to aid for minority students.

In spite of these successes, Johnson felt that he was not successful in securing "major investment" in graduate education at the University and that such an investment was never a priority for the University during his time as dean (Johnson, 2/11/91). His perception was that the major initiatives during the period went to the undergraduate programs and the professional schools, especially law, medicine, and business. "There is only so much money to go around" he acknowledged (Johnson). A common limitation faced by graduate schools, according to Johnson, is that they do not have a loyal body of graduates to whom to appeal for financial support in the way that law and medical schools do. Many alumni of graduate schools do not have the financial resources which are more typically acquired by lawyers and physicians.

During the Johnson years, the Graduate School did mount significant outreach programs off campus, especially in the fields of education and business. The Air Force bases in Grand Forks and Minot, in addition to the UND Graduate Center at Bismarck, were the locations of these programs. These efforts enjoyed the solid support of Clifford, who frequently provided significant funding for the programs administered by the Division of Continuing Education. The president viewed these programs as vital to the state-wide mission of the University. The programs provided service to many students who were place-bound and unable to come to the main campus. The fact that they provided visibility for the University, especially in Bismarck, was seen by Clifford as no small benefit.

The on-campus enrollments of the Graduate School during this period were 1,088 in 1971-72, reached a peak of 1,337 in 1982-83 and declined to 1,269 in 1988-89. There were few new graduate programs introduced during this period. The declines during the 1982-89 period, while not large, took place at the same time the undergraduate enrollments continued to increase. Those fluctuations were influenced by many factors, perhaps by changing student financial aid policies during the Reagan era which shifted funding from direct grants to loans, by shifts in job markets, and by competition from new graduate programs within the state and surrounding region.

Johnson recounts his experience with efforts to gain approval for a new doctoral program in physics at the University, a story which reveals a persistent problem for higher education in North Dakota. The University had gone to considerable effort to develop a doctoral degree program in the Physics Department. When it came time to secure approval from the North Dakota State Board of Higher Education, a "real battle" ensued, according to Johnson. He and others from UND traveled around the state attempting to gain support for the program over the opposition of North Dakota State University in Fargo. According to Johnson, NDSU was "afraid of getting locked out" though their institution did not even have a Physics Department. The end of the story is that two years later the State Board of Higher Education approved a program for NDSU. Robinson's "too much" theme seemed evident once again.

A major change in the gender of graduate students took place during this period. Because the change was gradual, it was little recognized on the campus. In 1971 there were 834 men (77 percent) and 254 women (23 percent) enrolled in graduate programs, including the military programs. By 1989 the enrollments had shifted to 520 men (46 percent) and 609 women (54 percent), not counting the military programs (gender could not be extrapolated from the off-campus data). Dean Johnson was successful in securing federal fellowship support for women students, especially at the doctoral levels. This "silent revolution" at UND was reflective of the same trend across the nation as more women entered higher education. A growing literature on the differences between the educational experiences of men and women, and of "women's ways of knowing," will give some faculty and administrators adequate reason to ponder the implications. This issue is certain to become more urgent during the 1990s.

The implementation of academic program review was a major achievement of the Johnson years. The policy required periodic review by a faculty committee, appointed by the Graduate Committee, of every graduate program. In the reviews, strengths as well as weaknesses were identified and recommendations for changes were made in formal reports. Johnson credits these reviews with providing the motivation and justification for significant program improvements over the years. In addition, the review reports were helpful in documenting facility needs to the North Dakota State Board of Higher Education when requests for funding for remodeling and construction were presented. Johnson is pleased to point out that UND was one of the first Graduate Schools in the nation to implement the program review policy which is now standard practice in higher education.

Dean Johnson was viewed by many as a guardian of academic standards and a champion of quality. He was experienced by some as a stern and sometimes even unyielding enforcer of Graduate School policy and regulations. These qualities combined with his sometimes direct and even caustic letters and memos did not endear him to some faculty and students. Nevertheless, he was widely respected as a person of great integrity, someone who paid careful attention to detail, and one who possessed considerable knowledge about graduate education. He was an opera "buff" and announced a regular opera program on KFJM, the University radio station. Over these years Johnson demonstrated a tireless devotion to the Graduate School. There can be no doubt that the quality of graduate education at the University improved markedly during this period.

The Engelstad Gift and Controversy

In early February of 1988 the University announced a ceremony to be held later that month to honor alumnus Ralph Engelstad by naming the Winter Sports Arena after him. Engelstad, a former Sioux hockey player, a Sioux Award recipient, and a successful businessman and owner of the Imperial Palace Hotel in Las Vegas, had given a donation of $500,000 to the UND Foundation to establish the Ralph and Betty Engelstad Endowment. Engelstad acknowledged that his past donations and future gifts would easily be in the millions and the local press reported the amount at $5 million (Hand and Bonham, 1988). By the next fall, however, the University and Grand Forks community were concerned to learn that the Las Vegas press were reporting that Engelstad had a collection of Nazi memorabilia and had held Adolph Hitler parties in the Imperial Palace. Engelstad issued an apology to those who had been offended by his actions and he also sent a letter of explanation and apology to the University. Engelstad explained that he was a collector of World War II memorabilia but went on to say that "I despise Adolph Hitler and everything he stood for" (Hand and Bonham).

The revelations from Las Vegas raised serious questions on the UND campus about the propriety of the relationship between Engelstad and the University. Engelstad invited a delegation from UND to visit the hotel and inspect the Nazi collection which included about 20 automobiles. President Clifford quickly appointed a team of seven persons: David Vorland, executive assistant to the president and director of University Relations; Elizabeth Hampsten, English professor and president of the University Senate; D. Jerome Tweton, history professor; Vernon Keel, communications professor; Barry Vickrey, law professor; David Glessner, student body president; and Marijo Shide, North Dakota Board of Higher Education member. The team concluded that the collection was certainly not a Nazi shrine but could be open to misunderstanding (Schmidt, 1988).

Back at the Grand Forks campus, a group of concerned faculty and students took the controversy as an opportunity to educate people about the Holocaust. In the weeks and months to follow, a number of special events were held on campus and efforts were made to incorporate material about the subject into appropriate courses. The controversy subsided with everyone learning some important lessons. Later, Engelstad brought an Imperial Palace entertainment team to the Chester Fritz Auditorium for a benefit program.

All Time Enrollment Reached

The 1988-89 academic year was noteworthy in that this was the year the freshman class reached an all time high of 2,173 students. That increase was more than the enrollments at each of seven of the other campuses in the state. The record held through the 1991-92 academic year and may well stand for several years to come. Some higher education prognosticators estimated that enrollments across the nation would move up again in the middle to late nineties. Enrollment limits adopted by the North Dakota University System, however, might prevent the University from ever reaching that peak again.

A New Dean for the Graduate School

During the 1988-89 academic year a national search was mounted to find a replacement for A. William Johnson, dean of the Graduate School. Several excellent candidates were interviewed. There was some concern about whether the University could offer a competitive salary in order to attract one of these candidates. However, the position was offered to and accepted by Duncan Perry who was serving as an associate dean of the Graduate School at the University of Maryland at College Park. Perry came with considerable experience in the administration of graduate education. After he became familiar with the campus during the fall term, he began to make changes. It became evident that Perry's philosophy was that more of the decision making should be decentralized and should take place at the program or departmental level rather than in the Graduate Committee or the office of the Graduate Dean.

Perry was a historian with a specialization in Eastern Europe, specifically the Balkans. He took special interest in the efforts to internationalize the UND campus. He made three trips to Eastern Europe during the next two years in part to establish contacts with universities there to begin the process of developing cooperative programs.

A Strategic Plan for the 90s

Perry quickly gained recognition on the campus and the following year was named by the president to chair a new strategic planning effort. The Strategic Planning Council was appointed by the president and was composed of representatives from the various campus constituencies. This time, however, it was a much smaller group than in some previous instances. Of the 21 members, 11 were administrators, eight were faculty, and two were students. The council met throughout the 1989-90 academic year. Their report, "A Strategic Plan for the 90s," was circulated during the spring. Public hearings were held, but, unfortunately, were poorly attended, perhaps because of the low morale resulting from the vote on December 5 when several tax measures had been defeated. The plan was presented to the president late in the spring and was accepted without significant change.

The plan included a newly revised mission statement for the University which was subsequently revised by the Council of Deans. The recommendations in the plan included endorsement of the admissions standards and enrollment limitations which were being advocated by the North Dakota State Board of Higher Education. However, the Planning Council emphasized that these policies must be accompanied by a transition from the budgeting formula based on student enrollments (FTEs) to a programmatic budgeting policy whereby budgets would be based upon actual costs of delivery of academic programs (A Strategic Plan . . ., p. 5). The plan contained few specific recommendations beyond these. It called instead for review and evaluation of many University programs and units. The Planning Council did recommend that the title of the Vice President for Academic Affairs should be changed to Senior Vice President or Provost to emphasize "the primacy of the academic mission of the University" (A Strategic Plan . . ., p. 12).

In the spring of 1990, Dean Perry was offered and accepted a one-year position with the Voice of America program in Germany for the 1990-91 academic year. The fact that the Iron Curtain was crumbling all across Eastern Europe must have made the opportunity irresistible. Perry requested and was granted a one-year leave of absence from the Graduate School post. After an internal search, Harvey Knull, professor of biochemistry and molecular biology, a Chester Fritz Distinguished Professor, and a former chair of the Graduate Committee, was selected to serve as acting dean while Perry was on leave.

Accreditation

During the latter half of the 1980s, the efforts to achieve accreditation or reaccreditation of the professional schools and other programs continued with determination. Those which were achieved were the School of Law by the American Bar Association (1986), the baccalaureate program in the College of Nursing by the National League of Nursing (1986), Theatre Arts Department by the National Association of Schools of Theatre (1986), Computer Science Department by the Computing Science Accreditation Board (1987), Counseling Department by the American Psychological Association (1987), Clinical Psychology Department by the American Psychological Association (1988), and Industrial Technology Department by the National Association of Industrial Technology (1988).

The Centennial of the State of North Dakota

UND was to play a special role in the North Dakota Centennial during the week of April 1989. It was a time of remembering and celebrating for the people of the state. April 3-9 was declared Native American Week and Native American Day was set for April 5 — both received the endorsement of the State Legislature and the governor. A $60,000 grant was awarded by the North Dakota Centennial Commission to assist with the cost of the Native American Week celebration at UND. Tribal leaders from the reservations within the state were involved in the planning. The week-long celebration included a University Convocation on April 5 featuring Steven Emery, a Cheyenne River Sioux musician, at the Chester Fritz Auditorium. The 20th annual UND Indian Association Wacipi (Powwow) ran from April 7-9 at the Hyslop Sports Center. A noon awards luncheon on April 5 was a highlight of the week with the presentation of awards by Governor Sinner to recognize several outstanding Indian leaders in the state. Pemina Yellow Bird of Fort Berthold received the Indian Citizen of the Year Award. Cornelius P. Grant and Clark J. Wold, both of Bismarck, and Christopher "Kip" Quale of New Town, and Art Raymond of UND, all received Meritorious Service Awards. At a ceremony later in the day, three outstanding Native American teachers were recognized, Viola Carlson of Bottineau, Gretta White Calf of White Shield, and Don Yellowbird of White Shield. Outstanding American Indian school administrators recognized were Marlene Ward and Karen Swisher. The Sioux Award, a distinction given by the Alumni Association also was presented to Ward and Swisher.

A project undertaken as part of the celebration, which would continue to make an impact well into the future, was a new Native American curriculum. The curriculum was developed by the Center for Teaching and Learning and the North Dakota Department of Public Instruction for use in all public schools in the state. The development of the curriculum had been supported by a grant of $30,000 from the Centennial Commission to match funds contributed by the Center for Teaching and Learning, the North Dakota Department of Public Instruction, Exxon Foundation, and Mountain West Equity Center. When the new curriculum materials arrived from the printer, the boxes filled the dean's office and the conference room of the Center for Teaching and Learning. A cadre of volunteers was required to mail the materials to the schools.

All of the nearly 3,000 Native American graduates of the University were invited to return to the campus for the centennial celebration and many did. President Clifford commended Leigh Jeanotte of the UND Native American Program and his staff for their role in this historic event. It was a time when the state and the University recognized the contributions of the first citizens of the place which came to be known as North Dakota. The University expressed its pride as the campus in the North Dakota higher education system with a special mission to serve the American Indian people of the state.

By the late 1980s, several American Indian student organizations had been organized on the campus including Seven Fires, Strengthening of Spirit, American Native Student Association, American Indian Student Law Association, and Indians Into Medicine Student Association (Jeanotte 2/1/91). Even so, a downturn in the enrollment of American Indian students occurred in the late 1980s and early 1990s. In 1982 the enrollments stood at 195 students for the fall semester and rose to a high of 311 students by the 1986 fall semester. Thereafter, the fall enrollments were 276 (1987), 271 (1988), 267 (1989), 216 (1990). In part, these declines reflected the general reductions in undergraduate enrollments. However, additional factors were at work, according to Leigh Jeanotte, assistant to the vice president for student affairs for Native American programs. Federal Funds, from Title V of Indian Education Programs for Personnel Development, U.S. Department of Education, were reduced and many of the programs supported by those funds declined or were eliminated. Higher education budgets at the tribal level, which were supported by federal funding, did not keep up with inflation. Within North Dakota, tribally supported community colleges were recruiting more high school graduates and retaining more students, which Jeanotte regarded as a positive trend. In addition, more Native American students were enrolling at other campuses within the state. North Dakota State University and Minot State University had made extra efforts to attract more Native American students. While Jeanotte viewed this latter trend as a valuable one for those campuses, he did express concern about the diffusion of Native American students throughout the campuses in the state because a substantial core of students are necessary to both justify and support the extensive and costly services required to sustain a quality program (Jeanotte, 2/1/91). Once again, the practice within the state seemed to be that if one institution developed a successful program, other campuses attempted to develop their own similar programs. While that response is understandable, the state does not have the resources to support a multitude of quality programs that serve the same purpose. One is reminded again of Robinson's "Too Much Mistake" as the state has often attempted too much with too little. As the decade of the 1990s began, it seemed that Native American programs would become one more example of this problem which continued to plague higher education in North Dakota. Many hoped that the new "system" approach at the state board level would address such issues.

Earth System Science

During homecoming of the same year, 1989, a groundbreaking ceremony was held for another impressive new facility in the Center for Aerospace Sciences complex on the west side of the campus. North Dakota Senator Quentin Burdick and other dignitaries attended. The new facility, which was named the Earth System Science Building, would cost $8.4 million, and was funded by a grant from the U.S. Department of Agriculture. As the name suggests, the facility will house multidisciplinary instruction and research programs which will focus on the complex earth systems which interact to produce the planet's weather and ecosystem. An important element of the new program will be the acquisition of a "super computer" which would analyze the vast quantities of data required for such complex research. In a news story, University officials explained that efforts were under way to secure federal funding for the acquisition of the super computer (Schmidt, 7/14/91).

Some elements of the higher education community began to emphasize in the late 1980s that economic development was a major contribution of higher education to North Dakota. The Center for Aerospace Sciences calculated that its 600 employees with a payroll of $6 million annually, its research programs and grants, and the cost of its construction projects, contributed $84 million to the Grand Forks regional and North Dakota economy during 1988-89. The remarkable growth of CAS was quite evident by the end of the 1980s.

The North Dakota Museum of Art

A wonderful addition to the campus in the fall of 1989 was a new home for the North Dakota Museum of Art. The museum, previously housed in the Memorial Union, did not require a new facility, however, as it found a home in the old West Gym. The worn and dreary old gymnasium was transformed into a bright and impressive art gallery. Large windows, running from floor to ceiling, were installed on each end of the building and a large skylight was installed on the roof. The inside is bathed in natural light during the day. The old gym floor was refinished, a gift shop installed and the entire interior refurbished and transformed. Most of the $1,000,000 cost was donated by Laura Christenson specifically for a museum. Other funding came from private citizens and corporate gifts. With expansive display areas and superb illumination, the museum greatly enriched the cultural opportunities of the region. Noted artists from literally all over the world were featured at the museum which was administered by director Laurel Reuter.

A New Dean for the School of Engineering and Mines

During the 1988-89 academic year, Alan Fletcher, dean of the School of Engineering and Mines since 1969, announced his retirement. Associate Dean Tom Owens and chair of the Chemical Engineering Department was named acting dean for the 1989-90 academic year. Owens would have been a strong candidate for the permanent position but decided to withdraw his application. Mogens Henriksen from Northern Colorado University in Greeley, was selected after a national search, and assumed the deanship in the fall of 1990. In an interview, Henriksen explained that one of the reasons he decided to come to UND was because of the Energy and Environmental Research Center (EERC) "and its potential — not only financial, but intellectual" (Phillips, 1991). The EERC had become a centerpiece of the University research effort.

In reflecting upon Alan Fletcher's contributions as dean of the School of Engineering and Mines, President Clifford noted that Fletcher was instrumental in initiating Project Lignite at the University. That project, according to Clifford, was essential in developing the research potential of the University, the expertise on campus, and the credibility of the University as a research center. "The vision and persistence were Alan's," Clifford stated (2/26/92).

Athletics

Intercollegiate sports continued in importance at the University during these years but the Fighting Sioux teams met with mixed success during the late 1980s. In 1986 Pat Behrns, head football coach, departed the campus and was replaced by Roger Thomas but progress was slow. Likewise, in basketball, these were not outstanding years. The hockey team made a comeback for the 1987 season by winning titles in both the National Collegiate Athletic Association (NCAA) and Western Collegiate Hockey Association (WCHA) with a 40-8-0 season, establishing a new record for wins in one season by a college hockey team. It was also a record for season attendance for a sport at UND. Three Sioux made all American — Tony Hrkac, Bob Joyce and Ian Kidd. It was an excellent team. Individual skaters made All American in subsequent years — Steve Johnson (1988) and Russ Parent (1990). By the late 1980s legendary basketball coach Dave Gunther decided to step down but remained at the University and was appointed assistant athletic director.

Rich Glas, a native of nearby Bemidji, Minnesota, began UND basketball coach duties April 7, 1988, coming from an assistant athletic directorship at the University of Hawaii. Glas coached basketball for eight years in the 1970s at the University of Minnesota-Morris, where he was known as the "Little Wizard," but his first team at UND finished with a 8-20 record. Glas was not despairing, however, as he continued to tell the team "Hey, we're going to Springfield," a reference to the location of the National Collegiate Athletic Association Division II Elite Eight Tournament each year (Fee, 1991). The 1989-90 season was one to behold as the team completely reversed its previous record and ended with a 28-7 record and finished third at Springfield. What's more, it was the first team since 1925 to move from last spot in the North Central Conference (NCC) to the first spot in a single season. Outstanding performances were given by players Dave Vonesh, recognized as an All American, and Rico Burkett, Mike Boschee, and Solomon Ayinla.

The women's basketball team under Coach Gene Roebuck had a tremendous season. The women won the North Central Conference championship, the

NCAA Division II North Central Regional Tournament, and finished third in the nation with a 27-4 record. Durene Heisler was recognized as an All American, and Jenny Walter and Whitney Meier gave outstanding performances. Sioux basketball fans had a banner year!

December 5, 1989

The 1989 legislative session was one of the best for higher education in recent years. The Legislature had responded to the case which had been made by the higher education community for urgently needed faculty salary increases and other important needs. A state-wide opinion poll produced results which indicated that the people of the state would support increases in their taxes to support education. A series of tax measures were passed including an increase in the state income tax, the state sales tax, and a gasoline tax. These measures would generate additional state revenue which would largely support elementary, secondary, and higher education as well as human service programs and other vital governmental functions. Few worked harder to make these gains than President Clifford and the team from UND. But danger loomed on the horizon.

The Legislature had hardly adjourned when efforts were mounted to refer the taxes, along with several other matters, to a vote of the people. The leadership for the anti-tax movement seemed to be centered in the communities of Bismarck and Minot. The referral efforts proved to be successful and the petitions were certified and filed. It fell to Governor George Sinner to call a special election. The governor received conflicting advice about when to schedule the election. Some favored an early election, as soon as possible, they argued, to let the people have their say. Others urged a delay to allow enough time for the forces on both sides to take their case to the people and allow for a public debate on issues of such importance. The governor finally took what may have been a middle-ground position and announced that the special election would be held on December 5, 1989.

Those who favored sustaining the tax measures approved by the Legislature organized a coalition which was identified by the word YES which urged the voters to vote yes on the appropriate measures — measures numbered 3, 5 and 7 on the ballot. At UND the YES campaign was led by faculty member Thomas Potter and executive director of University Advancement David Vorland. Vorland took a temporary leave from his University post to assist with the campaign. On a state-wide level, a relatively sophisticated television campaign was organized and funded by donations from YES supporters. The opposition relied heavily upon printed materials such as tabloids and inserts in local newspapers and free media interviews with opposition leaders.

There were many unknowns involved in attempting to predict the outcome. There were factors which would most likely strengthen the opposition. Much of the state continued to suffer from a lengthy drought. The drought inflicted more suffering on the already devastated economy in the "oil patch." Many small communities in the state were suffering economically. Other ballot measures were unpopular and would attract "no" votes. Especially unpopular was the new retirement plan for members of the Legislature. The mandatory seat belt law, the health curriculum for school children, and a gambling measure were also unpopular issues which would draw contingents of negative voters to the polls. Would these measures taken together produce an overall "no" vote? On the other side, would the people of the state really fail to support their schools as well as reject support for programs for the needy and the elderly? Would citizens vote against state taxes if that action would almost certainly result in increasing their local property taxes?

The YES coalition mounted an enormous effort which was especially well organized in Fargo and Grand Forks. President Clifford made over 200 appearances all across the state. He was joined by Senator Evan Lips from Bismarck, one of the most respected senior Republican leaders of the Legislature. The Governor campaigned day and night. Local parent and student groups organized, operated telephone banks, and distributed literature. It was a rather remarkable show of support. But as the month of November waned a sense of impending peril began to emerge. Polls indicated that the YES votes were limited to pockets of urban support in the Red River corridor but were not to be found in much strength elsewhere in the state. Senator Lips, in describing his experience during the campaign noted that many people asked him why they should pay to educate the young people of the state when so many of them left North Dakota. Lips replied, "Should we send them out dumb — so they can't get a job anywhere?" (Lips, 10/19/91). Lips went on to point out that the UND Foundation, with assets of $35 million, had received a large share of those funds from people who left the state but sent their contributions back to help North Dakota students.

As the results began to come in on election eve on December 5, it was clear from the outset that a groundswell of negative votes was going to be the result that night. As the evening wore on, measure after measure went down to defeat. Not a single one of the legislative actions put to the test was sustained by the voters. As for the efforts of the YES coalition, Grand Forks, Fargo and a few pockets of support were maintained in the eastern part of the state but virtually all of the remainder of the state voted "no." The two largest urban and higher education centers in the state outside of the Red River Valley, Bismarck and Minot, were carried by the "no" movement.

The mood on campus after the election was grim. In some ways the psychological impact was more damaging than the economic impact, though the latter would be real enough. Many in the educational community took the vote personally. Many faculty talked openly about their feelings of being unappreciated by the people of the state. Some even felt that the citizens of North Dakota were openly hostile to education. The future looked bleak for higher education.

Some faculty threatened to leave the state. In the following months the actual number of faculty who left was not as great as the immediate reactions might have suggested. The full impact was not evident until the following year when resignations increased from 31 (1989-90) to 39 (1990-91) (Testimony before the Appropriations Committee, Academic Affairs, March 4, 1991, p. 6). But something more important than an increase in the number of resignations began to develop. A different type of faculty member began to leave — not the junior, assistant professor type. Faculty who had been at the University for many years, who were at the full professor rank, who were established in the community, these were the people who began to leave. Those who resigned in the following months included Vernon Keel, professor and director of the School of Communication; William Dando, professor of Geography; Charles Turner, associate professor of Engineering; Ronald Kutz, professor of Elementary Education; Frederick Peterson, professor of Secondary Education; Lewis Oring, professor of Biology and director of the EPSCoR research program, and a Chester Fritz Distinguished Professor; and Stephen Wikel, professor of Microbiology and Immunology and a Chester Fritz Distinguished Professor.

No doubt, there were probably other factors which contributed to faculty decisions to leave the University. Clearly, the vote on December 5 did nothing to encourage a hopeful view of the future. These resignations represented a depth of erosion in the University faculty which would take years to overcome. They represented the loss of a considerable investment by the University and the state over many years. These were faculty who were productive, often generating substantial research grants, faculty who were at a point in their careers where they felt they could not risk the prospects of a bleak future. Their replacements would almost certainly come with a lower level of experience. While the president reminded the University community that there had been equally difficult times in the past and the University had prevailed, that was not enough to sustain some senior faculty. The winter and spring of 1989-90 was one of the darkest times for the University in recent memory.

The task before the University administration was to reduce the budget by $6.7 million during the remainder of that biennium, not including the Medical School budget (Crow, 12/18/91). Of that amount, $4 million was made up by increases in student tuition. The Medical School was especially hard hit with a loss of general fund appropriations of $2,611,956 for the remainder of the biennium. Clifford's strategy was to absorb the reductions which would be required even after the tuition increases by leaving vacant positions unfilled and not replacing those who retired or resigned and by making cuts in the operations side of the University. He met with the Council of Deans and explained that he was determined to preserve the "academic core" of the University. In spite of this strategy, rumors began to circulate on campus about how the reductions would be made. In an effort to reassure the faculty and staff, Clifford scheduled a series of open meetings. Finally, a small group of faculty led by Thomas Potter, who had led the YES campaign, called for a meeting of the University Council.

Clifford responded by announcing a meeting of the University Council, the "town meeting" and ultimate legislative body of the University. Clifford opened the meeting before several hundred persons gathered in the Chester Fritz Auditorium. He offered a brief explanation, without notes, of the circumstances which had led to the budget crisis, including a recitation of the correct budget figures and how he intended to respond. He then turned the meeting over to Potter. Potter made a rather personal statement and called upon an ad-hoc committee which had drafted a set of recommendations. Copies of the recommendations had not been prepared and the situation quickly became confusing as recommendations were read and discussed and counter proposals and modifications were offered from the floor. The outcome of the session was that the recommendations were largely rejected by those present. This action or, more correctly, inaction by the Council gave Clifford an indirect vote of confidence. It became clear to most present, if it had not been before, that the University could be effectively led in such a circumstance by the president and not by a mass meeting.

The North Dakota State Board of Higher Education, acting in the aftermath of the vote on December 5, announced the extent of budget reductions to be absorbed by each campus and also announced tuition increases which would be effective for the following Fall term. The tuition increases would raise the costs of attending the University closer to those of attending a private school, especially for out-of-state students. Governor Sinner rescinded the salary increases of 3.5 percent which had been authorized by the Legislature.

The staff of the North Dakota State Board of Higher Education drafted a directive which was intended to address the issue of program duplication on the campuses. The Board seemed concerned that the negative vote was an expression of the view that some programs on the various campuses were unnecessary duplications and were, therefore, wasteful of state resources.

Each campus was required to respond to a proposal from the Board staff which suggested the possible elimination of certain programs. At the University, the proposal called for the possible elimination of the School of Engineering and Mines, Home Economics and Nutrition Department and the Communication Disorders Department. The faculty and administrators of the University responded quickly with convincing reasons why these programs should not be eliminated or relocated to a different campus. The Board was persuaded and the entire proposal was dropped. However, the negative publicity and uncertainty which resulted from this strategy created difficulty for the targeted programs in the months which followed. Parents and prospective students called the University to ask if the programs were still operating and, if so, how long they might remain at UND. Rather than helping the situation, the Board had inflicted another wound on an already afflicted University.

It is interesting to note that there was no discussion by the State Board of reducing the number of campuses within the system even though that was clearly the single most frequent criticism made by the public about higher education in North Dakota. Instead, the Board restated its position that each campus served a useful purpose, that closures would not save that much money, and that there was no practical or economical way to dispose of the facilities.

The YES strategy had been to warn the public that quality on the campuses would deteriorate if the tax measures were not sustained. Now that prediction would come back to haunt the campuses. With predictions of slippage of quality and, at the same time, the reality of tuition increases, the outlook for the following year was uncertain. The Fall enrollment in 1990-91 came in at 11,885, down from 12,321 the previous year. Undergraduate enrollment was 10,104, down from 10,650 the previous year. Graduate enrollment declined, for the second year in a row, to 1,194, down from 1,240 the previous year. Monty Nielsen, registrar, was quick to point out that the lower enrollments were consistent with national trends which reflected smaller numbers of graduating high school students. The lower numbers were most probably the result of several factors working in concert. The North Dakota State University (NDSU) enrollment fell even more sharply than it did at UND, but nearby Moorhead State University in Minnesota registered a substantial increase in enrollment. The increase in the Moorhead enrollment raised further concern about whether the fear of reduction in quality at North Dakota institutions had led some students to go elsewhere.

The University certainly had undergone difficult times in the past, some more difficult than this one. For example, the terrible influenza epidemic of 1918 resulted in a general quarantine of the campus and necessitated the conversion of the Phi Delt house and top floor of Budge Hall to temporary hospitals. The war had already drained the campus of many students and faculty. A total of 320 of the 470 male trainees in the Student Army Training Corps became critically ill and 29 died. It was a tragic time. The campus was actually closed for a brief period. According to historian Louis Geiger, many key faculty never returned to the University and more left after the war (Geiger, 1958, p. 299). Many must have wondered at that time how the University could ever recover from such adversity. Adversity struck again during the great depression when faculty were released and those who were retained received their pay checks late because the First National Bank of Grand Forks had closed and University funds were impounded. These difficult times were a reminder that adversity was not new to the University. It there was a need to prove the point that the fortunes of the University were directly tied to the economy of the state, the election on December 5 made the case. At least two of Robinson's themes, economic disadvantage, and the "Too Much" mistake, seemed to be at work in the minds of the voters.

THE THIRD DECADE BEGINS: 1990-1992

PRECEDING PAGE: The increasing pace and expansion of the University on many fronts as the 1990s began did not detract from the enduring beauty of the wooded campus. The English Coulee which winds through the central area has long been one of the most remembered UND features by the nearly 170,000 students who have attended UND in its 109-year history.

CHAPTER **9**

A TIME OF TRANSITION

The beginning of the 1990s was a time of transition for the University. While President Clifford delayed his retirement by an additional year to come to the aid of the North Dakota State Board of Higher Education and serve as chancellor, the prospect of a new president, nevertheless, was beginning to loom on the horizon. The conventional wisdom on campus was that Vice President Clark would retire the year after Clifford and it was evident that at least two of the deans were approaching retirement, as well. Henry Tomasek, the first and only dean of the College for Human Resources Development, announced in the spring of 1991 that he would retire as soon as a replacement was secured. New policies advanced by the State Board of Higher Education were changing the tradition of open admissions at the University and, at the same time, enrollment "caps" or "ceilings" were being considered. Concerns about slipping quality, combined with smaller numbers of high school graduates and increases in tuition, resulted in enrollment declines, something the University had seldom experienced. Change is always a reality in higher education but it was clear that the 1990s would bring more than ordinary change to the University of North Dakota.

A Tribute: When Irish Eyes Are Smiling

On Saturday, October 20, 1990, at 6:30 p.m. nearly 500 people gathered in the Civic Auditorium in Grand Forks for a banquet to honor Tom Clifford.

109

It was Homecoming weekend and many of his friends from across the nation returned for the special "Thank Tom" event which was being sponsored by the UND Alumni Association. It was Clifford's 20th year as president of the University. Tickets were sold out days before the event. The theme for the tribute was "When Irish Eyes Are Smiling."

The evening began with a presentation of the colors by the U.S. Marine Corps, a fitting tribute to the honoree, an ex-Marine. The menu featured Irish corned beef, cabbage and boiled potatoes. Mayor Mike Polovitz presented Clifford with a key to the city and a citation. Clifford quipped that he had been looking for such a key but noted that it was welded to the plaque. Governor George Sinner spoke on behalf of the citizens of the state, as well as the many governmental officials present, including members of the State Legislature, the Board of Higher Education, and several constitutional officers of the state. Sinner had been the chair of the State Board of Higher Education when Clifford was selected to succeed George Starcher as president of UND. President Gordon Olson of Minot State University spoke for the Council of Presidents, Tom's colleagues in higher education. Other campus presidents attending were President Jim Ozbun of North Dakota State University, President Albert Watrel of Dickinson State University, Garvin Stevens, the executive dean of the UND branch campus at Williston, and Sharon Etemad, the executive dean of UND Lake Region at Devils Lake.

Earl Strinden, executive vice president of the UND Alumni Association, the sponsors of the event, noted to the crowd that many groups across the state had requested a spot on the program that night but time would permit remarks from only a select few. Representatives from 18 organizations proceeded to pay tribute. They included several Grand Forks organizations (Chamber of Commerce, United Hospital, First Bank), state-wide groups such as the Greater North Dakota Association (GNDA), Vision 2000 (an economic development task force), and the Boy Scouts of America. Harold Schafer, founder of the Gold Seal Company spoke on behalf of the Teddy Roosevelt Medora Foundation. Regional interests were represented by the Bush Foundation and Otter Tail Power Company. Speakers from the Alumni Association and Foundation paid tribute for the many graduates who had been helped and befriended by Clifford over the years. One of the most moving statements was delivered by UND Academic Vice President Alice Clark, who spoke for faculty and staff of the University and expressed the depth of respect and affection felt for the president. Clark closed with the sentiment, "Long live the president!"

Jim Siefert spoke for a group of alumni and announced the beginning of a Tom Clifford endowment fund. Over $250,000 had been pledged by a planning group which had met for the first time the day before. According to

Siefert and Alumni Association Executive Vice President Strinden, the goal was to raise a total of $25 million, all of which would be used for special needs of the University. Two projects would bear Clifford's name, a Clifford Scholarship Endowment and a Clifford Endowed Chair.

In his remarks to the crowd, Clifford expressed gratitude and noted that having so many friends had made his life worthwhile. In his response to the announcement of the endowment, Clifford said, "One couldn't ask for a better gift. It will last forever. And the thing I appreciate about it is you gave it to me while I was still living" (Schmidt, 1990, October 21). Clifford expressed words of appreciation to his family, several of whom were present. His wife Florence had died in 1984 and he expressed his gratitude for her support over the years. He had married Gayle Kielty Kenville in 1986 and expressed gratitude for her support, as well.

The formal celebration concluded with everyone singing "When Irish Eyes Are Smiling," and everyone was invited to remain for an evening of dancing and further celebration. It was an evening to remember. Few people ever receive or have earned such a tribute.

The President as Chancellor

North Dakota Commissioner of Higher Education John Richardson had pushed hard for many months for a plan to upgrade his position to chancellor. He had argued that elevating the position and requiring that all of the presidents of the campuses report directly to the chancellor, rather than directly to the North Dakota State Board of Higher Education, would streamline the management of higher education in the state. This change in lines of authority would give the chancellor more ability to "manage the system" according to proponents. One could argue, on the other hand, that the existence of strong presidents who could relate to the Legislature and the Board are what had enabled higher education in North Dakota to survive as well as it had. In order to remove the element of self-promotion from the deliberations, Richardson finally announced that if the plan was adopted, he would resign and not seek the new position. During the spring, the Board adopted the plan in spite of almost universally unenthusiastic and often quite negative responses received at public hearings on the campuses. The Board seemed to sense that it had to do something dramatic in response to the vote on December 5 and the chancellor plan was something concrete, if not dramatic. Richardson announced that he would leave the position on or before August 1, 1991. The Board asked him to serve as chancellor until that time. During the early summer it became evident that Richardson's time-line would be even shorter and he notified the Board that he would be leaving as of October 1, 1990.

Another element of the new strategy emerging from Bismarck was that the larger campuses, specifically UND and North Dakota State University, should have admission standards and enrollment limits. The rationale was that these two measures would induce students to attend the smaller institutions for the first year or two and then transfer to one of the larger campuses, if they wished to, for their upper division work. The new strategy seemed similar in many respects to the California system which had been developed during the 1960s. The California system consisted of three levels of higher education. The first level was the community college system which allowed open access for students, especially the less well prepared. The second level included the four year comprehensive colleges which were somewhat selective in admissions practices and the third level was composed of the highly selective research universities. While this strategy seemed logical in many respects, it was an open question as to whether it would work in North Dakota which had a long-standing tradition of open access for students to attend any institution they chose and a system of relatively autonomous campuses with strong presidents. Other important differences were that California is a large state, a rapidly growing one at that, with exceptional resources. North Dakota is a small, rural state with a declining population and inadequate resources.

President Clifford had long opposed both of these concepts —imposition of admission standards (beyond a high school diploma) and centralization of authority in a staff person in Bismarck. Clifford may have acquiesced to the new strategy based upon some assurances that an effort would be made to shift the funding for the University from an enrollment-driven formula to program budgeting, an approach which based the budget upon actual costs of the delivery of academic programs. Such an approach to budgeting would protect the University from the drastic income losses which could follow the imposition of enrollment limits. However, the Board seemed intent upon making these changes regardless of opposition from the campuses.

With the adoption of the chancellorship plan an accomplished fact, speculation began at once about who would become the new chancellor. There was an instant move by some on the Board to put Clifford's name forward for consideration. Clifford resisted those urgings for several months before they became public. In late July, the *Grand Forks Herald* issued a front-page story speculating on Clifford's future (Schmidt, 1990, July 26). Clifford continued to express the view that he was probably "too long in the tooth" to make such a move. The *Herald* also reported that Clifford, while on retreat with the University vice presidents, had discussed his tentative plans to retire as president of the University in July of 1991.

At the August meeting the State Board announced that Clifford had agreed to serve as interim chancellor, beginning October 1 and serving until a new chancellor was employed. Board President Marijo Shide of Larimore said,

"He did not seek the position, the position sought him." Lee Christensen of Kenmare, president-elect of the Board, explained that there had been some "arm twisting and some compromising" which resulted in the Board agreeing that Clifford would remain president at UND while serving as interim chancellor. Christensen further explained that the Board was especially concerned about the approaching biennial session of the Legislature and that "It was the Board's feeling that we needed a person of Tom's stature and ability and prestige around the state to get us through the next few months" (Lee, 1990, August 15). Those who knew Clifford were sure that he had agreed to such a compromise because of his loyalty to UND as well as his concern that the entire higher education system needed his help in making a strong appeal to the Legislature. A successful legislative session for higher education was crucial in light of the demoralization of the December 5 referral. In his remarks at the news conference held to make the announcement of his appointment as interim chancellor, Clifford noted that a factor in his decision was that "time was of the essence" (Lee). There were skeptics, however, including the editorial staff of the *Grand Forks Herald*, who questioned the wisdom of Clifford serving in both posts.

Clifford also attempted to dispel any uncertainty about his own intentions at UND by announcing at the same news conference that he would not seek the full-time chancellor position and that he would retire from the presidency of the University on June 30, 1991, and, he said with emphasis, "You can count on it" (Lee). It appeared that this strategy would give him one final year to complete his presidency after the new chancellor was selected. He also noted that he had thought it would be difficult for the State Board to have to find a new chancellor and a new president for UND, the system's largest university, during the same year.

One of the first items on Clifford's agenda when he assumed the chancellor's position on October 1 was to begin a series of meetings around the state with legislative leaders. The relationship between the Legislature and the State Board of Higher Education was in need of mending after several years of tension with former Commissioner Richardson. Clifford knew that it was important to begin the mending process well in advance of the next legislative session. He used these sessions with legislative leaders to begin to lay the groundwork for an appeal for the needs of higher education, especially in the areas of faculty salaries and operational expenses. Operations and equipment had been short-changed on a regular basis in the past. Equipment replacement, for example, was on a 200 year replacement cycle in North Dakota higher education. A second round of meetings across the state was held with newspaper editors, other media representatives, and key community leaders.

It had been a busy summer for Clifford on another front. During the late spring and early summer, reports from the state government began to indicate that the revenue picture for the state was going to be much better than expected. Projections were for a surplus in the general fund of from $90 to $150 million by the end of the biennium. Oil prices were up and some areas had better crops than expected. In private, Clifford and others began to urge Governor Sinner to restore some of the funds which had been cut from education as a result of the December 5 referral. At first the Governor made small restorations to only the state Tax Department and one other agency. But finally, late in the summer, the governor announced that $5 million would be restored to higher education. Clifford had hoped that a first priority for restored funding would be to replace the faculty salary increases which had been approved by the Legislature but rescinded by the governor after the vote on December 5. By the time the issue officially reached the North Dakota State Board of Higher Education in November, Clifford was the interim chancellor and the Board adopted a revised budget which provided $4 million in statewide faculty raises and over $1 million in operating and equipment funds to the campuses. UND officials announced that much of the operating and equipment funds which would come to their campus would go to the Chester Fritz Library in keeping with an earlier decision. Raises for faculty at UND averaged 8 percent.

In one additional matter, Clifford remedied a complaint from the Dickinson area about the Chancellor Search Committee membership, originally named by out-going Chancellor Richardson. The Committee did not include representation from the southwestern section of the state. Clifford recommended that a citizen-at-large member from that area be added to the membership to correct that problem and the Board agreed to do so.

In December of 1991, Governor Sinner announced his new proposed budget for the state. Revenue forecasts had been upbeat and the governor proposed an increase of 10 percent in higher education spending. That would translate to $45 million for UND, a 14 percent increase and the Medical School would receive $27.5 million, a 9 percent increase. The governor's budget proposed a 4 percent increase in faculty salaries; whereas, the State Board of Higher Education had requested a 9 percent increase for each year of the biennium. But these were figures which would certainly receive a critical eye from the Legislature.

As the 1991 legislative session got under way, Clifford was surprised to discover that the State Board of Higher Education had no funds for providing a social gathering for members of the Legislature. Such things are very important in the political world and Clifford knew just how important. With his usual sense of confidence he indicated that he would "pass the hat" to a few who could well afford to support the event. It was something that had to be done.

Clifford began to work closely with the Office of Management and Budget, the governor, and legislators well before the legislative session began. The typical process by which the Legislature considered appropriations bills was to alternate between the Senate and House from session to session (Strinden, 1992). In the 1991 session, the higher education appropriations were considered first in the House. Clifford worked with members of the House appropriations committee, especially those from Grand Forks, to keep the cuts in the budget to a minimum. Clifford invited the leadership from the House to the commissioner's office to "iron out any difficulties" (Clifford, 5/23/91). This strategy was successful, in part, because some members of the House thought that they could have another opportunity to make more cuts when the measure went to a Conference Committee after the Senate had acted on the bill. Traditionally, the other chamber would make further cuts and changes in the appropriations once the bill had passed the first chamber. These actions would require a conference between the two branches of the Legislature to reconcile the differences in the bills. In this session, Clifford worked with the leadership in the Senate to get the bill passed on that side without any changes. He was successful. The higher education budget passed both houses three weeks before the end of the session and went to the governor for his signature. The House was unable to make further cuts, if they had desired to do so. Clifford's strategy broke the typical pattern of the Legislature working on the higher education budget, along with other large budget items, making cuts and adjustments right up to the final moments of the session. It was a masterful strategy. A number of smaller projects from several of the campuses were placed in a separate bill which was considered later. The core budget for higher education, however, was secure. In reflecting upon the session, Clifford observed that he had taken a cooperative rather than a confrontational approach to the Legislature and "that worked a lot better!" (Clifford, 5/23/91).

As for the substance of the appropriations, the Board, with Clifford's leadership, had proposed a 9 percent increase in faculty salaries, or 4 1/2 percent for each year of the biennium. What the Legislature passed was 4 1/2 percent for the first year and raises of $40 per month for all full-time employees for the second year. The higher education formula was funded at 100 percent for the first time in years, perhaps in history. Operating budgets were increased. Additional resources were acquired for the Chester Fritz Library at UND. All in all, it was a remarkable turn-around from the December 5 election the year before. In fact, no one would have predicted at that time that such gains could have been possible in the next session of the Legislature. Tom Clifford, working with Governor Sinner and key legislative leaders, helped make it happen.

Clifford's term as chancellor ended July 1, 1991. A new chancellor had been selected by the State Board — Douglas Treadway, president of Southwest State University at Marshall, Minnesota. In August Clifford was invited to return to Bismarck for a special "thank you" party sponsored by the Board and friends of higher education. Clifford had pulled it off. He had managed both positions. He was the first to admit that the staff at Bismarck and at Grand Forks put forth extra effort to make it work. While certain matters on campus may have needed more of his attention during this period, nothing he could have done could have been more important to the health of the University, not to mention the state system, than his work in Bismarck. At 70 years of age, he had simultaneously managed both of the toughest jobs in North Dakota higher education.

Sponsored Research and Other Grants

As the University attempted to strengthen its position as a research institution in the late 1980s and early 1990s, success at receiving outside support had never been better. The total sponsored support for the 1989-90 academic year leaped to $32.92 million, compared to $25.12 million the previous year. Sectors of the University which registered the largest increases were the Energy and Environmental Research Center (EERC) with an increase of $5.5 million and the Center for Aerospace Sciences with an increase of $1.57 million. While the dollar amounts were not as large, the Colleges of Arts and Sciences, Nursing, and the School of Medicine all registered significant gains. The lion's share of the total increase, $23.82 million (72.4 percent) came from the federal government with $3.14 million from industry, $2.84 million from foundations, and $1.70 million from state agencies. The 1990-91 year was even better with a total of $39.8 million received. The amount and proportion received from the federal government increased to $30 million and 75.7 percent of the total. While the role of state agencies in providing various kinds of support to this research effort was important, the amount remained rather modest at $2.3 million which was 5.9 percent of the total. It would seem that, if the past was any indication, the future of support for research at the University would continue to lie outside of the state. This record of steady growth was one of the brighter signs on the horizon as the University entered the decade of the 1990s. (A table illustrating growth of sponsored support from 1977-1990 is provided in the appendices.)

The research effort at the Energy and Environmental Research Center (EERC) had expanded considerably by the 1990s. The annual income of the Center approached $20 million in 1990 with about 65 percent of that coming from federal sources and about 35 percent of that coming from the private sector. By 1991 the Center employed some 250 people representing a total of 12 countries. The list of clients in 1991 numbered over 200 U.S. firms, many of them major corporations, and nearly 20 foreign clients.

International contracts were the focus of much effort in the early 1990s. Visitors from several governments were guests at the Center during this period averaging two international visitors each week. Many of these guests were given tours of the coal and oil development in western North Dakota as well as of the UND facilities. The development needs in Eastern Europe were especially attractive and in November of 1990 the EERC announced the signing of an agreement with the Power and Research Institute of Prague, Czechoslovakia. By 1991 plans were under way for an international conference to be sponsored by UND in Czechoslovakia. The Center had also established offices in Germany and Hong Kong, and was in the process of establishing one in Czechoslovakia.

Plans were moving ahead for the construction of expanded facilities at UND which would cost in the range of $7 million. The funding for the facilities represented another example of cooperative and creative financing. In addition to $3.5 million from federal funds, the UND Foundation guaranteed $2.5 million in bonds, and the city of Grand Forks approved a $1 million grant from the city economic development fund. The expanded facilities would do much to keep EERC at the forefront on energy research issues, especially on the cleaner use of coal (EERC Facts, 1991).

The organizational structure which had placed EERC within the School of Engineering and Mines in 1987 opened up much more cooperation and collaboration between the two. Faculty and students in the School of Engineering and Mines had access to EERC for research. In turn, the staff of the EERC had access to the faculty and facilities of the School of Engineering and Mines. The complete integration of EERC into the University and especially into the School of Engineering and Mines would take time. The extent to which that would be successful would be more evident by the conclusion of the 1990s. In a relatively brief period of time the EERC had emerged as a major research program which rivaled The Center for Aerospace Sciences and the Medical School in terms of generating external income.

An academically significant grant received during this period was a grant for $300,000 from the Bush Foundation for a faculty development program in Writing Across the Curriculum (WAC). The grant was written by the director of the Office of Instructional Development, Daniel Rice, and a faculty planning committee. Elizabeth Rankin, director of Freshman Composition, was especially instrumental in the selection of writing as the focus of the grant and was heavily involved in the writing of the proposal, as well. The new writing program assisted faculty with developing both more frequent and more effective writing experiences for students. The poor quality of student writing had long been a concern at UND as at all colleges and universities in the country. Joan Hawthorne was selected as the coordinator of the new WAC program.

A grant from the Indian Health Service of $549,525 to the College of Nursing to establish a program similar to INMED was announced in January of 1991. The goal of the new program was to increase the number of American Indian students who enter the field of nursing. The program was designed to work closely with INMED, as well as the Native American Program at UND, and to build on the experience gained in these successful programs. LaVonne Russell served as the director of the project.

Accreditation Up-Date

The goal of achieving and retaining accreditation for all of the professional programs continued to receive attention as the new decade began. The reaccreditation of the Center for Teaching and Learning by the National Council for Accreditation of Teacher Education (NCATE) was undertaken beginning in 1988 with a site visit taking place in October of 1990. Dean Mary Harris had arrived at UND from Kansas State University in 1986 following the departure of Vito Perrone to join the Carnegie Endowment for the Advancement of Teaching. Dean Harris led the effort to retain NCATE accreditation and the effort was successful. Other programs which were successful with accreditation during this period were the Music Department by the National Association of Schools of Music (1990), and Occupational Therapy Department by the American Occupational Therapy Association and the Council on Allied Health Education and Accreditation of the American Medical Association (1990).

The accreditation of the Master of Business Administration (MBA) program was an especially difficult goal for the University to reach. Dean W. Fred Lawrence and the faculty of the College of Business and Public Administration prepared the self-study report, an exhaustive report required prior to a site visit by a team from the American Assembly of Collegiate Schools of Business (AACSB). The report was submitted, the team made its visit, and a period of many weeks passed while word was awaited on the recommendations. When word finally came it was not all bad news but neither was it all good news. The MBA program was close to the mark but had yet to meet several conditions and would be given a period of time to make the necessary improvements. Concerns noted by AACSB included faculty salaries, scholarly production of the faculty (publications), work loads of the faculty (too high), and the inadequate level of financial support provided by the state. Lawrence and the faculty, with the help of the president and the UND Foundation, made another determined effort to meet the conditions of accreditation. Incentives were put in place to reward faculty for the successful publication of articles in professional journals, salary adjustments were made, work loads were reduced (business faculty were withdrawn from involvement in the correspondence study program). The UND Foundation provided significant financial resources to support the expenses required. The total expenditures over and above the normal state appropriations to the program were in excess of $500,000, according to President Clifford (2/27/92). It was a major effort, the extent of which was little understood by most of the public.

The AACSB team made a return visit and once again those most concerned waited for word on whether these renewed efforts would result in success. When word came this time, it was good news — accreditation had been achieved. It was May of 1990. It had taken many years, a tremendous effort by many people, and the support of the UND Foundation, in addition to the support of the state, to finally reach the goal. The UND program remains the only business program in the state of North Dakota to be fully accredited by the AACSB.

The accreditation of the entire University would be up for review by the North Central Association (NCA) in 1993. President Clifford and Vice President Alice Clark once again turned to the dean of the Center for Teaching and Learning and appointed Dean Mary Harris to chair the accreditation committee. Considerable work would be required to develop a self-study report prior to the site visit in 1993.

Faculty Achievements

The quality of the faculty was outstanding during the Clifford years. A *Directory of Scientists, Artists and Scholars at UND* was published in 1990 and 1992 by the Graduate School and Office of University Advancement. A listing of the faculty authors of books and the titles of their works, as listed in the directory, is provided in the appendix. It is an impressive body of scholarly work by any standard. However, most faculty publish their work as journal articles. The University was also served by many faculty who were excellent teachers during this period. A listing of those faculty who have won awards for teaching, as well as those who have won for research, service or advising, is also provided in the appendix.

The Writers Conference

A significant cultural and educational event which took place on campus every year during the Clifford years was the UND Writers Conference. Each conference focused on a particular theme and five or six noted authors were invited to participate in the week-long event. The campus originator and coordinator for the highly successful conferences for a number of years was John R. Little, associate professor of English. The first conference was held when Little, a graduate of Southern universities, decided to invite some Southern writers to come to UND for a conference in April 1970 (Anderson, 1989). That first conference was so successful that another followed the second year. The theme for the second conference was "The Northern Plains." A partial listing of the over 100 authors who have participated in 21 conferences includes Edward Albee, John Barth, Robert Bly, Joseph Brodsky, Truman Capote, James Dickey, Louise Erdrich, Richard Ford, Allen Ginsberg, Alex Haley, John Houseman, Ken Kesey, W.P. Kinsella, Norman Mailer, Thomas McGrath, Jay McInerney, Larry McMurtry, N. Scott Momaday, William Least-Heat Moon, Leslie Silko, Susan Sontag, Alice Walker, Will Weaver, Eudora Welty, Tom Wolfe, and Tobias Wolff. The conferences received financial support from several sources including the North Dakota Humanities Council, student fees, the president's office, and private donations. When John Little decided to step down as the coordinator of the conference, the English Department kept the conference alive. The conferences were popular not only with faculty, staff and students, but with people from the local community. Many others traveled to the campus from across the region to attend.

International Programs

The international programs on campus were bolstered by receiving a priority recommendation in the strategic plan "Strategy for the 90s." Subsequently, two full-time positions were funded for the 1990-91 academic year. Sharon Rezac-Anderson was employed as the student affairs administrator and Mary Grisez-Kweit as the academic affairs administrator in the International Center. The Center, located on University Avenue opposite the Memorial Union, became the focus for much more activity for both international students and the University community at large. President Clifford allocated additional funds to be administered by the international program for foreign travel.

Distance Learning

The great distances and sparse population in North Dakota have always created difficulty for many citizens, especially the place-bound, in their efforts to gain access to educational programs. In response to this need, the Division of Continuing Education had developed a very extensive and successful correspondence program over the years. Many of UND's finest faculty served as instructors in this program at various times. However, the development of technology offered new opportunities in the 1990s. For many years educators in the state had discussed the potential of technology for improving access to education in North Dakota. The cost of developing such a system beyond the interactive telephone network (ITN), however, had been prohibitive. But, thanks to a large grant from the U.S. Department of Agriculture (USDA), which covered about half of the total cost, a start was made in the late 1980s on developing an interactive television network (IVN). The North Dakota University System provided the balance of the needed funds. UND played a major role in the development of the new system.

By the 1990-91 academic year, 10 campuses in the state were connected to the new IVN system. The USDA project supported the offering of courses over IVN in nursing, social work, and medical technology. By the beginning of the 1991 academic year, UND had approval from the North Dakota University System to offer a Master of Business Administration (MBA) degree over the IVN network. Some technical and policy questions remained to be resolved but the IVN system was operational and delivering educational courses and degree programs across the state. There could be little doubt that the new technology would assist many students who otherwise would probably never reside on a campus. The effectiveness of this new delivery method would become more apparent during the 1990s.

New Graduate Programs

A significant new graduate program was implemented with the beginning of the fall term for the 1990-91 academic year. The Master of Social Work (M.S.W.) degree program had been approved by the North Dakota State Board of Higher Education, new faculty had been recruited, and students admitted. The program was the culmination of an extended and extensive period of planning by the faculty of the Social Work Department chaired during this period by Robert Klinkhammer and, subsequently, by Kenneth Dawes. The MSW program was the only one available between the Twin Cities to the east and Washington State to the west.

An unusual new doctoral program was approved during 1991, a Ph.D. in energy engineering. This degree was made possible by the combined resources of the School of Engineering and Mines and the Energy and Environmental Research Center. It was another indication that the University was positioning itself to be on the cutting edge of emerging technical disciplines. The program could also provide research and technical skills of critical importance to this region of the country. It was the first interdisciplinary doctoral program.

The Chester Fritz Library

The Chester Fritz Library came in for some special attention and support during this period. Under a new director, Frank D'Andraia (replacing Ed Warner), the Library moved fully into the new ODIN system, a computer-based reference system which replaced the old card catalog. Thanks to a grant from the 3M Company to cover one-half of the $160,000 cost, the Chester Fritz became one of 67 federal patent and trademark depository libraries. The new service assisted faculty researchers in the new "patent or perish" climate, according to Bruce Gjovig, director of the UND Center for Innovation and Business Development (Schmidt, 1991, October 15).

After many years of objection within the University to the installation of a security system in the Library, one was finally installed. While the loss of materials at UND was not as serious as at many universities, the matter was creating enough difficulties that such measures finally seemed justified. Library materials were marked by a process which allowed them to be detected by the electronic security system located at the exits, if the materials were passed through without being properly checked out.

The Library received a significant allocation of discretionary funds from the president during the 1990-91 academic year to increase acquisitions. The Library was also placed high on the priority list for funding for the 1991-93 biennium and received an increase in appropriated funds for that period. This focus on the Library was an important aspect of improving the overall quality of the University. The Law Library received some additional funding to bolster its collections, as well.

A Change in the Deanship of the Graduate School

During the 1990-91 academic year, word came from Duncan Perry, dean of the Graduate School, that he had been offered a permanent position with the Voice of America in Germany and that he would not be returning to the University the following year. He would resign as the dean of the Graduate School. Perry's announcement was met with genuine disappointment across the campus. His contributions during his brief tenure had been significant. He brought a new vision to the Graduate School and provided leadership on campus for the strategic planning activity and for international exchange programs. The latter effort would be seriously impeded by his absence. A national search was undertaken for a new graduate dean and Harvey Knull continued as the acting dean. Knull had earned the confidence of many on campus during the interim period and emerged from a pool of local and national candidates to be selected as the replacement for Perry. The appointment was made before the 1991 fall term began.

Service to the State

The service activities of the University were extensive and multifarious during the Clifford years. Departments which received recognition or had a reputation for their service activities included aviation, music, early childhood education, industrial technology, accounting and business law, communication disorders, social work, educational administration and the Law School. These and many other departments and individual faculty reached out to the public in various ways to strengthen services to the public and private sectors and generally make life better for people in the region.

One of the most remarkable public service efforts of the University was the establishment of an entire unit in the middle of the 1980s to assist with small business development in the state and region. Known as the Center for Innovation and Business Development (CIBD) and founded by director Bruce Gjovig, the unit was described as one which "helps inventors, entrepreneurs and small manufacturers develop new products, start businesses and create jobs and wealth for the state" (Center for Innovation . . ., 1990). One venture which received significant assistance from the CIBD was Steffes ETS, a small manufacturing operation which produced electric thermal storage heaters and was owned by Paul Steffes of Dickinson. By 1990 the Center had assisted with over 100 start-ups. A few examples of projects included Agvise Inc., Northwood; Boat-Lift, Bismarck; Protein Lick Block, Walhalla; 4th Corporations, New Rockford; Technology Applications Group, Grand Forks; and Buxton Hartz Store, Buxton.

President Clifford attempted to further economic development for the state while also opening new contracts for the University by inviting representatives from foreign embassies to visit the state during the 1989-90 academic year. The invitations were accepted by representatives from the Netherlands, Germany, Finland, Australia, South Africa and France. The guests were typically given a tour of the campuses at UND and North Dakota State University, were flown to Bismarck for meetings with state officials, and toured several business and cultural sites at various places around the state. The visitors were impressed by what they saw in the "heartland of America" (Christenson, 1990).

Cultural Events on the Campus

The campus continued to be a wellspring of cultural activity and entertainment for the community and region. During a brief period in the fall of 1991, for example, performances at the Chester Fritz Auditorium included world-renowned violinist Itzhak Perlman; a full production by the Community Theatre group of the musical, "Camelot"; a show by television personality and comedian Jay Leno; and a production by the American Indian Dance Theatre. The Burtness Theatre featured a production of "MacBeth," directed by Dan Plato of the Theatre Arts Department and "A Tribute to Mozart" directed by Daniel Jacobson and John J. Deal of the Music Department. A performance in the Memorial Union was presented by the Russian Dmitri Pokrovsky Ensemble. At the North Dakota Museum of Art an exhibition titled, "The Artists Who Live Among Us," showcased six regional artists. The Museum also hosted a lecture and slide presentation by Peter Gold, an expert on Tibet who was a guest lecturer for the Religion and Philosophy Department; a week-long program featuring Tibetan Monks making one of their first stops in the country; and "An Afternoon with Herman Melville" featuring George Frein of the Religion and Philosophy Department. The quality and variety of events were ample to suit every taste and rivaled most metropolitan areas.

Varsity Bards, the University's all-male chorus, prepared to celebrate its 40th anniversary in 1992. The Bards were known all across the region as they sang and represented the University. Luther Bjerke, alumnus, former staff member and regional personality, agreed to be the honorary chairperson for a fund drive to enable the Bards to accept an invitation to the National Convention of Music Educators in New Orleans. The Bards were one of only four collegiate groups invited to perform at the convention. Bjerke reported that the Bards was the "single most important thing" to happen to him while he was a student at the University (Liffrig, 1992). No doubt, many other Bard members from the past 40 years would echo that statement.

Greek Life at UND

Many alumni of the University look back with fondness on their years as fraternity or sorority members. Several attractive Greek houses line the north side of University Avenue and other streets near the campus. Membership in the Greek chapters rose and fell over the years (see the next chapter), but remained relatively stable. By one account, there were 13 fraternity chapters and seven sorority chapters on campus in the fall of 1991, for a total of 1,280 members (Schmidt, 1991, November 3). In the past, Greek life on many campuses was associated with the "animal house" image which included wild parties, alcohol abuse, sexual escapades, and sexual abuse. Many at UND worked to improve both the practices and the images associated with Greek life. The Division of Student Affairs employed a staff person to serve as the coordinator of Greek Life. The policy of "dry rush" banned the use of alcoholic beverages from the activities associated with "rush," the time when new pledges are recruited. Many fraternities and sororities sponsored charitable fund raisers and community projects. A fund drive was organized to establish an endowment. While one chapter was closed for violation of national standards and two closed due to financial and membership problems, most chapters at the University continued to function well. Two chapters were considering the construction of new houses in 1991. While Greek life was the focus of campus discussion and a topic of debate in the *Dakota Student* from time to time, it remained a traditional element of student life at UND.

Housing Wins Award

University Housing, led by Director Terry Webb, gained a national reputation and an award for the high quality of services and programs offered to students. Unlike most campuses where the housing program is located in the student affairs unit, at UND it was located in the operations unit. However, the professional staff of both units worked well at cooperating and coordinating services to serve students. The housing and food services operations at the University constituted the largest "hotel" and "restaurant" operations in the state.

Human Nutrition Research Center
The Grand Forks Human Nutrition Research Center opened in 1970 as a laboratory of the U.S. Department of Agriculture. While it was not officially a part of the University, an important relationship existed between the two. The Center was originally brought to Grand Forks by the joint efforts of Senator Milton Young and William Cornatzer, UND professor of biochemistry. Young sponsored the bill which established and funded the Center and Cornatzer went to Washington several times to testify and lobby for the project. Cornatzer reported that many UND graduate students have conducted research in the Center. The facility, located on the east side of the campus on Second Avenue near the hockey arena and initially 20,000 square feet, grew in 1991 to over 80,000 square feet. In 1991, the Center had an annual operating budget of nearly $7 million and employed 175 people, 130 of whom were University staff members. The Center was one of only two laboratories in the country which was conducting nutritional research of healthy subjects. The research focused primarily on establishing the Recommended Dietary Allowances (RDAs) for minerals in the human diet. The Grand Forks Center did much to improve the understanding of RDAs (Liffrig, 1991). The Center was another example of the benefits of a close working relationship between the University, the U.S. Congressional delegation, and the local community.

Athletics
A significant transition came to the athletic program on June 25, 1990. At a news conference with President Clifford at his side, Athletic Director John "Gino" Gasparini announced that he was stepping down from the athletic director position. He would remain as the head coach for the hockey program. He explained that after serving in both posts for six years he found that he "was being consumed" by the two jobs. Later in the week, in an interview with the *Grand Forks Herald*, Clifford recalled a moment from March 11. UND had just lost the Western Collegiate Hockey Association (WCHA) playoff game to Minnesota after controlling the game for two periods. Clifford went down to console Gasparini.

> "'John was sitting by himself, his head down,' Clifford
> said. 'You can tell by a man's jaws, looking grim like
> that, that not a lot of good things were going through his
> head. I felt very badly about that'" (Foss, 1990).

Clifford went on to describe how he had suggested to Gasparini that it seemed that the dual jobs were taking a terrible toll on him and that he should think it over when the hockey season had ended. It seemed that Gasparini had taken the president's advice.

At another news conference on October 1, 1990, President Clifford introduced the new athletic director, Terry Wanless, a South Dakota native, who had recently resigned as the athletic director at Western Carolina University. The *Grand Forks Herald* chided the UND administration for not giving an interview to one of the candidates, UND Assistant Director Dave Gunther (Durkin, 1990). Clifford noted during the news conference that one of the reasons for choosing Wanless was the perception that athletic programs would be facing more scrutiny by the National Collegiate Athletic Association (NCAA) and Wanless had recently been offered a position with the NCAA. It should be noted that Gunther remarked about Wanless in an interview, "... I'm going to be 100 percent behind him and work with him" (Durkin).

The basketball teams had another very good season during the 1990-91 academic year. The women's team finished with a 28-2 win-loss record and won the North Central Conference championship for the second year in a row. While the team was ranked number one in the nation for several weeks, it ended with a number four ranking in the nation. Individuals with outstanding records included Whitney Meier who was named to the American Basketball Coaches Association-Kodak All-American first team. Meier, Nadine VanDeKerckhove, Beth Ihry, and Jenny Walter all made the All Conference team. Gene Roebuck, coach of the women's team, was selected as the conference coach of the year.

The men's basketball team won both the conference championship and the Division II regional tournament for the second year in a row and played in the national Elite Eight championships. Everyone watching the first game of the Elite Eight must have been stunned as the Sioux were upset and eliminated. Senior Dave Vonesh turned in another remarkable year as he captured the UND career records for scoring and rebounding. He was named the Outstanding Player for the conference and to the All-American first team. Scott Guldseth was also named Outstanding Player in the conference with Vonesh. Rich Glas was named the conference coach of the year.

The football team ended the season with a 7-3 record for second place in the conference. Strong performances were given by quarterback Todd Kovash who achieved the career passing record. Dean Witkowski won the defensive back of the year in the conference, was named an All-American, and was drafted by the Green Bay Packers. Tim Gelinske won a spot on the Region VII All-American team and coach Roger Thomas was honored as the conference coach of the year.

The hockey team suffered a number of injuries and ended the season at fourth in the Western Collegiate Hockey Association (WCHA). Greg Johnson and Russ Romaniuk were named to the all conference team and Johnson to the All-American team.

The swimming and diving team, which had a long-established regional and national reputation for quality and success under coach Mike Stromberg, had another outstanding year. The women's team shared the conference championship with Northern Colorado, UND's 10th title. The women won the 200-yard medley relay for the third year in a row. The men's team won the conference title for the sixth straight year. Outstanding performers included Marion Warner, Janine Etchepare, Katie Stephens, Wade Ritter, Dave Bolitho and Brian Strom.

In other sports, Jair Toedter and Kris Presler were named All-American wrestlers. Sheila Pexsa, Steph Bruening, and Chris Carbonneau ran in the Division II Cross Country meet. Rory Beil won the 55-meter dash at the North Central Conference (NCC) Indoor Track championships and Scott Jemtrud captured third place in the nation in pole vaulting. Mark Johnson and Dan Tannahill received all-conference recognition in golf. The volleyball team ended the season with the best record ever at 26-11.

Vice President Clark's Legacy

Alice Clark continued as the vice president for Academic Affairs for the remainder of the Clifford years. After the controversial and change-intensive term of Conny Nelson, Clark brought a period of stability to the Office of Academic Affairs. She presided with dignity and quiet confidence as she worked with the council of deans, testified before the Legislature and North Dakota State Board of Higher Education, and carried out her duties. While she was a very compassionate and patient person, she could stand her ground when necessary. She was highly visible on campus, regularly attending both athletic and cultural events. She gave most of her career to UND and served with tireless devotion and loyalty. She will be remembered, certainly, as the first woman to achieve the role of chief academic officer of the University, but beyond that, she will be remembered for her professionalism and absolute integrity. She deserves much credit for the stability, maturity and improvement in quality which characterized the academic sector during her tenure as vice president for Academic Affairs.

Part Five

A SUMMATION

PRECEDING PAGE: A collaborative management style was a key to the success of President Clifford in dealing with varied constituencies in his 21-year UND presidency. Here, he addresses a meeting of the State Board of Higher Education in 1980.

CHAPTER **10**

AN OVERVIEW OF THE CLIFFORD YEARS

The nature and extent of change at the University during these years can be illustrated by a closer examination of several important indicators. It was a time of tremendous growth in enrollments. But the growth was uneven. The total enrollment grew by 42 percent, from 8,395 (1971) to 11,940 (1991). The undergraduate enrollment grew by 3,015, a 43 percent increase. The graduate school enrollment, on the other hand, grew by only 113 students from 1,088 (1971) to 1,201 (1991), a 10 percent increase (excluding extended degree enrollments, which were not included in 1971). While many graduate programs have enrollment limits, the level of increase was very modest for a 20 year period.

Students

The University student population changed in important ways. One of the most dramatic changes was an increase in the numbers of women students at all levels. In 1971 there were a total of 4,898 men and 3,231 women on campus. In 1991 there were 6,156 men and 5,575 women, a 26 percent increase in men but a 73 percent increase in women. The number of undergraduate men in 1971 was 3,821 and the number of women was 2,929. In 1991 the number of undergraduate men was 5,304 and the number of undergraduate women was 4,753, a 38.8 percent increase for men but a 62 percent increase for women. But, more dramatically, in 1971 the number of men in graduate school was 828

131

and the number of women was 294. By 1991 the number of men in graduate school had actually dropped to 541 and the number of women had risen to 666, a 35 percent reduction in men but a 127 percent increase in women. The changes in gender in the two professional schools (law and medicine) were even more dramatic. In 1971 there were 280 men in the two professional schools and a mere 15 women. In 1991 there were 327 men in the two professional schools and 176 women, a 16.7 percent increase in men but an amazing 1,073 percent increase in women. (All data from the annual enrollment summaries of the Office of the Registrar and the Student Profiles released by University Advancement). The gender shift at the University was nothing short of remarkable. Yet in 1991 women were still under-represented in many disciplines and were still far from parity in the professional programs.

The student population had changed in other important ways. The age distribution had shifted to older students, following national trends in that direction. In 1971 students 18-23 years of age accounted to 76.3 percent of the enrollments; 24-29 years of age, 17 percent; and older than 29 years of age, 6 percent of the total. In 1991 students 18-23 years of age declined to 65.7 percent of the enrollments, 24-29 years of age was down slightly to 15.8 percent, and older than 29 years of age increased considerably to 16.9 percent of the total. Contrary to what one might expect, the actual number of married students was greater in 1971 (1,982) than in 1991 (1,735) even though the total enrollment was much larger.

The residence of students changed significantly, as well. In 1971 North Dakota residents accounted for 77.5 percent of the enrollments, Minnesota residents for 9.8 percent. In 1991 North Dakota residents accounted for a smaller ratio of 56.8 percent of the enrollments and the percent of Minnesota residents had increased considerably to 25.7 percent. This was a change of major significance as the University came to depend heavily upon the enrollments and reciprocity tuition from Minnesota students.

The number of students affiliated with Greek organizations fluctuated some during these years, remaining at about the same overall in number but declining as a portion of the student body. In 1971, 1,231 students were Greek (14.7 percent) and in 1991, 1,290 were Greek (10.8 percent). As a percent of the student body, Greek affiliation was at the highest in 1971, the beginning of this 20 year span, when it reached 14.7 percent of the student body and 1,231 students. Greek affiliation declined in the mid-1970s to a low of 836 students. This decline may have reflected the social and political attitudes of students during that period. Affiliation rose somewhat during the late 1970s and early 1980s but then declined again to reach the lowest percent during this period, 8.9 percent in 1985. The largest number of students affiliated with Greek organizations during the entire period, 1,425, was reached in 1989.

The racial composition of the student body changed little during these years. In 1973, the first year when race was included in the student profile reports, Native Americans numbered 177 or 2.1 percent of the enrollments, African Americans numbered 30 or .4 percent of the enrollments, Asian students numbered only 8, and Hispanic Americans only 2. In 1991, Native Americans numbered 264 or 2.2 percent of the enrollments, African Americans numbered 46 or .4 percent of the enrollments, but the number of Asian students numbered 111, though they still accounted for only about .9 percent of the student enrollments, and Hispanic Americans numbered 100 for .8 percent (Office of University Advancement). While there were increases in the numbers of under-represented students, these were minimal gains in the overall diversity of the University. As noted earlier, the number of American Indian students had actually started to decline in the late 1980s. The University student body remained a very homogeneous population. As cultural diversity becomes more important in higher education, it will continue to be a challenge to pursue that goal at UND.

The internationalization of the student population of the University increased modestly in actual numbers but declined slightly as a proportion of the total student body. The actual number of students from other countries was 291 in 1971 and 403 in 1991 but the percent declined slightly from 3.5 percent to 3.3 percent. This was a difficult issue for the University for several reasons. At various times the University had been criticized by some in the state for having too many non-North Dakota students. President Clifford and other University officials explained that having a diverse population on campus was essential for educational reasons including the social and cultural development of students. Recruitment of international students was difficult because of limited resources for scholarships and, of course, foreign nationals were not eligible for U.S. government student aid. And there were not strong efforts to recruit international students for other reasons, including the fact that at times the University had more students than it could accommodate. A challenge for the future will be to find ways to increase international student enrollments. The Center for Aerospace Sciences (CAS) SPECTRUM program brought international student pilots into that program, but they were not integrated into the campus because they did not take regular University courses, for the most part. (All enrollment data came from official reports of the Office of the Registrar.)

Enrollments within the colleges shifted some during these years. The most dramatic shift was within the Center for Teaching and Learning. In 1971 the School of Education had 1,169 enrolled for 13.9 percent of the University enrollments. In 1991 the Center for Teaching and Learning had 578 enrolled, a 50.5 percent decline in actual numbers and only 4.8 percent of the total enrollments. A major reason for the shift, however, was the movement of several programs out of education to the College of Business and Public Administration and the new Colleges of Human Resources Development and Fine Arts. The movement of these programs greatly distort any enrollment comparisons. A shift which did represented significant change during this period was the proportion of enrollments in the College of Arts and Sciences. In 1971 Arts and Sciences had 1,870 enrolled for 22.3 percent of the total enrollments. That proportion fell to 16.9 percent by 1981 and rose to 18.1 percent with 2,167 enrolled by 1991 for an overall loss of 4.2 percent for the period. Another college which experienced a loss was Business and Public Administration which had 1,019 enrolled for 12.1 percent in 1971, rose to 1,484 enrolled for 13.8 percent by 1981, but fell to 1,083 enrolled for 9.1 percent by 1991, an overall loss of 3 percent. One reason for this change was a new policy to delay enrollment of students in that college until the junior year. The Graduate School, as noted earlier, decreased as a portion of total enrollments from 13 percent in 1971 to 11 percent in 1991. Finally, University College actually increased from 1,888 enrolled for 22.5 percent of total enrollments in 1971 to 3,420 for 28.6 percent in 1991. It should also be noted, when considering these shifts, that the Center for Aerospace Sciences, which did not exist in 1971 or 1981, enrolled 917 or 7.7 percent of all enrollments in 1991. One conclusion to draw from these data is that a somewhat smaller proportion of University students were enrolling in the traditional liberal arts programs which are located in the College of Arts and Sciences. While this change followed a national trend, it gave concern to those who valued the historic liberal arts mission of the University.

Vice President for Student Affairs, Gordon Henry, in assessing the Clifford years, described the importance of the development of the Centers for African American, American Indian, and women students. The president gave enthusiastic support for all of these efforts. In addition, Clifford won North Dakota State Board of Higher Education support for special initiatives at UND for disabled students. All of these efforts were supported by the president, according to Henry, before many other campuses in the region and across the nation gave these issues much attention. This gave the University a head start over many campuses by 10 to 15 years. Also noteworthy, according to Henry, Clifford provided "real leadership for equality for women in athletics" (Henry, 1/28/91).

Finances

On the financial side, total University expenditures increased from $24,450,000 (1971) to $173,671,935 (1991), a 610 percent increase. Total revenue for 1991 was over $180 million compared to $25 million for 1971.

State general fund appropriations, however, actually declined as a percent of the total revenue of the University from 28 percent in 1971 to 25.7 percent in 1991, while there was a tremendous growth in the actual dollars generated by outside grants and contracts from $6.4 million in 1971 to over $40 million in 1991. As a percent of total University revenue, however, the proportion declined from 25 percent in 1971 to 22 percent in 1991. Because of significant tuition and fees increases to students during the period, the share of tuition and fees as a portion of the University revenue increased from 14 percent to 16 percent. In other words, student tuition and fees increased while state appropriations actually declined as a proportion of total revenues. Put differently, students were asked to carry a larger share of increased costs while the state contributed a smaller share. In February of 1992 a report given to the North Dakota State Board of Higher Education indicated that students at UND and North Dakota State University were paying 24 percent more in tuition than students at comparable universities in the region. While tuition in the past seven years in the region had increased by 50 percent and at the national level by 75 percent, at North Dakota's two universities it had nearly doubled (Wheeler, 1992). The remainder of the revenue for the University came from sales and services of approximately $64 million which accounted for 35.5 percent of the revenue, and endowment income of $788,000 for approximately .5 percent of the revenue.

An examination of expenditures by function, when viewed as a proportion of total expenditures, produced some interesting comparisons. Instructional expenditures are of special importance. During the period instructional expenditures actually declined from 43.3 percent of total expenditures in 1971 to 34 percent in 1991. Research expenditures, on the other hand, increased from 3.7 percent of total expenditures in 1971 to 7.6 percent in 1991. Academic support expenditures increased from 4.2 percent to 7.6 percent. Student services as a share of expenditures increased modestly from 2.2 percent to 2.6 percent for the period. Physical plant expenditures, contrary to some impressions, actually declined a bit as a portion of expenditures from 6.8 percent to 5.7 percent. That decrease may have been because that sector absorbed more of the belt-tightening measures. Auxiliary enterprises declined slightly as well, from 20.7 percent to 18.5 percent. Student financial aid declined from about 10 percent to 6.7 percent in spite of sharply rising tuition costs to students during the period. (Data on University finances are taken from reports provided by the Office of the Controller.)

The value of the facilities of the University was reported at $57,987,276 in 1970 (Robinson, p. 36). The Office of the Assistant to the President for Facilities reported in 1991 that the value of the facilities was $223,923,844. The office listed 29 major building projects between 1971 and 1991 with a total expenditure of $96.98 million, approximately 43 percent of the total value of all University facilities (a complete list is provided in the appendices).

Faculty and Library

In the fall of 1991, the University had 458 full-time faculty, excluding medicine, at the instructor level and above, up from 427 in 1982, the year of the last institutional accreditation report. Women held 146 of these positions for 31.8 percent of the total, up from 25 percent in 1982 and 20 percent in 1973. The doctoral degree was held by 291 or 57 percent of these faculty, down slightly from 58 percent in 1982. The average salary in 1991 for full-time faculty (followed by the 1982 amount) at the full-professor rank was $45,430 ($33,050), at the associate professor rank $33,049 ($22,341), and at the instructor rank $26,771 ($19,318). The Chester Fritz Library held a total of 554,368 books, up from 436,229 in 1982 (Data from Richard Balsley, Office of Institutional Research).

Peer Institution Comparison

In 1991 the Office of Institutional Research at the University released an analysis titled "Peer Institution Comparison" which compared UND to universities in the immediate region utilizing data from 1988-89 (Balsley, 1/29/91). UND compared very favorably in some respects and not so well in others. For example, the only other institution to spend more on instruction than UND was the University of Wyoming and on a percentage basis, UND spent 59 percent of the budget on instruction, the third highest in the comparison group (these rates differ with those reported elsewhere in this account because the Peer study considered only unrestricted funds). The only other North Dakota university in the comparison study was North Dakota State University (NDSU) which was last in percent expended on instruction. UND did well in academic support, ranking third in actual dollars expended and fifth in percentage for this category. Only the University of Northern Colorado had a larger percentage of women faculty than UND. NDSU had the lowest percentage of women faculty. UND ranked fifth in percentage of women faculty with tenure and NDSU ranked ninth. UND ranked first in the number of librarians and library staff and the library budget was second only to that at the University of Wyoming. If both libraries at the two South Dakota universities were combined, they would nearly equal the UND library staff and budget. Total cost to students continued to be below the average in spite of tuition increases in North Dakota. On the other hand, NDSU spent more on research and public service than any other institution, in part because of the large extension program at that institution. The two North Dakota schools were near the bottom in the amount expended for student services; however, they were above the two South Dakota universities and the University of Northern Iowa. Most disappointing, faculty salaries at UND were below the average for the peer institution group.

Faculty Salaries

Because faculty salaries have been mentioned at several points in this account, the record of increases for the last decade of the Clifford years is noteworthy. From the years 1981 to 1991, there were four years with no increases at all (1983-84, 1984-85, 1987-88, and 1988-89). The highest level of increases came in 1981 with average increases of 20 percent, with 11 percent given in January and another 8 percent in July of that year. Faculty received a 9 percent increase the following year in 1982-83, an 11.5 percent increase in 1985-86, and a 4 percent increase in 1986-87. Increases of 8 percent were received in 1989-90 and 7 percent in 1990-91. Increases of 4 percent were given in 1991-92. Salaries for staff members at the University became a serious problem during this period, as well. In testimony to the legislative session in 1991, the University presented a survey which indicated that wages for staff at UND had fallen below those of virtually all other major employers in the city of Grand Forks.

An Academic Assessment

One of the most seasoned and sage academic administrators at the University during this period was dean of Arts and Sciences, Bernard O'Kelly, appointed in 1966 by President Starcher. In making an assessment of the changes during the Clifford years, O'Kelly pointed first to the development and implementation of several academic programs. Specifically, he mentioned the elevation of archeology and anthropology to a separate department. It had formerly been within the Sociology Department and had only two faculty. The program currently has four and one-half faculty positions. Especially important, in O'Kelly's view, were five interdisciplinary programs which were developed during this period: Indian Studies, Women Studies, Integrated Studies, Peace Studies, and most recently, International Studies. All of these programs, according to O'Kelly, had the support of the president. At least two of the programs went to the North Dakota State Board of Higher education more than once before they were finally approved. More generally, O'Kelly concluded that these "years were marked by strengthening and consolidation of existing programs. The research intensive doctoral programs are all stronger, significantly stronger over the past 20 years . . . they have been wonderfully strengthened" (O'Kelly, 1991). He went on to point out, for example, that "There were questions about English in the early 1970s but now we can't accommodate all the graduate students who want to enter . . . they come from all over the United States, Canada, and other places in the world, as well as locally" (O'Kelly, 1991). He pointed further to the accreditation of programs such as communication disorders, and the doctoral program in clinical psychology. He was pleased by the development of the School of Communication which was formed by the combination of the Journalism Department with the Speech and Communication Department.

The Mission of the University

The most significant change during the Clifford years was probably a shift in the focus of the mission of the University. This shift actually began during the Starcher years but was accelerated during the Clifford years (Robinson, 1973, p. 44). It became increasingly evident over these years that considerable effort was being made to emphasize the research mission. In an interview in 1986, President Clifford indicated that one of his long-term goals was to improve the research mission of the University (Rice, 1986, p. 99). Official publications from the University Advancement Office, the Alumni Association Office, and public statements by the president tended to focus increasingly on research and the economic development potential of University projects. The acquisition of the Energy and Environmental Research Center, the expansion of the Center for Aerospace Sciences, the new Earth System Sciences building, the success of the medical school in securing research funding, all of these developments moved the University toward that emphasis.

In the fall of 1991 the University brought an expert on "research parks" to Grand Forks to provide advice on the development of such a "park" on the western side of the campus. President Clifford saw these developments as the hope for the future of the University. He concluded that state government was not going to be the source for the resources needed to carry the University forward. As noted above, the proportion of the University budget provided by the state was on a downward trajectory. He concluded, therefore, that the University would be required to seek outside funding just to stay even, not to mention to make any progress (Clifford, 11/4/91).

In this sense, the shift to more emphasis upon research was a survival strategy. At the same time, UND was historically the "flag ship" doctoral degree granting institution in the state and this, in itself, provided the basis for such an emphasis. The change, therefore, was a gradual and natural progression rather than a dramatic change in direction.

The implications of this change in emphasis have only been alluded to up to this point. The issue faced by most if not all institutions which follow this path is the role which undergraduate education will play within a research university. Far too often at other research universities, that role has been minimized (Kerr, 1982). On these campuses, as the focus has been placed increasingly on graduate education and research, less attention has been paid to undergraduate education and to teaching, in particular. As higher education in the United States entered the 1990s, this tension within research universities was being addressed with renewed concern at Harvard, Stanford, and other prestigious universities. David Kennedy, president of Stanford University, for example, announced a $7 million initiative to revitalize undergraduate teaching at that campus (Kantrowitz, 1991).

As the University of North Dakota moves into the 1990s and into the next century, this internal tension will be of concern. The issue is especially difficult for an institution like this one. Faced with limited resources to begin with, in a rural state with an economy dependent upon agriculture and energy, maintaining quality in undergraduate education will be a major challenge if more resources are placed at the disposal of graduate programs and research. On the other hand, a strong, vital undergraduate program is necessary to provide both the resource and the intellectual base for graduate education and research.

Clifford, to his credit, was largely successful in efforts to maintain balance in the mission of the University. His skill at generating external funds, the support of the UND Foundation, and the entrepreneurial efforts of John Odegard, dean of the Center for Aerospace Sciences, and Gerald Groenewold, director of the Energy and Environmental Research Center and many others, kept this tension from being severe. And yet, as the Clifford years drew to a close, the ultimate resolution of this issue would pass to other hands. A new chancellor of higher education and a new president of the University would have much to do with shaping these future directions.

North Dakota State University and Minot State University

A word should be added about the role and mission of the other major university in the state, North Dakota State University, and also about Minot State University. North Dakota State University, the only other doctoral granting institution in the state, began as a land-grant institution with a focus on agriculture and technical studies, as mandated by the federal government. Over the years, however, NDSU grew and expanded its programs and extended its mission beyond the earlier parameters of an agricultural school. This development led to predictable areas of competition with UND. Each university had a strong and influential political base in the two communities involved, Fargo and Grand Forks, and loyal alumni throughout the state. The state governing board, while somewhat removed from direct political influence because members were not elected, was, nevertheless, pressured and persuaded in ways which allowed programs to develop at each campus which probably should not have been allowed. The Legislature also contributed to this problem over the years by advancing certain issues and blocking others. The failure of the state to resolve this situation was, in the minds of some observers, one of the reasons for the public reaction to the tax measures on December 5, 1989.

The development of the North Dakota University System and the chancellorship position was the State Board's answer. It will be a major challenge to make the new system work. The old political alliances and interests will not suddenly disappear from the North Dakota scene. Minot State University, for its part, has attempted to move beyond the old teacher's college tradition from which it came. Both Clifford and Minot President Gordon Olson were powerful and popular figures for many years. Long-time NDSU President Laurel Loftsgard died October 1, 1987. New presidents at UND and Minot will further weaken the "old guard" and this tradition of strong and popular presidents. At the same time, the future will be fraught with some danger. It is evident that a strong president at each campus has, in fact, made those campuses as strong and effective as they are today. The temptation in the years ahead will be to reduce all campuses to a lowest common denominator. Should that happen, the people of the state will be the losers. Wise planning, strong leadership, and considerable diplomacy will be required over many years to improve the entire system. It seems reasonable to predict that the economic fortunes of the state will not change greatly in the coming years. That reality dictates continued attention to Robinson's "too much" theme in North Dakota. Clearly, North Dakota will not be able to provide the resources necessary for excellent higher education within the present configuration of institutions and programs.

University System Enrollment Comparisons

An examination of the headcount student enrollment changes at each of the four-year public campuses in North Dakota during this period is instructive. The total enrollment at UND increased by 34.9 percent, at North Dakota State University by 30.9 percent, at Minot State University by 35.8 percent, at Dickinson State University by 6.4 percent, at Mayville State University by 7.7 percent, and at Valley City State University enrollment declined by -8.9 percent. Likewise, the enrollments at the individual campuses changed as a portion of the total enrollments in the state system. In comparing 1971 to 1991 enrollments, UND had 29.2 percent of the total system enrollments in 1971 but by 1991 had 34.9 percent of the total. NDSU had 23.3 percent of the total system enrollments in 1971 but by 1991 had 25.7 percent of the total. Minot State had 9.5 percent of the total system enrollments in 1971 but by 1991 had 10.9 percent of the total. Dickinson State had 4.9 percent of the total system enrollments in 1971 but by 1991 had slipped to 4.4 percent of the total.

Mayville State had 2.4 percent of the total system enrollments in 1971 but by 1991 had slipped to 2.2 percent of the total. Valley City State had 4.1 percent of the total system enrollments in 1971 but by 1991 had slipped to 3.1 percent of the total.

Put in a different perspective, the enrollment increase at UND between 1971 and 1981 was 2,355 students, which was more than the combined enrollment at Dickinson State and Valley City State in 1981 (2,301 students). During the same decade when UND grew so dramatically, Dickinson State, Minot State, Mayville State, and Valley City State all declined in enrollment. By the end of the next decade, Minot State and Dickinson State, as well as UND, had increased significantly. The enrollment at NDSU increased by just over 1 percent during the decade from 1981 to 1991 while at UND enrollment increased by 10 percent.

An examination of the headcount enrollment data for the two-year campuses during the same period indicates that only two of the campuses made significant gains in enrollment. Bismarck State increased from 1,632 to 2,374, an increase of 45 percent. UND-Williston increased from 481 to 760 students, an increase of 58 percent. The North Dakota State College of Science declined from 3,047 to 2,144, a drastic 29 percent drop. NDSU-Bottineau declined from 529 to 368, a drastic 30 percent drop. UND-Lake Region increased from 638 to 663, a modest increase of 3.9 percent. The combined enrollments of the five two-year campuses represented just 18 percent of the total system enrollments in 1991. (All enrollment data from *Fall 1971 Enrollments . . . , Fall 1981 . . . ,* and *Fall 1991 . . .*).

One conclusion which might be drawn from these data is that enrollment increase seemed to be associated with the location of the campus. The largest numbers of students seemed to be drawn to the campuses in Grand Forks, Minot, Fargo, and Bismarck.

These figures seem to indicate that during this period students were increasingly selecting the larger of the four-year campuses, especially UND and Minot State. The policy of the North Dakota University System, however, seemed designed to counter student preferences by advocating enrollment limits at the three largest institutions.

The Campus

The campus dramatically changed in appearance during these years. The campus now extended from the Energy and Environmental Research Center, on the east, to the Center for Aerospace Sciences complex beyond 42nd Street to the west (see map provided in the appendix). Clifford recalled from time to time that President West, Starcher's predecessor, used to say that he doubted that the campus would ever extend beyond the English Coulee! By 1991 the

Hughes Fine Arts Center, virtually all of the student residence facilities, the Chester Fritz Auditorium, the operations complex, as well as the extensive Center for Aerospace Sciences complex, all were located west of the coulee.

One of the most frequent comments from visitors to the campus was about the excellent facilities, how well maintained they were, and how attractive the grounds were, especially the large, gorgeous flower beds which blossom in the summer. Many people did not expect to find such a lovely campus in North Dakota, or in most states, for that matter, and they were pleasantly surprised. The excellent condition of the campus was a tribute to the operations staff under the leadership of Vice President Al Hoffarth. It was well known that President Clifford took a special interest in the appearance of the campus. Someone once remarked that there wasn't a tree removed without his permission. In fact, one year some students foolishly cut down a small evergreen tree on campus, rather than purchase a Christmas tree for their room. An investigation was launched and the culprits were tracked down. They found themselves in the president's office, offering an apology and making restitution.

Al Hoffarth, vice president for Operations, gave much of the credit to President Clifford for the vision and foresight which made most of the expansion possible. Clifford's strategy from the very beginning had been for the University to acquire any land which became available in the vicinity of the University. This strategy was assisted by support from the UND Foundation and the resources of another private foundation known as the Fellows of the University of North Dakota. The Fellows was organized in 1970 with the charter members being two Grand Forks business people, Fred Orth and Edgar Berg, and three administrative officers of the University as ex officio; at that time they were the president, George Starcher; the vice president for Academic Affairs, William Koenker; and the vice president for Finance, Tom Clifford. The Fellows was established to give non-alumni who were friends of the University an avenue by which they could make gifts which would be administered to the benefit of the University. Membership was open to anyone who made an outright gift of $10,000 or more or a deferred gift of $15,000 or more. With careful nurturing, the Fellows grew over the years to over 70 members and the total assets grew to over $4 million. The resources of the Fellows allowed the University to do many things which would have otherwise been very difficult if not impossible.

Illustrative of the projects supported by the Fellows, in addition to the purchase of land, and scholarships for students were projects for the Center for Aerospace Sciences such as the Arthur Anderson Atmospherium; two projects in the Memorial Union, the Edgar Berg Computer Learning Center and the Fred Orth Lecture Bowl; and awards and prizes for outstanding faculty. The

Fellows also provided the University with discretionary funds when unusual situations or emergencies arose. An important example in this regard was the guarantee of the Fellows for the fees for the final preparation of the blue prints for the addition to the Chester Fritz Library. The immediate completion of those plans enabled the construction to begin and eventually saved the university several hundred thousand dollars in construction costs because of the bidding climate at that particular time (A Special Organization for Friends of UND, undated; Beiswenger, 10/22/91).

The University was both a much larger, more comprehensive, and stronger institution in 1991 than it had been in 1971. A much larger student body and faculty, a host of new buildings, a greater focus on research, and the full accreditation of all the professional programs attested to these strengths. While the University experienced economic stress during these years, this had always been the case in North Dakota. Although dramatic retrenchment was taking place in many states in the early 1990s, North Dakota was at least spared that kind of trauma. North Dakota did not seem to experience either the peaks or the valleys in state support which many other higher education systems did. The North Dakota system functioned at a relatively stable, though always modest, level.

The University ended the Clifford years with an array of interdisciplinary programs which did not exist in 1971 and which strengthened the liberal arts core. At the same time, student enrollments had shifted somewhat out of the liberal arts areas into the technical and professional programs. The student population had changed in two important respects, age and gender. The athletic program had expanded to provide more opportunities for women students. The 20 year span saw several championship teams in several sports. The hockey team, the only Division I sport at the University, had produced 14 All-Americans and 43 former UND "fighting Sioux" had skated in professional hockey. Four new colleges were in place which did not exist in 1971, Fine Arts, The Center for Teaching and Learning, Human Resources Development, and Aerospace Sciences.

The Energy and Environmental Research Center, formerly a federal facility, was now a research program within the School of Engineering and Mines. The School of Medicine was now a full-fledged degree-granting program with area centers located throughout the state, a growing research program and plans for expanded facilities. The Law School had a larger faculty and a new library and it continued to be fully accredited. The University was probably as actively engaged in public service and economic development as it had ever been in its history.

CHAPTER **11**

THE CLIFFORD STYLE

Tom Clifford brought to the presidency an open, personal, congenial way of relating to everyone — faculty, staff, and students. His administrative approach was an interesting mixture of direct, hands-on control in some areas and a relatively loose, hands-off approach in other areas. For example, it is quite clear from interviewing those in his administration that all of the major financial decisions were made by the president. Advice might be sought from various quarters, but everyone knew who would make the final decision. Clifford left his imprint on some details, as well. Dormitory and food rates had to receive his personal approval, as did the profit margin in the University Bookstore. These matters reflected his persistent concern about the direct costs to students. As mentioned earlier, his attention to the grounds was keen. Plantings and landscaping conformed to his wishes. He could probably tell how much coal was in the coal pile at the power plant at any given time. The coal pile was often the target of discretionary spending, no small cost in North Dakota.

Contrasted with these examples of his hands-on approach, was his general hands-off approach to the academic sector of the University. He seemed to wish to create a climate of freedom which would encourage risk-taking by those who were willing to do so. In this kind of organizational environment, those who were "self-starters" and possessed a good deal of drive and initiative could thrive and even prosper. On the other hand, those who followed a more low-key approach to academic work were left to their own devices. One can speculate about the reasons for these approaches. The most logical explanation may be Clifford's business perspective. He seemed to approach many issues from a business or corporate perspective. His support for the entrepreneurial efforts of people such as John Odegard is probably a reflection of this perspective. His predisposition to promote from within the organization also reflects a corporate perspective. From this perspective one views promotions as a means to solidify organizational loyalty and enhance morale. When asked about the issue of internal promotions Clifford explained that the external candidates were "not any better and — all things being equal — I went inside" (Rice, 1986, p. 163). At the same time, the tendency to promote from within may also reflect the difficulty the institution had in attracting and keeping excellent people from the outside, usually because salaries were often uncompetitive.

The president generally kept himself apart from the internal decision making within the bureaucratic structure of the University, especially during the later years. However, Clifford was noted for his willingness to overturn a decision made at a lower level if he felt that an individual had been treated unfairly or deserved special consideration. The person who had been helped was extremely grateful but the official who had been overturned was sometimes displeased. Yet, Clifford's style may have had a preventative influence on the bureaucratic structure because those in the various offices knew that students, faculty and staff could always have recourse to the president. Most observers agreed that Clifford had more of an open-door policy than did Starcher.

Sharon Etemad, executive dean of UND-Lake Region College, described the way President Clifford related to that branch campus:

> The strong relationship which has developed between the university and the community college can be attributed in large part to the leadership style of President Thomas J. Clifford. He provides a supportive environment, encourages creative local leadership, and recognizes the teaching excellence at the college. (Etemad, 1991).

Dean Etemad believed that the alignment of UND-Lake Region with the University has improved both the quality and the image of the College. Clifford gave her wide latitude in administering the campus and was available for consultation and support when he was needed.

Clifford was known for his generosity, sense of fair play, and his support for almost any good cause. If the cause could not be supported by University funds, for whatever reason, he usually reached into his own pocket and made a contribution. He walked the full distance for the CROP Walk for Hunger for many years. He appeared at a multitude of fund raisers. Privately, he was known to have helped many with their business and financial problems.

Within his own "cabinet" of vice presidents, Clifford seemed to place high value on personal and institutional loyalty. He surrounded himself with people who were team players and who understood his values and approach. All of the vice presidents were internal appointments during the last years of his presidency. The "cabinet," with whom Clifford met regularly, included the vice president for Academic Affairs (Conny Nelson and then Alice Clark), the vice president for Health Sciences (Tom Johnson and then Edwin James), vice president for Student Affairs (Bill Bryan and then Gordon Henry), vice president for Operations (Loren Swanson and then Al Hoffarth), vice president for Finance (Gerald Skogley and then Lyle Beiswenger), and executive director of University Advancement (Harvey Jacobson, and then David Vorland). In the early years John Penn served as assistant to the president. While the president was known to consult widely with many people, depending on the issue, if there were those who served as his informal advisors, they were probably Henry Tomasek and Loren Swanson during the early years, and David Vorland during the later years. Some observers have concluded that no single person could be identified as the president's "chief advisor."

Some faculty thought that the president was more interested in the professional programs and research and less interested in some of the liberal arts disciplines. Yet, it seems clear that Clifford cared deeply about the entire University. He was an extremely well-read person with broad interests in many fields. This breadth of interest enabled him to "speak the language" of almost any academic field, which he did with considerable effectiveness. He made a serious effort to support all of the cultural and artistic activities of the University. His enthusiasm was evident, however, when he talked about the growing research capacity of the University and the expansion of the Center for Aerospace Sciences (CAS) and the Energy and Environmental Research Center (EERC). He loved sports and took a special interest in all of the teams. He was an excellent handball player, himself. He took special pride in the University having a "clean" athletic program which conformed to all of the regulations promulgated by the various athletic associations. To insure that reputation, Clifford relied upon George Schubert, a trusted associate, to serve as his official institutional representative to the athletic associations.

Clifford was pre-eminently a people person. He could remember people from many years in the past. For example, while visiting with someone in the parking lot in front of Twamley Hall one day he saw a young student who had just registered at the University. He recognized her, called her over and asked how she was doing. In the conversation he asked the student how her mother was doing and commented that she had been a good student when attending the University. It is likely that he even knew the mother's mother! Not only did he remember people by sight, he almost always remembered their names and from where they came.

A tragic incident involving a medical student is illustrative of Clifford's care for individual people. Lynn Meier had diagnosed his own leukemia. Clifford learned of the situation. Lynn was taken to the Mayo Clinic at Rochester. His parents, Ben and Clara, were taken there as well. Clifford made all the arrangements, himself. Sadly, the student did not live long (Skogley, 1991).

The annual Founders Day banquet and program was especially noted for the personal touch of the president. Each February on the appointed evening, the ballroom in the Memorial Union was filled to capacity. A splendid meal was served at a price subsidized by the President's Office in order to insure that everyone could afford to attend. Retired University staff and spouses turned out in especially large numbers. Awards were presented to outstanding individual faculty and academic departments for teaching, service and scholarly activity. More recently the student government presented an award for the outstanding faculty advisor. A slide show prepared by Richard Larson and members of the staff of the University Advancement Office featured all faculty and staff who were being recognized for length of service or retirement. All were given equal time whether they were employed as a cook, a painter, a grounds keeper, a secretary, a faculty member, or an administrator. Prior to Clifford's presidency, only people from the academic sector had been featured at Founders Day (Skogley, 2/2/91). After the slide show, which provided a brief but personal portrait of the honoree and her or his family, each was called forward to receive a certificate, a gift, and a handshake from the president. The president almost always had a personal comment to make, a brief story or a joke about the honoree. It seemed that no one knew what he was going to say, including sometimes the president, himself. These spontaneous remarks evoked many smiles and chuckles and even tears of laughter. And, perhaps, the most moving aspect of this was that he knew almost everyone on a first-name basis and knew about their work. This personal touch made this a memorable occasion for people who had given many years of faithful service to the University. The president knew them and he knew what they had done. He cared.

A measure of the regard in which he was held was a surprise 70th birthday party in Twamley Hall on March 16, 1991. Clifford had been in Bismarck much of the time while serving as the chancellor. Room 305, a large conference room, had been secretly decorated with green decorations denoting the president's Irish heritage and a large white cake trimmed in green and a large bowl of green punch punctuated a table at one end of the room. As the appointed hour drew near, the room swelled with people from Twamley Hall and all across the campus. Clifford was led to the room, unsuspecting, and was greeted with the "Happy Birthday" song. In typical fashion, he made his way around the room with a twinkle in his eye, shaking every hand, and thanking each person for coming. And, again, he greeted nearly everyone by name.

Clifford's care and even compassion for people should not suggest that he could not be firm or persistent when it was necessary. He never displayed his anger in public but he could be angered, especially by someone's hurtful actions toward another or toward the University. At the same time, he was not a vindictive person. In fact, he generally served as a peacemaker in conflict situations.

The president's ability to handle controversy was severely tested during the 1970s when UND was often the primary target of self-styled "Referral King," Robert P. McCarney. In 1975, only a ruling by the State Supreme Court prevented UND's legislative budget from being referred to a vote of the people. Clifford's approach to dealing with McCarney was unvarnished and direct, unlike that of some North Dakota leaders, who handled the maverick politician with kid gloves. In one memorable scene, Clifford responded to a charge that UND was concealing travel records by personally piling several boxes of documents in the middle of McCarney's office at his Ford dealership in Bismarck.

Eventually, McCarney and Clifford settled their differences. In the last years of his life, McCarney made several contributions to UND's scholarship funds in journalism, medicine and law. (Vorland, 1992).

The president's style with external constituencies, such as the Legislature and other public officials, reflected his personal style. Henry Tomasek, dean of the College for Human Resources Development, a member of the legislative team from the University for many years, described the president's relationship with the state's governors as "extremely close" (Tomasek, 1/7/91). Clifford's role in maintaining stable support for higher education has certainly been significant. His personal, quiet, non-confrontive style with legislators, governors and board members has certainly averted some disasters and maintained general good will in the political community in the state. Tomasek noted that "Clifford could speak to them as a farmer, businessman, and educator. He would use analogies that they could understand. . . . He never pressured or threatened anybody" (Tomasek, 1/7/91). Sometimes legislators would tell Clifford privately that if he really needed their vote that he would get it. But if something wasn't going to pass anyway, not to be surprised if they voted "no" in order to appease their constituencies (Tomasek, 1/7/91). In short, there was a great deal of mutual respect between Clifford and individual members of the Legislature. Vice President Henry, also a frequent member of the legislative team from the University, described the president as "a master at understanding the needs of all sides. He doesn't shoot from the hip. He has compassion and caring for everyone. He listens and communicates in an honest way" (Henry, 1/28/91). And Clifford relished a challenge. Vice President James noted that the president had great "tenacity. . . . he knows something needs to be done and he does it . . . He is a tremendous problem solver. He grasps a situation quickly and makes a determination about what needs to be done" (James, 1/28/91).

Vice President James of the Medical School provided a description of Clifford's typical approach to a hearing before a legislative committee:

> He knows what to say and what should be said in a way which gets across with a fair amount of humor. He is so relaxed. He uses practically no notes, he makes a few key points, perhaps with a small slip of paper. He always begins with brief introductions, renewing his acquaintances with the committee . . . He puts people at ease immediately. He allows the vice presidents and others to testify. When all is said, he gets up and summarizes . . . It's like he's one of them. . . . To them he's "Mr. UND."
> (James, 1991)

This typical Clifford approach utilized the skills of each member of the UND team. Clifford would prepare the committee and get them in a receptive mood. The vice presidents or a dean would present the factual data and make a case for a particular issue. Clifford would summarize, emphasize the key points, and urge their support. It was a most effective approach and served the University well.

The president had to attend to matters at both Bismarck and at Grand Forks when the Legislature was in session. At times this proved to be a challenge. One evening, during the 1989 session, the Legislature was still meeting at midnight. A member made a motion to delete the Abbott Hall and North Unit (Medicine) UND building projects from a piece of legislation. The UND team phoned Clifford, who was back in Grand Forks, to inform him of this dire development. Clifford was in Bismarck at 7 a.m. the next morning. The projects were restored (Beiswenger, 10/23/91).

A Study of Clifford's Style

A doctoral dissertation study of Clifford's administrative practices produced an analysis in three areas, agenda setting, network building, and task accomplishment (Rice, 1986). In the area of agenda setting, which included formal and informal planning and priority setting, Clifford was rated on a scale from number one (spontaneous "muddle through" planning) to a number four (rational "strategic planning"). His rating was 2.4 (p. 105). An interviewee commented, "He likes to leave a lot of flexibility but knows what his goals are" (p. 105). Another reflected the complexity of Clifford's approach:

> Certainly not a #1 — he is not a muddler. He's very decisive and though he may not have the #4's rigid objectives and standards and goals but he knows where he is going and he knows how to get there. He knows the implications of the decisions he has made. . . . In some ways I'd put him on a #3 but a 3 might mean he has more of it written down. If you put him on a #2 it sounds more like the haphazard, spontaneous person and I don't see him like that at all. He is spontaneous but it is not spontaneity out of nothing. It is spontaneity out of long hard thinking and information gathering that's incredible. He has a tremendous capacity to integrate and put things together and see their relationships. (p. 106)

The general consensus from those interviewed was that the president utilized the formal planning process extensively and, at the same time, had his own very personal yet extensive, informal way of proceeding.

In the area of network building Clifford's rating on a scale of -3 (very negative relationship) to +3 (very positive relationship) was +2.5 or higher for nine out of 10 constituencies. The only rating below +2.5 was a +2.0 for the governor at that time, still a very positive rating. These ratings were very high by any standard. The lengthy duration of his relationships as well as his congenial personality were certainly important factors. Yet, he devoted considerable time and energy to attending to the many constituencies of the University.

In the area of task accomplishment, interviewees were asked to distribute 100 percent of the president's actions across three administrative types: the bureaucratic, the individualistic, and the entrepreneurial. The mean percent for each was bureaucratic 16 percent, individualistic 22 percent, and entrepreneurial 62 percent. Interestingly, the president's self-assessment was bureaucratic 15-20 percent, individualistic 45-50 percent, and entrepreneurial 35 percent (p.

125). In part, this difference between the assessment by the interviewees and the president's own assessment may reflect the extent to which certain activities are more visible than others i.e., entrepreneurial efforts produce visible results while individualistic efforts often are more low-key and behind the scenes. The different assessments may also reflect how much differently the president's role may appear from the outside as compared to how it appears from the inside. In some respects, Clifford did not fit the "model." While he was often perceived as an entrepreneurial type, such leaders usually function with a large staff of technical experts. The president's office at UND had a relatively small staff for the size of the University. When asked about this, Clifford reported that he found it bothersome to have to brief others and delegate tasks which he would prefer handling himself. In this respect, he was an individualistic type, which probably accounted for the high rating he gave himself in that category.

Some of the particular skills which were identified in the same study included Clifford's "Information Gathering," "Idea Testing," and "Stage Setting." Information gathering was an ongoing activity for the president to the extent of being "second nature" (p. 94). He was described as having an amazing memory for detail and a "sponge-like mind" (p. 96). In addition to being an avid reader, he used his vast network to keep informed. His travels and service on various committees and boards were sources of information and trends in education, government and business. Sometimes his knowledge was uncanny. A faculty member reported that sometimes he "tells you about your own department and you don't know how he knows!" (p. 95).

Idea testing took place in both formal and informal ways. During the meetings of the "cabinet" Clifford often discussed ideas he was considering. Commissioner of Higher Education John Richardson reported that Clifford frequently conferred with him about issues well in advance of taking them to the State Board of Higher Education. In addition, Clifford consulted with individual members of the Board. If his ideas received a warm reception he proceeded but if not, he waited or changed plans. Clifford suggested that normally he did not take matters to the Board if he thought they would not pass (p. 97). Not only did his methods of idea testing improve his ideas, it enhanced the credibility of both himself and the University.

Stage setting was the method Clifford employed with considerable skill in preparing for future eventualities. As Clifford moved closer to retirement, Commissioner Richardson noticed that the president was working hard to generally "shore things up financially" (p. 98). Steps were taken to secure the financial base of the Center for Aerospace Sciences (CAS) by allocating for the first time a considerable amount of state appropriated funding to that college for faculty salaries. Richardson thought the president was delegating more tasks to the vice presidents and others as a way of preparing them for his retirement and a new president. The commissioner was highly complimentary and regarded these moves as signs of good management (p. 98). Clifford seemed to have an intuitive sense about what others might do and about which strategies would best serve the University.

One of Clifford's greatest strengths, as should be evident from this account, was his financial acumen. He was clearly a master at managing the extensive resources of the University. He put in place several special foundations which allowed the University to seek, accumulate, and expend private funds. The president's skill at investing expanded the funds even further and his skill at refinancing saved the University money. These foundations served as sources of necessary venture capital for important new projects and provided discretionary spending which the state could not fund and sometimes would not allow with state funds. Clifford's quick grasp of financial matters was another reason for his credibility with legislators, governors, and the North Dakota State Board of Higher Education. Individually and collectively, they often sought his advice on such matters. Dean Tomasek noted that Clifford was a master at reading complex budgets and he "could just glance at something and would know where the problems were" (Tomasek, 1/7/91).

Tom Clifford was a team builder. He worked very well not only with his own cabinet but with key faculty and other administrators in forging effective teams within the University. He assisted with the linking of these campus teams with external persons. The linkages with the Congressional delegation in Washington proved to be especially effective in securing federal funding for key projects at UND during these years.

The president was also a risk taker. He did not take foolish risks. He was what someone has called a "conservative risk taker." He generally avoided risks which gave evidence of probable failure or which could greatly weaken or embarrass the University. On the other hand, he was willing to take calculated risks as he did with the development of the Center for Aerospace Sciences (CAS), Energy and Environmental Research Center (EERC), and to some degree, with the four-year medical program. Many of the major developments during these years might not have come to fruition if Clifford had been unwilling to take risks.

The job of a college or university president, with the demands of long days, short nights, and endless travel, requires great physical stamina. Clifford was easily recognizable on campus with his broad shoulders and measured, confident gait. He always seemed to have a ready smile and a twinkle in his eyes. He was an avid and excellent handball player, worked out regularly at the YMCA, and never seemed to be ill. His days were usually filled with appointments and meetings and his evenings with various events yet he never seemed to be hurried or stressed. He told a group that his days averaged 12 working hours and while he was chancellor, they averaged 17 working hours. He told the same group that he had reviewed his calendar from the past year and, of a possible 104 days of weekends, he had had only seven free from official duties.

No description of Clifford's presidency would be complete without reference to two additional characteristics — his sense of humor and his eternal optimism. Both were unshakable. His ability to see the humor in almost any situation relieved the tension in many a difficult moment. This was the case in informal settings as well as at more formal, public occasions. On one occasion the University was seeking approval from the State Board of Higher Education for an academic program which had stirred some opposition at another campus. When it came time for President Clifford to make his presentation to the Board, he surprised everyone in the room by simply saying, "Well, are there any questions?" The room erupted in laughter. The tension broken, the discussion proceeded in a more receptive climate (Skogley, 2/2/91). His humor often disarmed his critics and smoothed the way for a more congenial and productive discussion.

Likewise, his optimism enabled him to see some good in most situations and some hopeful prospects for the future. He always assumed that the Legislature would provide as much support for higher education as it could, given the available resources. His sense of the history of the University enabled him to remember earlier times of adversity which had been overcome. This perspective enabled him to escape the despair which sometimes comes from a short-term view. When the University lost its bid for a federal training program, Clifford explained to the vice presidents, "that may be the best thing that could happen to us." (Rice, 1986, p. 184).

The president liked to tell a story about an incident during the Second World War. Intense combat was taking place on a small Pacific island. The U.S. troops were surrounded by the Japanese. As the U.S. forces pondered what to do, their commander finally said to the other officers, "Well, we've got them right where we want them! We can attack in any direction!" This story typified Clifford's own unfaltering optimism. These two characteristics, humor and optimism, are so essential to an effective leader and Clifford possessed both in abundance.

Clifford's effectiveness as a president was recognized by others beyond the campus. He was identified in a national survey as one of the 100 most effective presidents in the nation, a select group considering the fact that there are more than 3,000 colleges and universities in the country. Commissioner Richardson described Clifford as one of the two or three most effective presidents he had ever known. Richardson had worked for governing boards in three states and knew many presidents across the nation.

As the Clifford years drew to a close, it was clear that he had been a faithful steward of the trust given into his charge. And he would certainly be remembered with great affection by many people inside and outside of the University. In many respects, he was a product of the institution to which he had, in turn, given so much, an entire career and a distinguished record of service. He had learned much from his professors as a student. As a young administrator he was influenced by President John West who had been a public school administrator and who led the University through the Great Depression. West was effective with the Legislature and some of those lessons, no doubt, rubbed off on the young Clifford. Clifford would share with West the longest tenure as the University president — 21 years. George Starcher was an academic and was a president who had a clear vision for the University, especially the enhancement of its academic quality. Clifford learned important lessons from Starcher, as well. Tom Clifford, more than any other president of the University, was identified intimately with the institution, itself. This distinction will most likely remain uniquely his, well into the future. Perhaps forever.

On September 28, 1991, the new chancellor of higher education, Douglas Treadway, visited the University for the first time. The occasion was used to announce the membership of the search committee which would make recommendations on Clifford's replacement. Treadway spoke to an open meeting in Burtness Theatre at noon. He noted that he was being asked rather often the question, "How are you going to replace Tom Clifford?" Treadway had obviously given this more than a little thought as he told the audience, "We're not." And then he added, "In athletic terms, we're going to retire that jersey" (Schmidt, 9/28/91). Tom Clifford must have enjoyed that metaphor. The University will go forward. The truth is, Tom Clifford will not be replaced.

REFERENCES

Balsley, R.D. (1991, January 29). Memorandum to Alice Clark. Grand Forks: University of North Dakota, Office of Institutional Research.

Basic institutional data for North Central Association review. (1974). Grand Forks: University of North Dakota, Office of Academic Affairs.

Bohnet, L.K. (1983). Athletes. In Wilkins, R.P. (Ed.) *A century on the Northern plains: The University of North Dakota at 100.* Grand Forks: The University of North Dakota.

Brodshaug, J. (1981, May 28). Tin huts go, shed a tear for progress. *Dakota Student*, p. 2.

Buum, L.K., and Kozak, R.L. (1990, November). *Peer institution comparison 1990-91.* Vermillion: University of South Dakota.

Campaign for excellence: The University of North Dakota School of Medicine. (undated). Grand Forks: UND School of Medicine.

Carnegie Commission on Higher Education. (1970). *Higher education and the nation's health: Policies for medical and dental education.* New York: McGraw-Hill.

Center for aerospace sciences briefing paper. (1990, October 1). Grand Forks: University of North Dakota.

Center for innovation and business development seeks jobs, opportunities, new wealth for North Dakota. (1990, Fall). *Dimensions.* Grand Forks: University of North Dakota, Office of University Advancement, pp. 2, 3.

Christenson, W.J. (1990, Winter). Foreign officials discover opportunities in North Dakota. *Dimensions.* Grand Forks: University of North Dakota, Office of University Advancement, p. 4.

Clifford, T.C. (1986, October 9). Memorandum to vice presidents, deans, department chairs, unit heads re: President Reagan's visit. Grand Forks: University of North Dakota, Office of the President.

Clifford marks 15 years at the university's helm. (1986, Fall/Winter). *Dimensions.* Grand Forks: University of North Dakota, Office of University Advancement, pp. 2, 3.

Cory, M.H. (1982). *Nurse, A changing word in a changing world: the history of the University of North Dakota College of Nursing, 1909-1982.* Grand Forks: University of North Dakota, p. 51.

Data forms, North Central Association. *The University of North Dakota: Entering a second century. A decennial report to the North Central Association.* (1983, August). Grand Forks: Office of Academic Affairs, pp. 4, 7.

Davis, W.J. (1992, February 14). Memorandum to Daniel Rice.

Durkin, J. (1990, October 2). Treatment of Gunther lacked class. *Grand Forks Herald*, p. 3D.

Eken, R.S. (1991, February 1). Memorandum to Daniel Rice.

Energy and environmental research center, project plan and supporting documents. (undated). Grand Forks: University of North Dakota, Energy and Environmental Research Center.

Etemad, S.L. (1992, January 31). Memorandum to Daniel Rice.

Fall 1971 enrollments at North Dakota institutions of higher education. (1971). Bismarck: North Dakota Higher Education Facilities Commission.

Fall 1981 enrollments at North Dakota institutions of higher education. (1981). Bismarck: North Dakota Postsecondary Education Commission.

Fall 1991 enrollments at North Dakota institutions of higher education. (1991). Bismarck: North Dakota University System.

Fee, K. (1991, October 2). Timing right for Dakota-made Wanless. *Grand Forks Herald*, p. 1D.

Fee, K. (1991, February 13). Glas takes his Sioux to no. 1 *Grand Forks Herald*, p. 1D.

Fletcher, A.G. (1983, August 8). Memorandum to President Clifford.

Foss, V. (1990, June 28). Clifford saw the writing on the wall. *Grand Forks Herald*, p. 1D.

Fraternity house fire kills 2 U Students. (1971, October 19). *Dakota Student*, p. 1.

Fritz, C. (1972, April 13). Letter to President Clifford.

Fritz, C. (1972, May 12). Letter to President Clifford.

Geiger, L.G. (1958). *University of the Northern plains: A history of the University of North Dakota 1883-1958.* Grand Forks: The University of North Dakota.

Gobble unruffled in campaign. (1981, September 25). *Dakota Student*, p. 1.

Gornowicz, S. (1981, April 24). Minor fire in Budge results in extensive water damage. *Dakota Student*, p. 1.

Haga, C. (1971, January 19). Clifford named next president. *Dakota Student*, p. 3.

Haga, C. (1975, August 10). Koenker mourns trend away from broad education. *Grand Forks Herald*, p. 6B.

Hand, G.S., and Bonham, K. (1988, October 1). Flap over Nazi collection embroils UND benefactor. *Grand Forks Herald*, p. 1A.

Higher education and the nation's health: policies for medical and dental education. (1970). Princeton: *Carnegie Commission on Higher Education.*

International education task force final report. (undated). Grand Forks: University of North Dakota, International Education Task Force.

James, E.C. (1990). Dean's letter. *The Review: University of North Dakota School of Medicine, 15,* 3.

Kantrowitz, B., King, P., and Wingert, P. (1991, October 7). Showing its age: At 100 Stanford reflects the problems of higher ed. *Newsweek*, pp. 54-58.

Keller, G. (1983). *Academic strategy: the management revolution in American higher education.* Baltimore, Md.: Johns Hopkins University Press.

Kenner, H. (1976, August 15). New vice president for academic affairs brings own style to UND administration. *Grand Forks Herald*, UND Edition, p. 1A.

Kerr, C. (1982). *The uses of the university.* (3rd ed.). Cambridge, Mass.: Harvard University Press.

Koenker, W.E. (1971, June 1). Memorandum to President elect Clifford.

Koenker, W.E. (1971, July 21). Memorandum to President Clifford.

Koenker, W.E. (1972, October 2). Letter to President Clifford.

Laws of North Dakota, 1971. (1971). Bismarck: North Dakota Legislative Council, p. 1432.

Lee, S.J. (1990, August 15). Clifford will head higher education. *Grand Forks Herald,* pp. 1A, 7A.

Liffrig, J. (1991, September/October). Human nutrition lab helps set country's RDAs. *University of North Dakota Alumni Review*, p. 5.

Liffrig, J. (1992, January/February). Bards celebrate 40 years of music and fun. *University of North Dakota Alumni Review*, pp. 1, 2.

Lemon, D.K. (1988). Final Performance Report, Educational Personnel Development Project for Training Indian People in Educational Administration at the master's, specialist, and doctoral levels. Grand Forks: University of North Dakota, p. 42.

Medalen, J.I. (1991, November 9). Memorandum to Daniel Rice.

McCannel, A.D. (1956). *Medical milestones in North Dakota*. Bismarck: North Dakota Medical Association.

Merrill, L.J. (1991, February 28). Memorandum to Daniel Rice.

Munski, D.C., and Schubert, G.W. (1989). *A guide for parents and freshmen students*. Dubuque, Iowa: Kendall/Hunt Publishing Co.

Nelson, R. (1976, August 15). Project lignite seeks answers about energy needs from coal. *Grand Forks Herald*, UND Edition, p. 7C.

Perrone, V. Updated by Harris, M. (undated). *Teacher Education at the University of North Dakota: Highlights of a century-long history*. Unpublished manuscript. University of North Dakota, Center for Teaching and Learning.

Phillips, N.A. (1991, Spring). New leadership in the school of engineering and mines. *Grad Grapevine*. Grand Forks: University of North Dakota Graduate School, p. 3.

Redman, V.K. (Undated and untitled manuscript). Grand Forks: University of North Dakota School of Medicine.

Retallic, K. (1972, April 4). Clifford installed at UND. *Grand Forks Herald*, p. 1A.

Rice, D.R. (1986). *Selected administrative practices of a university president described and analyzed through the use of the Kotter/Lawrence Theory*. Unpublished doctoral dissertation, University of North Dakota, Grand Forks, ND.

Robinson, E.B. (1966). *History of North Dakota*. Lincoln: University of Nebraska Press.

Robinson, E.B. (Spring 1971). The Starcher years: the University of North Dakota, 19544-1971. *North Dakota Quarterly*, p. 5-44.

Rylance, D.F., and Fritz, C. (1982). *Ever westward to the far east: the story of Chester Fritz*. Grand Forks: University of North Dakota.

Rylance, D.F. (1983). Alumni. In Wilkins, R.P. (Ed.) *A century on the Northern plains: The University of North Dakota at 100*. Grand Forks: The University of North Dakota.

Sanborn, P.F. (1991, January 23). Memorandum to Daniel Rice.

Schieve, D., and Driscoll, T. (undated). *UND entering freshman 1987-88 and 1988-89: A composite picture based on ACT and ACE information*. (Report No. RR-SA-042889). Grand Forks: University of North Dakota, Division of Student Affairs.

Schmidt, S. (1988, October 10). Consensus: room isn't shrine. *Grand Forks Herald*, p. 1A.

Schmidt, S. (1990, July 26). As the chancellor churns: Will UND's Clifford leave? It's a university soap. *Grand Forks Herald*, p. 1B.

Schmidt, S. (1990, October 21). Banquet in Tom Clifford's honor kicks off major endowment drive. *Grand Forks Herald*, p. 1B.

Schmidt, S. (1991, February 2). UND to open patent, trademark library. *Grand Forks Herald*, p. 1B.

Schmidt, S. (1991, July 14). Earth system science institute: Once a dream it now is taking shape at UND. *Grand Forks Herald,* pp. 1B, 2B.

Schmidt, S. (1991, August 8). Med school expansion funds grow. *Grand Forks Herald*, p. 2B.

Schmidt, S. (1991, September 28). Treadway: we'll retire Clifford's jersey. *Grand Forks Herald*, p. 1A.

Schmidt, S. (1991, November 3). UND greeks battle image problem. *Grand Forks Herald,* p. 1B, 3B.

SCOPE report for the 70s. (1973, April). Grand Forks: University of North Dakota, SCOPE Planning Committee.

Special organization for friends of UND. (undated). Grand Forks: University of North Dakota, President's Office.

Stjern, B. (1981, September 1). VP calls on legislature to support academics. *Dakota Student*, p. 2.

Strategy for the 1980s. (1979, March). Grand Forks: University of North Dakota, Strategic Planning Committee.

Strinden, E.S. (1991, February 5). Memorandum to Daniel Rice.

Strinden, E.S. (1992, January 14). Memorandum to Daniel Rice, p. 9.

Stategic plan for the 90s, A. (1990, May). Grand Forks: University of North Dakota, Strategic Planning Council.

Testimony before the appropriations committee, North Dakota state senate. (1991, March 4). Grand Forks: University of North Dakota.

Toward the second century: A report of the president's planning council. (1980, January). Grand Forks: University of North Dakota, President's Planning Council.

UND: A centennial portrait. (1983, May). Grand Forks: University of North Dakota, Office of University Advancement.

Vanvig, J. (1983, November 11). Team endorses UND for full accreditation. *Grand Forks Herald*, p. 1A.

Vennes, J.W. (1991, November 15). Notes to Daniel Rice.

Vivian, J.F. (1983). The campus. In Wilkins, R.P. (Ed.) *A century on the Northern plains: The University of North Dakota at 100*. Grand Forks: The University of North Dakota.

Vorland, D.H. (1979, October 16). VP Conny Nelson is chief academic official. *UND Official Game Program*, p. 12.

Vorland, D.H. (1992, March 30). Notes to Daniel Rice.

Waldron, E.E. (1987). *From house calls to HMO's: A history of organized medicine in North Dakota, 1887-1987*. North Dakota Medical Association.

Wheeler, M. (1992, February 7). Survey says N.D. tuition outpaces regional schools. *Grand Forks Herald*, p. 3B.

Wilkins, R.P. (Ed.). (1983). *A century on the Northern plains: The University of North Dakota at 100*. Grand Forks: The University of North Dakota.

Youngblood, D. (1979, March 4). N. Dakota University's aviaton school is soaring. *Minneapolis Tribune*, p. 1D.

INTERVIEWS REFERENCED IN TEXT

All interviews conducted by the author unless otherwise noted.

Clark, A.T. (1/21/91). Vice President for Academic Affairs, University of North Dakota.

Clifford, T.J. (7/6/90). President, University of North Dakota.

Clifford, T.J. (1/23/91).

Clifford, T.J. (5/23/91).

Clifford, T.J. (8/8/91). Interview conducted by D. Bohn.

Clifford, T.J. (8/22/91).

Clifford, T.J. (2/26/92).

Crow, W.J. (12/18/91). Budget Director, University of North Dakota.

Beiswenger, L.W. (10/23/91). Vice President for Finance, University of North Dakota.

Davis, W.J. (1/29/91). Dean, School of Law, University of North Dakota.

Fletcher, A.G. (10/17/91). Retired Dean, School of Engineering and Mines, University of North Dakota.

Henry, G.H. (1/28/91). Vice President for Student Affairs, University of North Dakota.

Hoffarth, A. (10/24/91). Vice President for Operations, University of North Dakota.

James, E.C. (1/28/91). Vice President for Health Sciences and Dean of the School of Medicine, University of North Dakota.

Jeanotte, L.D. (2/1/91). Director, Native American Programs, University of North Dakota.

Johnson, A.W. (2/11/91). Professor of Chemistry and former Dean of the Graduate School, University of North Dakota.

Lips, E. (10/19/91). Business person and legislator, Bismarck, North Dakota.

Odegard, J.D. (2/5/91). Dean, Center for Aerospace Sciences, University of North Dakota.

O'Kelly, B. (1/29/91). Dean, College of Arts and Sciences, University of North Dakota.

Skogley, G. (2/2/91). Business Officer, The Bush Foundation and former Vice President for Finance, University of North Dakota.

Sondrol, L.S. (11/2/91). Director, Plant Services, University of North Dakota.

Strinden, E.S. (2/2/91). Executive Vice President, the University of North Dakota Alumni Association and Foundation.

Tomasek, H.J. (1/7/91). Dean, College for Human Resources Development, University of North Dakota.

Tweton, D.J. (10/22/91). Professor of History, University of North Dakota.

ENROLLMENT HISTORY
University of North Dakota — Fall Term, 1971-1991

Year	Total Students*	Graduate Students**	Undergraduate Students	Law and Medicine
1971-72	8,395	1,088	7,012	295
1972-73	8,282	1,171	6,816	295
1973-74	8,274	1,118	6,806	350
1974-75	8,171	1,083	6,671	417
1975-76	8,632	1,165	6,990	477
1976-77	8,858	1,282	7,116	460
1977-78	9,363	1,178	7,722	463
1978-79	9,505	1,291	7,729	485
1979-80	9,708	1,108	8,132	468
1980-81	10,217	1,240	8,474	503
1981-82	10,750	1,287	8,945	518
1982-83	11,103	1,337	9,256	510
1983-84	11,053	1,290	9.257	506
1984-85	11,060	1,206	9,358	496
1985-86	11,106	1,193	9,474	439
1986-87	11,006	1,148	9,438	420
1987-88	11,181	1,223	9,551	407
1988-89	11,860	1,269	10,166	425
1989-90	12,321	1,240	10,650	431
1990-91	11,885	1,194	10,104	495
1991-92	11,940	1,207	10,057	503

* *Includes off-campus*
** *On campus*

APPENDIX B

GRADUATE SCHOOL ENROLLMENTS BY GENDER

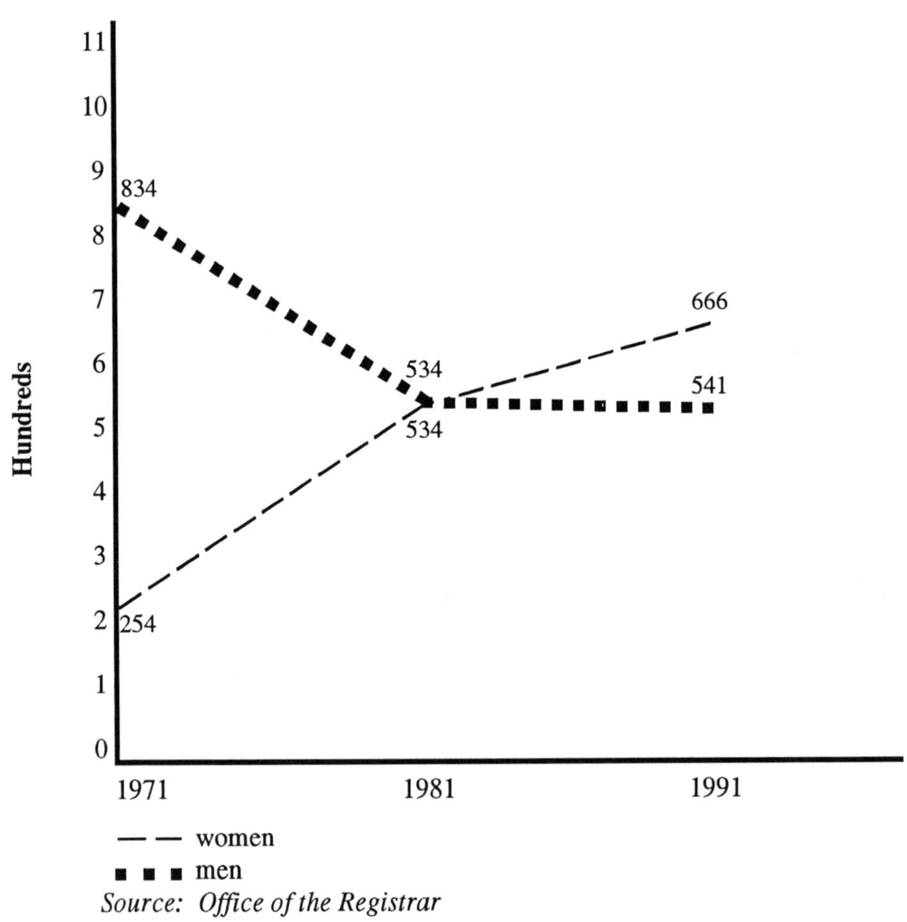

Source: Office of the Registrar

PROFESSIONAL SCHOOL* ENROLLMENTS BY GENDER

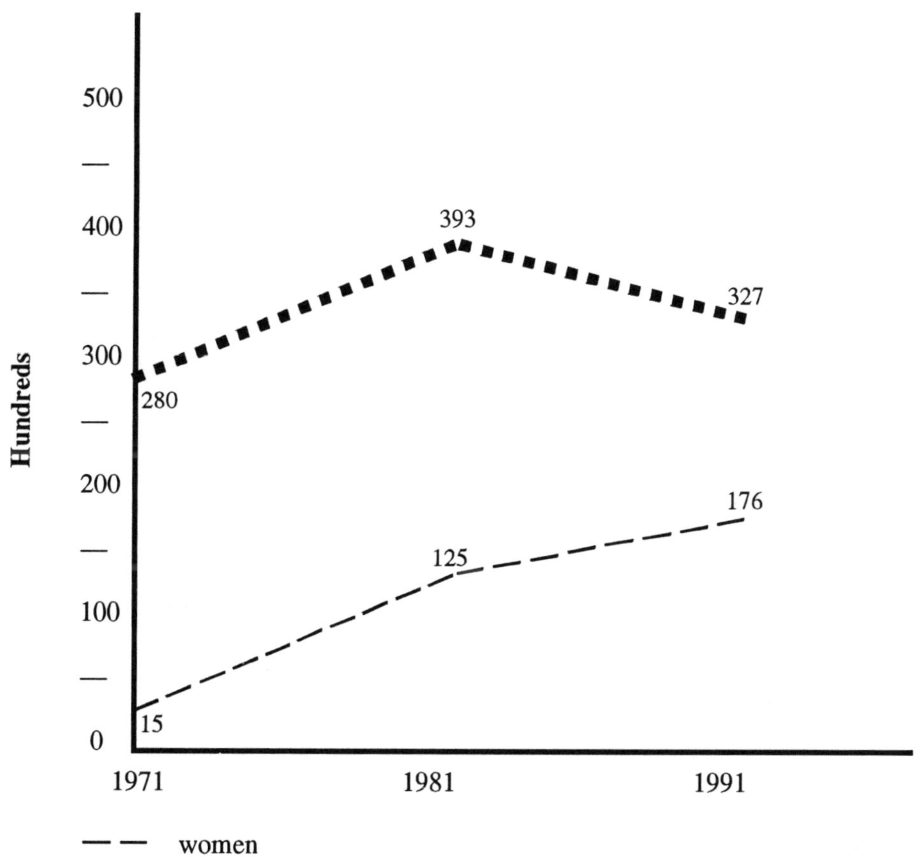

* *Law and Medicine*
Source: Office of the Registrar

APPENDIX D

FOUNDERS DAY AWARD RECIPIENTS

Listed are individual teacher awards which since 1967 for the most part have been determined by a University-wide committee of faculty and students. From 1967 to 1979, the awards were supported by the Amoco Foundation; in 1978, the Fellows of the University of North Dakota, Inc., began to sponsor an individual award, which in 1985 became a departmental citation. In 1980, the University of North Dakota Alumni Association and Foundation expanded and turned over to the committee its existing faculty recognition program and has supported individual and departmental awards since in the names of B.C. Gamble, Charles DeBruyn Kops, Edward and Lucille McDermott, Edgar Dale, and Lydia and Arthur Saiki. From 1985 to 1990, the Burlington Northern Foundation supported three faculty achievement awards for outstanding teaching, research and faculty development. In 1991, these awards were sponsored by the University. Beginning in 1992, Burlington Northern Foundation supported one award for overall excellence in teaching, research and service. In 1986, student government initiated an award for outstanding faculty advising, now supported in part by the UND Foundation.

The Fellows of the University Award for Departmental Excellence in Research and the University of North Dakota Achievement Award for Excellence in Research are determined by a committee composed of the director of research and program development, the dean of the Graduate School, and representatives from the Graduate and Faculty Research Committees. From 1968 to 1973, the departmental award was known as the McDermott Award for Departmental Excellence in Research, and was sponsored by the UND Alumni Association. The Achievement Award was sponsored by the Burlington Northern Foundation 1985 to 1990.

The Sigma Xi Faculty Award winner is selected by a special committee of that scientific research society. The UND Foundation/Student Government Faculty Adviser Award is selected by the Student Advisement Committee, appointed by the vice president for academic affairs.

Awards Since 1971 *(a complete list is maintained by the Office of University Advancement)*

Individual Awards for Teaching, Research, Service, Advising

1971 — Lloyd Jarman, Education; Robert W. King, English; Edward O. Nelson, Mathematics

1972 — Ruth MacKichan, Mathematics; W. Barnett Pearce, Speech and Journalism; Ruth Peterson, Occupational Therapy

1973 — Susan McIntyre, Occupational Therapy; Donald Poochigian, Political Science; Lydia Svetich, Nursing

1974 — Mabel Curry, Home Economics; Alan Meldrum, Industrial Engineering; Elmer Schmiess, Center for Teaching and Learning

1975 — Larry J. Dobesh, Economics; Olen Kraus, Physics; Ronald E. Pynn, Political Science

1976 — Suzanne Bennett, Theatre Arts; Robert Mullins, Philosophy; Glenn Prigge, Mathematics

1977 — Bruce Benner, Political Science; Michael Gregory, Mathematics; Carla Hess, Speech Pathology and Audiology

1978 — Kenneth Klabunde, Chemistry; Stephen Rendahl, Journalism and Speech; David Wiener, English

1979 — Carol Neuberger, Nursing; Fred Peterson, Center for Teaching and Learning

1980 — William Bolunchuk, Health, Physical Education and Recreation; Kenneth Dawes, Social Work; Louis Palanca, Languages; Marilyn Peterson, Health, Physical Education and Recreation

1981 — Omer Larson, Biology; Roy Miller, Chemistry; Clara Pederson, Center for Teaching and Learning; Scot Stradley, Economics

1982 — John Crawford, English; Joe Hootman, Electrical Engineering; Myrna Olson, Center for Teaching and Learning; Donald Smith, Aviation

1983 — Richard Crawford, Biology; Robert Nordlie, Biochemistry; Lawrence Loendorf, Anthropology and Archaeology; Randy Lee, School of Law; Thomas Robinson, Mathematics

1984 — Richard Molenaar, Aviation; William Beckwith, Psychology; Mark Langemo, Business and Vocational Education; Michael Ahlen, School of Law; Donald Lemon, Center for Teaching and Learning

1985 — James Boelkins, Pharmacology; Dale Fuqua, Counseling; Martin Jones, Chemistry; Marcia

O'Kelly, School of Law; Wan-Lee Cheng,
Industrial Technology; Leon Osborne,
Aviation; Lewis Oring, Biology
1986 — Nanak Grewal, Mechanical Engineering;
Steven Harlow, Center for Teaching and
Learning; Beverly Brekke, Center for Teaching
and Learning; Thomas Petros, Psychology;
Glenn Prigge, Mathematics; John D. Williams,
Center for Teaching and Learning, Sharon
Wilsnack, Neuroscience; Mary Lou Fuller,
Center for Teaching and Learning
1987 — Brad Stewart, Sociology; Duane Bartak,
Chemistry; Owen Anderson, School of Law;
Thomas Akers, Physiology; Mary Lou Fuller,
Center for Teaching and Learning; Dory
Marken, Occupational Therapy; Robert
Nordlie, Biochemistry and Molecular Biology;
Thomas Owens, Chemical Engineering
1988 — Douglas Munski, Geography; William
Schwalm, Physics; Surendra Parmar,
Physiology; Carla Hess, Communication
Disorders; William Dando, Geography;
William Beckwith, Psychology; John Salter Jr.,
Indian Studies
1989 — DuWayne M. Wacker, Accounting and
Business Law; James J. McKenzie, English;
Patti Ann Alleva, School of Law; Gerald C.
Lawrence, Humanities; Patricia F. Sanborn,
Humanities; Kenneth J. Dawes, Social Work;
Richard G. Landry, Center for Teaching and
Learning; Dale E. DeRemer, Aviation
1990 — William Borden, English; Kathleen Gershman,
Secondary Education; Douglas Munski,
Geography; John O. Oberpriller, Anatomy and
Cell Biology; B. Seshagiri Rao, Physics; L.
Elliot Shubert, Biology; Elmer Schmiess,
Elementary Education
1991 — William Beckwith, Psychology; William
Gosnold, Geology and Geological Engineering;
Diange Langemo, Nursing Professionalism and
Practice; Lyle Mauland, Mathematics;
Elizabeth Rankin, English; Beverly Uhlenberg,
Home Economics and Nutrition; DuWayne
Wacker, Accounting and Business Law
1992 — John Reid, Geology and Geological
Engineering; Graciela Wilborn, Languages;
Lynn Chalmers, Special Education; Elvira
Szigeti, Adult Health and Anesthesia Nursing;
Wayne Swisher, Communication Disorders;
David Hein, Pharmacology and Toxicology;
Craig S. Holman, Computer Science

**Fellows of the University Award
for Departmental Excellence in Research**

1971 — Department of Biology, accepted by Joe K.
Neel, Acting Chair
1972 — Department of Chemistry, accepted by
Roland G. Severson, Chair
1973 — Department of Chemical Engineering,
accepted by Donald E. Severson, Chair
1974 — Department of Microbiology, accepted by
Robert G. Fischer, Chair
1975 — Department of Anatomy, accepted by
Dwayne A. Ollerich, Chair
1976 — Program Area of Special Education and
Statistics, accepted by Steven Harlow, Chair.
1977 — Department of Physiology and Pharmacology, accepted by Stanley Brumleve, Chair
1978 — Department of Chemistry, accepted by
Roland G. Severson, Chair
1979 — Department of Visual Arts, accepted by
Jacquelyn McElroy, Acting Chair
1980 — Department of Anthropology and
Archaeology, accepted by Lawrence
Loendorf, Chair
1981 — Department of Biochemistry, accepted by
W.E. Cornatzer, Chair
1982 — Department of Biology, accepted by Richard
Crawford, Chair
1983 — Department of Anatomy, accepted by
Edward Carlson, Chair
1984 — Department of Sociology, accepted by Arne
Selbyg, Chair
1985 — Department of Geology, accepted by Donald
Halvorson, Chair
1986 — Department of Chemistry, accepted by
Roland Severson, Chair
1987 — Department of History, accepted by Glenn
Smith, Chair
1988 — Department of Atmospheric Sciences,
accepted by Cedric A. Grainger, Chair
1989 — Department of Biology, accepted by Richard
D. Crawford, Chair
1990 — Department of Biochemistry and Molecular
Biology, accepted by Robert C. Nordlie,
Chair
1991 — Department of English, Sheryl R. O'Donnell,
Chair
1992 — Department of Anthropology, John A.
Williams, Chair

**Fellows of the University Award
for Departmental Excellence in Public Service**

1985 — School of Law, accepted by W. Jeremy
Davis, Dean

1986 — Department of Aviation, accepted by William
Shea, Chair

1987 — Department of Music, accepted by James
Fry, Chair

1988 — Department of Early Childhood Education,
accepted by Mae Marie Blackmore, Director,
Children's Center

1989 — Department of Industrial Technology,
accepted by Myron Bender, Chair

1990 — Department of Accounting and Business
Law, accepted by Hans Johnson, Chair

1991 — Department of Social Work, Kenneth Dawes,
Chair

1992 — Department of Educational Administration,
Donald Lemon, Chair

**The Sigma Xi Faculty Award for
Outstanding Scientific Research**

1971 — Frank N. Low, Anatomy; George W.
Starcher, President, special award for interest
in and contributions to science

1972 — Joe K. Neel, Biology

1973 — Ya Pin Lee, Biochemistry

1974 — Virgil Stenberg, Chemistry

1975 — Mohan Wali, Biology

1976 — Roy Miller, Chemistry

1977 — John Duerre, Microbiology; Kenneth
Klabunde, Chemistry

1978 — Paul Kannowski, Biology

1979 — Surendra S. Parmar, Physiology; John D.
Williams, Center for Teaching and learning

1980 — None presented

1981 — Lewis Oring, Biology

1982 — Beverly Brekke, Center for Teaching and
Learning; Francis Jacobs, Biochemistry

1983 — William Dando, Geography

1984 — Paul D. Ray, Biochemistry and Molecular
Biology

1985 — Donald Bergstrom, Chemistry

1986 — Stephen Wikel, Microbiology and
Immunology

1987 — Harvey Knull, Biochemistry and Molecular
Biology

1988 — Neil Woolsey, Chemistry

1989 — Forrest E. Nielson, Human Nutrition
Research Center

1990 — Thomas Akers, Physiology

1991 — William Gosnold, Geology and Geological
Engineering

1992 — David O. Lambeth, Biochemistry and
Molecular Biology

**McDermott Award for Departmental
Excellence in Teaching**

1974 — Department of English, accepted by Robert
W. Lewis, Chair

1975 — Department of Political Science, accepted by
Stephen C. Markovich, Chair

1976 — Department of Mathematics, accepted by
Ronald Bzoch, Chair

1977 — Department of History, accepted by D.
Jerome Tweton, Chair

1978 — Department of Computer Science, accepted
by Mok Tokko, Chair

1979 — Department of Journalism, accepted by
Vernon Keel, Chair

1980 — College of Nursing, accepted by Nursing
Area Coordinators

1981 — Program Area of Educational Administration, accepted by Donald Piper, Chair

1982 — Department of Industrial Technology,
accepted by Myron Bender, Chair

1983 — Department of Economics, accepted by
Richard Kauffman, Chair

1984 — Department of Religious Studies, accepted by
George Frein, Chair

1985 — Department of Accounting and Business
Law, accepted by Ludwik Kulas, Chair

1986 — Department of Home Economics and
Nutrition, accepted by Joy Bostrom, Chair

1987 — Department of Occupational Therapy,
accepted by Sue McIntyre, Chair

1988 — Department of Elementary Education,
accepted by Mary Lou S. Fuller, Chair

1989 — Department of Aviation, accepted by William
F. Shea, Chair

1990 — Department of Electrical Engineering,
accepted by Sastry Kuruganty, Chair

1991 — Educational Foundations and Research, Ivan
Dahl, Chair

1992 — Department of Chemical Engineering,
Thomas C. Owens, Chair

FACULTY MEMBERS EMERITI

The University and the North Dakota University System bestow the title of Emeritus on those faculty who have given both lengthy and effective service to the University. The title is bestowed after the retirement of the faculty person.

AUSTIN, Alvin E., Professor Emeritus, Journalism

AUYONG, Theodore K., Associate Professor Emeritus, Pharmacology

BADER, Meinhardt, Associate Professor Emeritus, Accounting and Business Law

BAILEY, Beverly Brekke, Professor Emeritus, Special Education

BARNEY, William G., P.E., Professor Emeritus, Mechanical Engineering

BEHRINGER, Marjorie P., Professor Emeritus, Biology

BEHSMAN, Ervin A., Associate Professor Emeritus, Secondary Education

BLACKMORE, Mae Marie, Instructor Emeritus, Center for Teaching and Learning

BOEHLE, William R., Professor Emeritus, Music

BOGAN, Louis D., Associate Professor Emeritus, Health, Physical Education and Recreation

BROWN, Ralph C., Professor Emeritus, Geography

BRUMLEVE, Stanley J., Professor Emeritus, Physiology

BURRAGE, Ruth, Professor Emeritus, Nursing

CALDWELL, Mary Ellen, Associate Professor Emeritus, English

CAPE, Julia P., Assistant Professor Emeritus, English

CHRISTOFERSON, Lee A., Professor Emeritus, Neuroscience

COLLINS, Ben L., Professor Emeritus, English

CORNATZER, William E., University Professor Emeritus, Chester Fritz Distinguished Professor and Professor Emeritus, Biochemistry

CORY, Margaret Heyse, Dean Emeritus, College of Nursing

CRAWFORD, John C., Professor Emeritus, English

CURRY, Mabel L., Professor Emeritus, Home Economics and Nutrition

CURRY, Myron C., Associate Professor Emeritus, Speech

DeBOER, Benjamin, Professor Emeritus, Physiology and Pharmacology

DIXON, John, Professor Emeritus, Electrical Engineering

FISCHER, Robert G., Professor Emeritus, Microbiology and Immunology

FLETCHER, Alan G., Dean Emeritus and Professor Emeritus, School of Engineering and Mines

FOSSUM, Guilford O., Professor Emeritus, Civil Engineering

FOSTER, Keith G., Associate Professor Emeritus, Community Medicine and Rural Health

FRANK, Richard E., Associate Professor Emeritus, Chemistry

GAIDES, Glenn Edward, Associate Professor Emeritus, Elementary Education

GALLANT, Ruth, Professor Emeritus, Education, Elementary Education

GARD, William G., Associate Professor Emeritus, History

GROVOM, Dorothy, Professor Emeritus, Business and Vocational Education

HAGER, Oswald M., Associate Professor
Emeritus, Business and Vocational
Education

HALE, Richard O., Associate Professor
Emeritus, English

HAMMOND, George R., Assistant
Professor Emeritus, Aviation

HANKERSON, Kenneth, Professor
Emeritus, Mathematics

HILDEBRANDT, Bruno, Professor
Emeritus, Languages

HISEY, Philip D., Associate Professor
Emeritus, Music

HOLLAND, F.D., Jr., Professor Emeritus,
Geology and Geological Engineering

HOLLENBECK, Robert E., Associate
Professor Emeritus, Elementary
Education

JACOBS, Francis A., Professor Emeritus,
Biochemistry and Molecular Biology

JACOBY, Arthur P., Professor Emeritus,
Sociology

JENSEN, Ivan R., Professor Emeritus,
Civil Engineering

JOHNSON, Stanley O., Associate
Professor Emeritus, Visual Arts

JORGENSEN, LaVernia, Associate
Professor Emeritus, Health, Physical
Education and Recreation

KANNOWSKI, Paul, Professor Emeritus,
Biology

KEMPER, Robert W., Associate Professor
Emeritus, Accounting and Business
Law

KJELMYR, Helen, Associate Professor
Emeritus, Management

KOENKER, W.E., University Professor
and Vice President Emeritus for
Academic Affairs, University
Professor Emeritus, Economics

KOLSTOE, Ralph, Professor Emeritus,
Psychology

KORSMO, Richard G., Associate
Professor Emeritus, Accounting and
Business Law

KOTCH, Alex, Professor Emeritus,
Chemistry

KRAUS, Olen, Professor Emeritus,
Physics

KRUEGER, Jack N., P.E., Professor
Emeritus, Electrical Engineering

KULAS, Ludwik, Professor Emeritus,
Accounting and Business Law

LAIRD, Wilson M., Professor Emeritus,
Geology and State Geologist
Emeritus

LARSON, Edith E., Professor Emeritus,
Biology

LESER, Esther Hartley, Professor
Emeritus, Germanic, Romance and
Comparative Philology, Languages

LIND, Amy, Professor Emeritus, Occupational Therapy

LINKLETTER, C. Monte, Professor
Emeritus, English

LOW, Frank N., Chester Fritz Distinguished Professor and Professor
Emeritus, Anatomy

LUPER, Miltza, Assistant Professor
Emeritus, Biochemistry

MANZ, Oscar E., Professor Emeritus,
Civil Engineering

MARWIN, Richard M., Professor
Emeritus, Microbiology and Immunology

MAUCH, Patricia, Associate Professor
Emeritus, Health, Physical Education
and Recreation

McBRIDE, Woodrow, Associate Professor
Emeritus, Mathematics

MELDRUM, Alan H., Professor Emeritus,
Industrial Engineering

MILLER, Jack L., Associate Professor
Emeritus, Music

MORGAN, William I., Professor Emeritus, Languages

MULLINS, Robert J., Professor Emeritus,
Philosophy

NOLL, John O., Professor Emeritus,
Psychology

OECHSLE, Lois H., Associate Professor
Emeritus, Nursing

OSLUND, Valborg, Associate Professor
Emeritus, English

OWEN, John B., Professor Emeritus, Biology

PATTERSON, Channing F., Associate Professor Emeritus, Languages

PEDERSEN, Myrtle E., Professor Emeritus, English

PEDERSON, Clara A., Professor Emeritus, Center for Teaching and Learning

PENN, John S., Dean Emeritus, Summer Sessions and Professor Emeritus, Speech

PETERSON, Russell A., Chester Fritz Distinguished Professor and Professor Emeritus, Center for Teaching and Learning

POLOVITZ, Michael F., Professor Emeritus, Music

QUADAY, John, Professor Emeritus, Health, Physical Education and Recreation

QUERY, Joy M., Professor Emeritus, Neuroscience

READ, Tamar, Professor Emeritus, Music

RHONEMUS, Grace O., Associate Professor Emeritus, Health, Physical Education and Recreation

ROBERTSON, D.J., Dean Emeritus, University College

RODGERS, Marguerite, Assistant Professor Emeritus, German

ROGERS, John H., Professor Emeritus, Visual Arts

RUNDELL, Glenna, Professor Emeritus, Music

RUNDLE, Beulah, Assistant Professor Emeritus, English

RYKKEN, Marjorie B., Professor Emeritus, Nursing

SAINT CLAIR, Foster Y., Professor Emeritus, English

SCOTT, Rachel Shields, Associate Professor Emeritus, Adult Health Nursing

SCOTT, Thomas B., Professor Emeritus, Counseling Department

SEVERSON, Donald E., University Professor, Chester Fritz Distinguished Professor and Professor Emeritus, Chemical Engineering

SEVERSON, Roland G., Professor Emeritus, Chemistry

SHURR, Agnes G., Professor Emeritus, Nursing

SMITH, Glenn H., Professor Emeritus, History

SNOOK, Theodore, Professor Emeritus, Anatomy

STARCHER, George W., President Emeritus

STEINMEIER, Lyle, Professor Emeritus, Accounting and Business Law

STEWART, James A., Professor Emeritus, Chemistry

SUMMERS, Lawrence, Professor Emeritus, Chemistry

THOMFORDE, Clifford, Professor Emeritus, Electrical Engineering

URQUIAGA, Juana, Associate Professor Emeritus, Spanish

WEISSUR, Wilbur O., Associate Professor Emeritus, Physics

WHALEN, C.J., Professor Emeritus, Accounting and Business Law

WHITCOMB, John L., Associate Professor Emeritus, Mathematics

WILKINS, Robert P., Professor Emeritus, History

WILKINS, Wynona, Associate Professor Emeritus, Languages

WILLETT, Thelma E., Associate Professor Emeritus, Music

ZAZULA, Frank, Assistant Professor Emeritus, Health, Physical Education and Recreation

(Source: Official records, President's Office)

APPENDIX F

MAJOR BUILDINGS CONSTRUCTED 1971 - 1991

Year	Building	Sq. Ft. (1,000)	Cost (Millions)
1971	West Green #5	71	$1.38
1971	Upson I	47	1.34
1972	Chester Fritz Auditorium	82	3.09
1972	Winter Sports Center	91	1.96
1972	West Green #7	62	.95
1973	Law Addition	.8	.99
1973	Law Library	26	.97
1973	West Green #9	62	.90
1974	Rehab Hospital	132	4.10
1974	Fine Arts	91	2.90
1974	Upson II	42	1.22
1974	Plant Services	31	1.22
1976	Nursing	53	1.93
1978	Medical (Fargo)	25	1.50
1980	West Green #11	46	1.02
1980	Starcher Hall	85	3.79
1980	West Green #12	69	1.53
1982	C.F. Library Addition	80	4.48
1982	Memorial Union Addition	27	3.18
1983	Center for Aerospace Sciences I	55	4.37
1984	Hyslop Sports Addition	141	6.39
1985	Swanson Residence Hall	55	3.04
1985	Center for Aerospace Sciences II, Computer Building	26	1.64
1988	Center for Aerospace Sciences III	63	5.46
1989	Aviation Maintenance Hanger	25	1.63
1989	Aviation Administration	16	22.28
1989	Aviation Maintenance	29	1.32
1991	Earth System Science	76*	8.10*
1991	Abbott Hall Addition	33*	3.80*
	Construction Total	**1,641.8**	**96.48**

*　*Estimates, projects in progress at time of writing.*

Source:　UND Building Activity Report, Office of Facilities Coordinator, 2/4/91, updated 10/30/91.

174

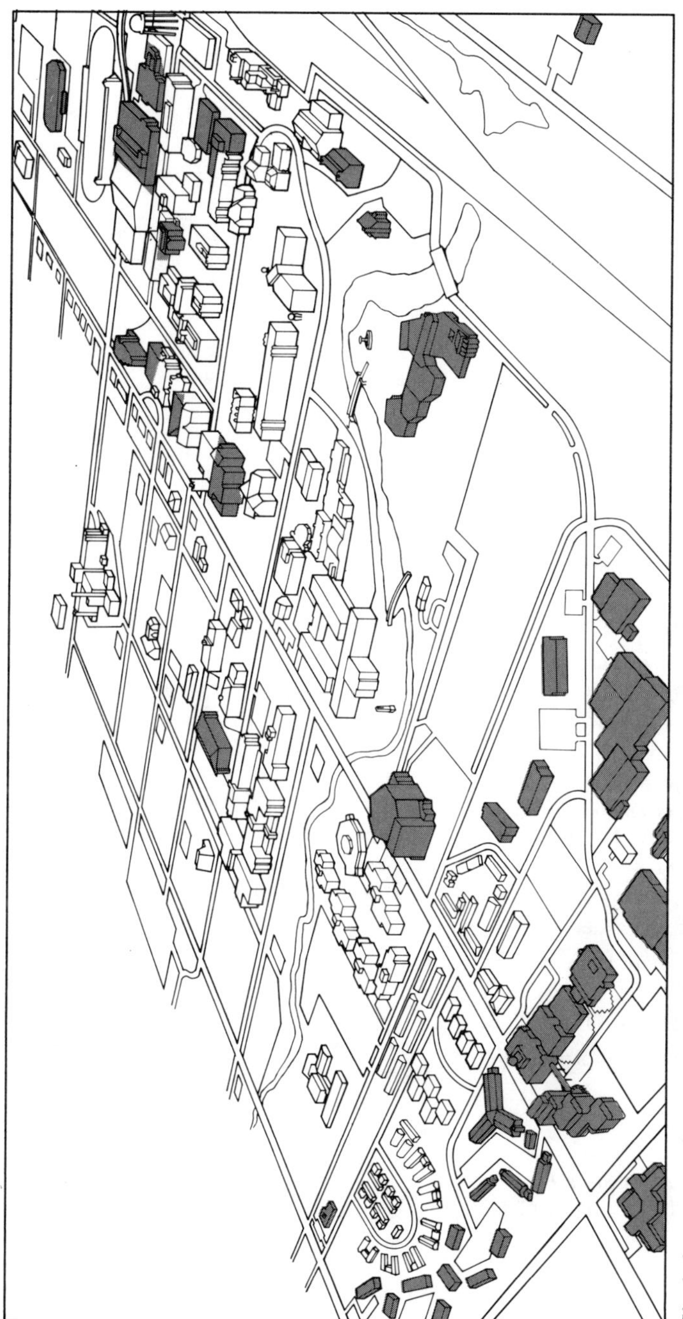

Shaded structures indicate the buildings which were erected during the Clifford presidency. Extensive construction also took place at the UND Aviation operation at the Airport.

APPENDIX H

FACULTY AUTHORS

Selected books authored by UND faculty.

The Role of Noncovalent Bonding in Coal, by Richard J. Baltisberger

Naked in Exile: Khalil Hjawi's "Threshing floor of Hunger," by Michael C. Beard (co-author)

Contact and Consequences: Over 300 Years of French Presence in North America, by Virgil Benoit

Why the South Lost the Civil War, by Richard E. Beringer (co-author)

The Last Prostitute (A Play), by William Borden

An Introduction to Quality Assurance and Quality Control in the Clinical Laboratory, by A. Wayne Bruce

The Michif Dictionary, by John C. Crawford

At the Waters Edge: Nature Study in Lakes, Streams and Ponds, by Alan M. Cvancara

Fantasia for Clarinet and Piano (music), by James Fry

Education, Modernity and Fractured Meaning: Toward a Process Theory of Teaching and Learning, by Kathleen W. Gershman (co-author)

Settlers' Children, Growing Up on the Great Plains, by Elizabeth Hampsten

Wildflowers of North Dakota, by Paul B. Kannowski

Pegged for Murder, by Norton D. Kinghorn

Standing Around Outside, by Robert W. King

Sex and Morality in the U.S. ..., by Albert D. Klassen (co-author)

History of the North Dakota State Psychological Association, by Ralph H. Kolstoe

The Vanitas Paintings of Harmen Steenwyck, by Kristine Koozin.

Concepts and Methods for Political Analysis, by Mary Grisez Kweit and Robert W. Kweit

Implementing Citizen Participation in a Bureaucratic Society, by Robert W. Kweit and Mary Grisez Kweit

Les Portes Secretes Du Reve, by Andre Lebugle

Hemingway in Italy and Other Essays, by Robert W. Lewis

American Political Economy: Using Economics in Politics, by Denise Markovich and Ronald E. Pynn

The Golden Age of Sound Comedy, by Donald W. McCaffrey

Stations, by Jay Meek

John Colet's Commentary on 1st Corinthians: An Edition of the Latin Text, with Translation, Notes and Introduction by Bernard O'Kelly (co-author)

Children Moving: A Reflective Approach to Teaching Physical Education, by Melissa Parker (co-author)

North Dakota's Ethnic History: Plain Folks, by Theodore B. Pedeliski (co-author)

The Politics of Terror: The Macedonian Liberation Movements, 1893-1903, by Duncan M. Perry

Women with Vision, by Susan C. Peterson (co-author)

NCPEA: The Fourth Decade, National Council of School Administrators, by Donald L. Piper

The Medea Myth (script) by Dan A. Plato

Invitation to Mathematics K-8 Series, by Glenn R. Prigge

This Business of Metrics, by Lila Prigge

American Politics: Changing Expectations, by Ronald E. Pynn

Economic Dimensions of Severance Taxation, by David Ramsett

Ever Westward to the Far East: The Story of Chester Fritz, by Dan Rylance

Jackson Mississippi, by John R. Salter

Sports Law, by George W. Schubert

Georges Perc: Traces of His Passage, by Paul Schwartz

The Law and Teacher Employment, by Gloria Jean Thomas

North Dakota's Ethnic History: Plain Folks, by Playford V. Thorson (co-author)

The New Deal at the Grass Roots, by D. Jerome Tweton

History of the President's Salary, by James F. Vivian

Horse, I Am Your Mother, by Ron Vossler

Walter White and the Harlem Renaissance, by Edward E. Waldron

North Dakota's Ethnic History: Plain Folks, by Robert P. Wilkins (co-author)

Alcohol Problems in Women: Antecedents, Consequences, and Intervention, by Sharon Wilsnack (co-editor)

Source: Directory of Scientists, Artists and Scholars at UND." 1992. UND Graduate School and Office of University Advancement.

APPENDIX I

UNIVERSITY OF NORTH DAKOTA CURRENT FUND
REVENUES AND EXPENDITURES

	1971	1972	1973	1974	1975
REVENUES BY SOURCE:					
Tuition and Fees	$3,574,925	$3,786,167	$3,856,250	$3,833,928	$3,824,800
State Appropriations	$7,162,200	$8,336,818	$8,422,339	$10,158,785	$11,386,794
Federal Grants & Contracts	$6,433,345	$6,510,026	$7,338,403	$7,997,987	$9,821,330
Other Gifts, Grants & Contracts					
Endowment Income	$135,621	$148,711	$155,965	$226,446	$247,711
Sales & Services, educ depts	$716,158	$746,954	$825,535	$961,587	$1,040,436
Sales & Services, auxiliaries	$6,396,771	$6,734,266	$7,009,023	$7,760,840	$8,841,298
Sales & Services, hospital	$1,058,641	$1,130,201	$1,314,289	$1,666,599	$2,645,582
Total Revenues	**$25,477,661**	**$27,393,143**	**$28,921,804**	**$32,606,172**	**$37,807,951**
EXPENDITURES BY FUNCTION:					
Instruction	$10,591,258	$11,263,299	$12,136,109	$12,641,187	$14,622,933
Public Service	$1,286,909	$1,375,863	$1,541,065	$2,482,079	$3,099,398
Research	$901,706	$980,028	$1,145,905	$1,618,624	$2,765,778
Academic Support	$1,031,178	$1,174,017	$1,280,148	$1,703,329	$1,988,289
Student Services	$543,022	$584,407	$784,433	$892,689	$1,123,088
Institutional Support	$925,509	$865,700	$979,395	$1,111,829	$1,328,899
Physical Plant	$1,667,579	$1,891,576	$1,846,253	$2,077,163	$2,325,413
Student Aid	$2,442,691	$2,174,052	$2,110,751	$1,959,514	$2,137,811
Auxiliary Enterprises	$5,060,350	$5,423,057	$5,842,047	$6,398,754	$7,211,206
Rehabilitation Hospital					
Total Expenditures	**$24,450,202**	**$25,731,999**	**$27,666,106**	**$30,885,168**	**$36,602,815**
EXPENDITURES BY OBJECT:					
Salaries and Wages					
Operating Expenses					
Equipment					
Student Aid					
Total Expenditures					

UNIVERSITY OF NORTH DAKOTA CURRENT FUND
REVENUES AND EXPENDITURES

REVENUES BY SOURCE:	1976	1977	1978	1979	1980
Tuition and Fees	$4,162,674	$4,358,481	$4,646,834	$4,910,429	$6,295.345
State Appropriations	$16,471,837	$18,264,572	$18,652,310	$24,731,033	$26,251,822
Federal Grants & Contracts	$10,693,102	$10,178,270	$9,620,641	$10,227,900	$12,637,921
Other Gifts, Grants & Contracts	$2,266,009	$2,548,859	$3,244,983	$3,182,624	$2,669,959
Endowment Income	$368,307	$146,624	$122,187	$154,813	$121,496
Sales & Services, educ depts	$1,551,243	$2,581,012	$3,624,152	$4,063,913	$4,961,805
Sales & Services, auxiliaries	$9,593,147	$10,342,700	$11,078,256	$11,693,335	$13,700,795
Sales & Services, hospital	$2,924,365	$3,840,075	$4,577,446	$5,638,565	$6,257,683
Total Revenues	**$48,030,684**	**$52,260,593**	**$55,566,809**	**$64,602,612**	**$72,896,826**
EXPENDITURES BY FUNCTION:					
Instruction	$18,841,006	$20,919,820	$22,990,423	$24,868,486	$28,735,484
Public Service	$776,425				
Research	$3,270,761	$3,436,036	$3,366,808	$3,510,210	$5,664,933
Academic Support	$2,630,256	$3,267,724	$4,095,731	$4,718,313	$3,951,048
Student Services	$1,295,576	$1,523,330	$1,581,741	$1,770,097	$2,144,759
Institutional Support	$1,420,974	$1,909,413	$2,189,300	$2,469,465	$4,025,844
Physical Plant	$3,215,102	$3,268,874	$3,897,436	$4,299,112	$4,884,150
Student Aid	$2,009,573	$2,073,240	$2,560,501	$2,586,511	$2,976,663
Auxiliary Enterprises	$8,300,888	$9,128,621	$9,745,781	$10,698,563	$12,533,909
Rehabilitation Hospital	$2,865,566	$3,552,402	$3,932,879	$4,944,941	$5,889,962
Total Expenditures	**$44,626.127**	**$49.079,460**	**$54,360,600**	**$59,865,698**	**$70,806,752**
EXPENDITURES BY OBJECT:					
Salaries and Wages	$27,207,890	$30,000,435	$32,302,821	$35,927,414	$41,692,577
Operating Expenses	$14,035,865	$15,755,236	$17,721,105	$20,202,667	$23,752,118
Equipment	$1,372,799	$1,250,549	$1,776,173	$1,149,106	$2,385,394
Student Aid	$2,009,573	$2,073,240	$2,560,501	$2,586,511	$2,976,663
Total Expenditures	**$44,626,127**	**$49,079,460**	**$54,360,600**	**$59,865,698**	**$70,806,752**

UNIVERSITY OF NORTH DAKOTA CURRENT FUND
REVENUES AND EXPENDITURES

	1981	1982	1983	1984	1985
REVENUES BY SOURCE:					
Tuition and Fees	$6,931,049	$8,011,823	$8,744,825	$13,646,765	$14,846,722
State Appropriations	$30,034,535	$36,218,276	$40,262,224	$39,204,212	$41,652,907
Federal Grants and Contracts	$13,873,686	$13,203,678	$15,224,847	$19,630,665	$22,862,289
Other Gifts, Grants & Contracts	$4,119,655	$4,731,379	$5,142,010	$6,521,495	$3,211,504
Endowment Income	$89,805	$103,446	$115,560	$108,333	$132,000
Sales & Services, educ depts	$6,509,929	$7,447,641	$7,617,082	$8,335,409	$9,414,386
Sales & Services, auxiliaries	$15,058,961	$16,584,110	$19,049,088	$20,167,026	$21,414,908
Sales & Services, hospital	$6,863,039	$7,838,492	$8,234,895	$8,956,133	$8,898,411
Total Revenues	**$83,480,659**	**$94,138,845**	**$104,390,531**	**$115,570,038**	**$122,433,127**
EXPENDITURES BY FUNCTION:					
Instruction	$33,033,696	$35,897,767	$36,872,580	$39,194,507	$41,050,270
Public Service	$243,763	$660,024	$800,156	$835,472	$1,115,044
Research	$6,449,065	$6,962,794	$8,291,037	$13,709,190	$13,406,299
Academic Support	$4,415,392	$6,330,605	$6,827,268	$7,974,543	$8,034,581
Student Services	$2,221,512	$2,801,468	$2,971,550	$3,020,779	$3,304,066
Institutional Support	$4,444,464	$5,233,989	$6,658,308	$7,313,866	$6,033,115
Physical Plant	$5,784,109	$6,872,910	$7,178,737	$7,620,062	$8,162,032
Student Aid	$3,425,944	$3,678,820	$6,632,703	$9,146,053	$9,077,536
Auxiliary Enterprises	$13,954,949	$15,610,739	$17,402,315	$13,612,216	$19,856,306
Rehabilitation Hospital	$7,094,777	$7,695,517	$7,995,854	$3,364,971	$9,181,780
Total Expenditures	**$81,067,671**	**$91,744,633**	**$101,630,508**	**$115,791,659**	**$119,221,029**
EXPENDITURES BY OBJECT:					
Salaries and Wages	$48,627,279	$55,999,841	$60,337,528	$65,958,810	$70,013,872
Operating Expenses	$26,651,774	$29,812,262	$31,146,118	$34,020,746	$35,963,764
Equipment	$2,362,675	$2,253,710	$3,514,159	$5,666,050	$4,165,857
Student Aid	$3,425,943	$3,678,820	$6,632,703	$9,146,053	$9,077,536
Total Expenditures	**$81,067,671**	**$91,744,633**	**$101,630,508**	**$115,791,659**	**$119,221,029**

UNIVERSITY OF NORTH DAKOTA CURRENT FUND REVENUES AND EXPENDITURES

	1986	1987	1988	1989	1990	1991
REVENUES BY SOURCE:						
Tuition and Fees	$14,256,811	$15,858,132	$18,408,184	$21,513,145	$25,562,383	$28,803,024
State Appropriations	$44,342,875	$45,657,929	$42,553,152	$43,429,445	$45,472,331	$46,392,789
Federal Grants and Contracts	$25,723,847	$24,739,545	$25,486,117	$27,182,003	$30,256,899	$30,720,591
Other Gifts, Grants & Contracts	$5,558,031	$4,860,391	$6,481,087	$7,315,691	$9,564,563	$9,551,774
Endowment Income	$132,000	$660,112	$611,180	$651,222	$712,346	$788,179
Sales & Services, educ depts	$12,532,618	$12,432,678	$13,294,683	$15,621,243	$19,191,504	$18,717,199
Sales & Services, auxiliaries	$23,441,718	$25,298,220	$27,787,263	$30,656,535	$34,763,791	$34,909,676
Sales & Services, hospital	$8,687,586	$10,130,541	$9,624,681	$10,622,257	$11,465,250	$10,427,518
Total Revenues	**$134,664,486**	**$139,637,548**	**$144,246,347**	**$156,991,541**	**$176,989,067**	**$180,310,750**
EXPENDITURES BY FUNCTION:						
Instruction	$44,176,010	$46,243,449	$48,099,932	$49,743,455	$56,216,400	$59,006,757
Public Service	$1,824,889	$3,063,951	$3,369,186	$3,070,144	$5,236,562	$6,577,868
Research	$15,602,022	$13,888,642	$14,888,979	$16,416,359	$17,204,798	$16,374,386
Academic Support	$9,149,456	$9,625,141	$9,887,944	$11,099,107	$12,801,833	$13,231,676
Student Services	$3,768,054	$3,894,425	$3,956,564	$3,958,781	$4,746,225	$4,517,507
Institutional Support	$8,802,334	$7,697,678	$7,376,184	$7,836,876	$10,929,406	$10,274,082
Physical Plant	$9,397,485	$9,031,805	$9,002,478	$8,948,759	$9,805,335	$10,013,266
Student Aid	$8,889,485	$8,522,094	$8,498,759	$10,190,277	$11,417,726	$11,647,693
Auxiliary Enterprises	$21,800,008	$23,219,842	$25,792,457	$28,334,275	$31,949,686	$32,150,744
Rehabilitation Hospital	$9,061,232	$9,518,654	$10,073,723	$11,431,587	$10,805,817	$9,877,956
Total Expenditures	**$132,470,975**	**$134,705,681**	**$140,946,206**	**$151,029,620**	**$171,113,788**	**$173,671,935**
EXPENDITURES BY OBJECT:						
Salaries and Wages	$76,064,206	$79,310,798	$80,936,422	$84,847,012	$96,117,373	$99,302,935
Operating Expenses	$42,777,314	$43,342,831	$47,704,686	$52,118,110	$57,602,382	$57,731,904
Equipment	$4,739,970	$3,529,958	$3,806,338	$3,874,221	$5,976,307	$4,989,403
Student Aid	$8,889,485	$8,522,094	$8,498,760	$10,190,277	$11,417,726	$11,647,693
Total Expenditures	**$132,470,975**	**$134,705,681**	**$140,946,206**	**$151,029,620**	**$171,113,788**	**$173,671,935**

APPENDIX J

SPONSORED PROGRAM ACTIVITY
AT UND, 1977-1991

Fiscal Year	Proposals Submitted (Number)	Amount Requested ($ Millions)	Awards Received	
			Number	Amount ($ Millions)
1977-78	185	$ — —	150	$10.30
1978-79	206	— —	168	9.80
1979-80	249	— —	170	12.60
1980-81	253	— —	189	12.85
1981-82	206	20.82	153	9.96
1982-83	284	31.86	179	13.56
1983-84	287	36.81	207	17.69
1984-85	402	69.66	272	23.56
1985-86	445	59.88	274	24.18
1986-87	445	54.58	290	22.65
1987-88	514	50.94	303	23.79
1988-89	520	46.53	344	25.12
1989-90	568	55.45	394	32.92
1990-91	560	62.77	416	39.80
TOTALS	**5,124**	**$ — — ***	**3,509**	**$278.78**

*   *No total is indicated since the data from all of the prior years are not available.*

Source: Office of Research and Program Development

182

A COMPARISON OF FACULTY SALARIES, 1980-1990

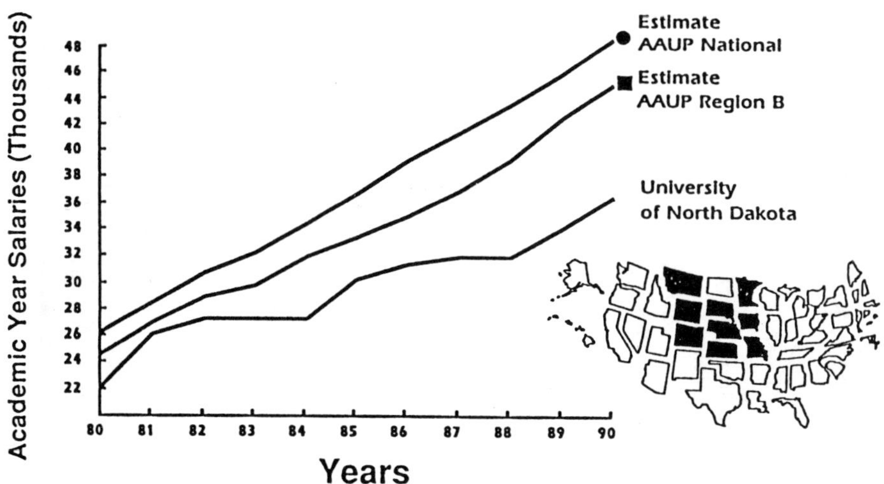

For academic year 1990-91 UND faculty salaries would need to be increased an average of $8,670 (24.1%) to reach the AAUP Region average.

For academic year 1990-91 UND faculty salaries would need to be increased an average of $12,200 (33.9%) to reach the AAUP National average.

**Region B consists of Montana, South Dakota, Wyoming, Nebraska, Minnesota, Iowa, Colorado, Kansas, and Missouri and excludes the University of Minnesota Main Campus.*

Source: *Testimony before the Appropriations Committee, North Dakota State Senate.* (1991, March 4). University of North Dakota.

APPENDIX L

HEADCOUNT ENROLLMENT COMPARISONS FOR FOUR-YEAR COLLEGES AND UNIVERSITIES, 1971, 1981, 1991

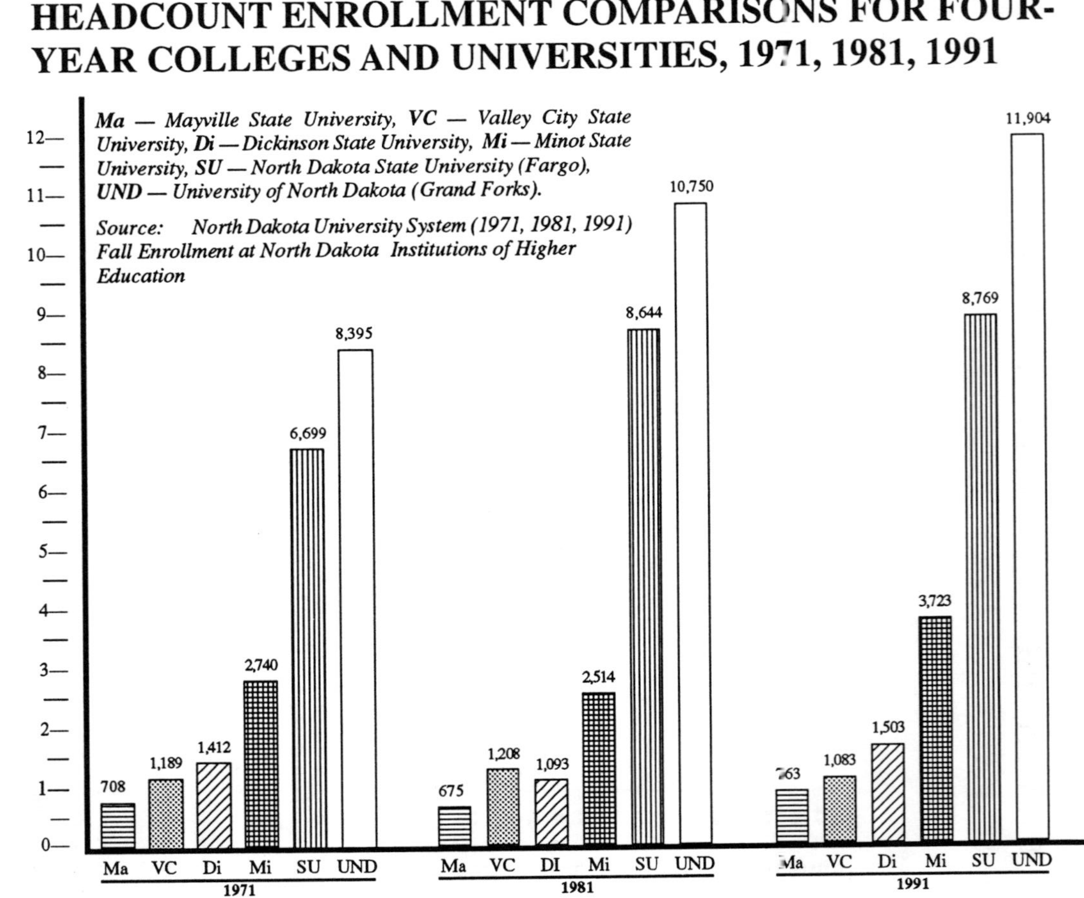

UNIVERSITY OF NORTH DAKOTA PRESIDENTS, 1884 to 1992

Name of President	Dates of Presidency	Length of Presidency Yrs. Mos.	Years at UND	Year and Conditions of Departure	Date, Place of Birth and Death	UND Enrollment Sept.-June, in first, last year of Presidency
1. BLACKBURN, William Maxwell	1884-1885	1 year	1884-1885	Summary dismissal	Born 12/30/1828 Carlisle, Ind. Died 12/1898 Pierre, S.D.	1884-85: 0 of college level, but 79 "preps" enrolled by end of year.
MONTGOMERY, Henry *(acting)*	1885-1887	2 years	1885-1889	Board considered his suitability for presidency limited to acting basis.	Born 11/11/1848 Cartwright, Ont. Died	1885-86: 8 1886-87: 25
2. SPRAGUE, Homer Baxter	Oct. 1887 - March 1891	4 years	1887-1891	Resigned March 1891.	Born 10/19/1829 Sutton, Mass. Died 3/23/1918 Newton, Mass.	1887-88: 29 1890-91: 24
3. MERRIFIELD, Webster	March 12, 1891- June 17, 1909	18 years	1884-1909	Retired from UND presidency, 1909, moved to California.	Born 7/27/1852 Williamsville, Vt. Died 1/22/1916 Pasadena, Calif.	1891-92: 37 1908-09: 422
4. McVEY, Frank LeRond	June 18, 1909 - Oct. 14, 1917	8 years	1909-1917	Resigned to accept presidency of Univ. of Kentucky (1917-1940).	Born 11/10/1869 Wilmington, Ohio Died 1/4/1953 Lexington, Ky.	1909-10: 485 1916-17: 868

Name of President	Earned Degrees	Honorary Degrees	Academic Specialty	Age When Term Began	Age When Term Ended	Age When Died
1. BLACKBURN, William Maxwell	BA, 1850, Hanover Col. DD, 1854, Princeton Theol. Seminary		Mental, moral & political science	55	56	69
MONTGOMERY, Henry *(acting)*	BSc, 1880, Victoria MA, 1887, Toronto PhB, 1903, Ill. Wesleyan		Natural sciences	36	38	
2. SPRAGUE, Homer Baxter	BA, 1852, Yale MA, 1855, Yale	PhD, 1893, NY Univ LLD, 1916, UND	Rhetoric & English literature	58	62	89
3. MERRIFIELD, Webster	BA, 1877, Yale MA, 1892, Yale		Greek, political & social science	39	57	63
4. McVEY, Frank LeRond	BA, 1893, Ohio Wesleyan PhD, 1895, Yale	LLD, 1910, O. Wesleyan; LLD, 1919, Alabama U; LLD, 1929, Transylvania; LLD, 1933, Berea; LHD, 1933, Rollins	Economics	40	48	83

Name of President	Dates of Presidency	Length of Presidency Yrs. Mos.	Years at UND	Year and Conditions of Departure	Date, Place of Birth and Death	UND Enrollment Sept.-June, in first, last year of Presidency
BABCOCK, Earle J. *(acting)*	Oct. 15, 1917 - April 8, 1918	5 months	1889-1925	Temporary position only	Born 6/11/1865 St. Charles, Minn. Died 9/3/1925 Bemidji, Minn.	1917-18: 711
5. KANE, Thomas Franklin	April 9, 1918 - June 30, 1933	15 years	1918-1933	Resigned	Born 5/5/1863 Westfield, Ind. Died 4/14/1953	1918-19: 858 1932-33: 1,610
6. WEST, John Chester	July 1, 1933 - June 30, 1954	21 years	1933-1954	Retired	Born 12/25/1885 Clearwater, Minn. Died 7/21/1961 Grand Forks, N.D.	1933-34: 1,580 1953-54: 2,708
7. STARCHER, George W.	July 1, 1954 - June 30, 1971	17 years	1954-1971	Retired	Born 1/14/1906 Ripley, W.Va.	1954-55: 2,976 1970-71: 8,129
8. CLIFFORD, Thomas J.	July 1, 1971 - June 30, 1992	21 years	1938-42, 1945-56, 1958-92	Retired	Born 3/16/21 Langdon, N.D.	1971-72: 8,395 1991-92: 11,940

Name of President	Earned Degrees	Honorary Degrees	Academic Specialty	Age When Term Began	Age When Term Ended	Age When Died
BABCOCK, Earle J. *(acting)*	BS, 1889, U of Minn.	DSc, 1914, UND	Geology & chemistry	52	52	60
5. KANE, Thomas Franklin	BA, 1888, DePauw MA, 1891, DePauw PhD, 1895, Johns Hopkins	LLD, 1911, DePauw LLD, 1933, UND	Classics	55	70	90
6. WEST, John Chester	AB, 1915, Fargo Col. MS, 1926, UND EdD, 1930, UND	LLD, 1944, Wesley College LHD, 1956, UND	Education	47	68	75
7. STARCHER, George W.	AB, 1926, Ohio U AM, 1927, U of Ill. PhD, 1930, U of Ill.		Mathematics	48	65	
8. CLIFFORD, Thomas J.	B.S., 1942, UND J.D., 1948, UND M.B.A., 1957, Stanford	LLD, 1973, Jamestown College	Commerce, law, business	50	71	

Source: H.K. Jacobson and Don Jacob, (1970, December 14), *Office of University Relations. Updated by Dan el Rice and Mavis Ness, 1992.*

GALLERY OF UND PRESIDENTS

William Maxwell Blackburn
1884-1885

Henry Montgomery (acting)
1885-1887

Homer Baxter Sprague
1887-1891

Webster Merrifield
1891-1909

Frank LeRond McVey
1909-1917

Earle J. Babcock (acting)
1917-1918

Thomas Franklin Kane
1918-1933

John Chester West
1933-1954

George W. Starcher
1954-1971

Thomas J. Clifford (right)
1971-1992

INDEX

196

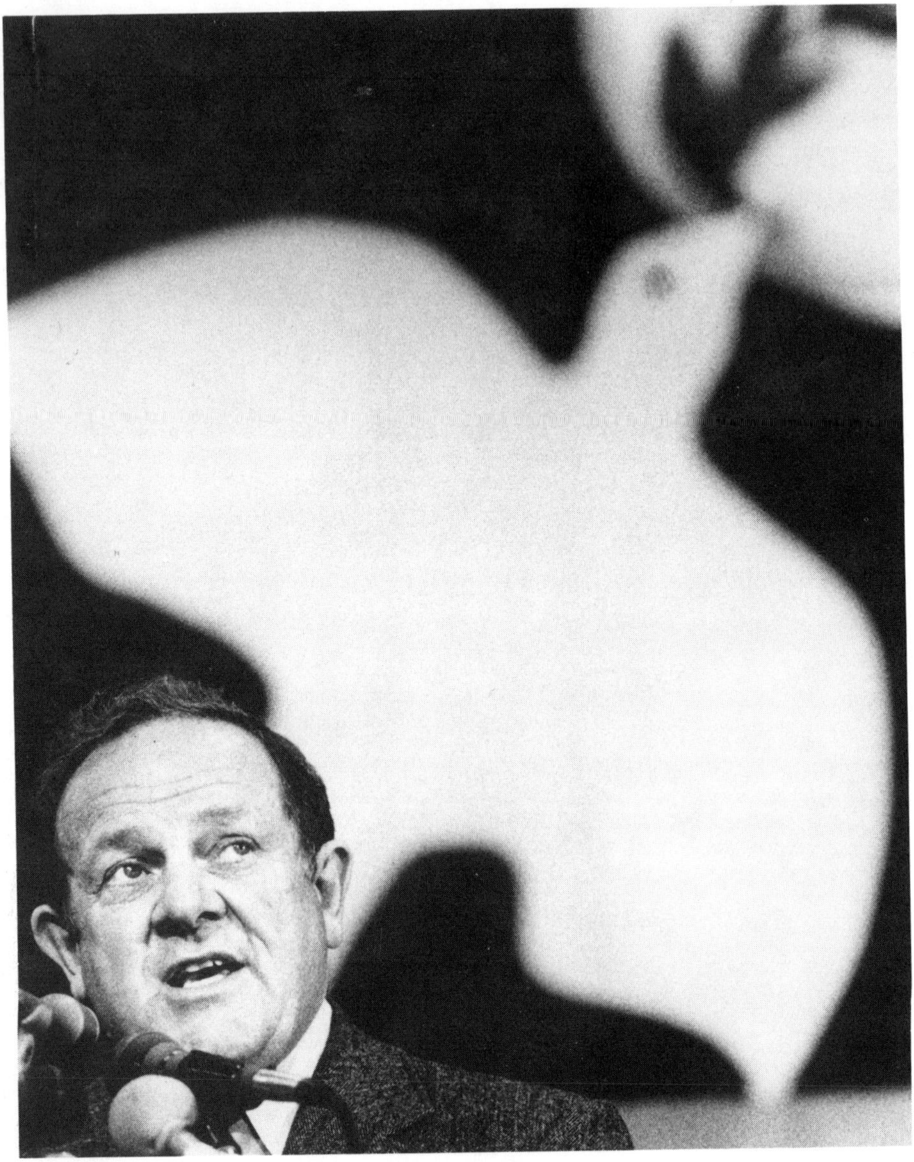

UNIVERSITY OF NORTH DAKOTA

1883

LUX ET LEX

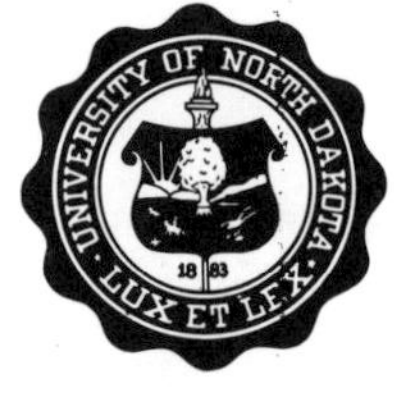